THE ILLUSTRATED HISTORY ENCYCLOPEDIA
EVERYDAY LIFE
IN THE
ANCIENT WORLD

THE ILLUSTRATED HISTORY ENCYCLOPEDIA
EVERYDAY LIFE
IN THE
ANCIENT WORLD

Consultant Editor: Dr. John Haywood

HERMES
HOUSE

CONTENTS
Great Themes of Everyday Life...6

HOME, FAMILY, & EVERYDAY LIFE
From Shelters to Homes...12

WORK, TRADE, & FARMING
From Survival to Specialization...72

ART, CULTURE & ENTERTAINMENT
Life, Leisure and Enjoyment...130

GODS, BELIEFS & CEREMONIES
Religion, Ritual and Myth...190

Great Themes of Everyday Life

When the ancient Chinese wanted to curse their enemies, they said to them: "May you live in interesting times". This referred to times of war and revolution, which, for ordinary people, meant suffering and destruction. Interesting times were bad times.

Ordinary people preferred to be left in peace, so that they could concentrate on making comfortable homes, working, having families and getting enough food to eat. This book explores the many ways of peaceful, everyday life that existed in the ancient world.

RURAL COMMUNITIES
The first nomadic peoples began to settle around 12,000BC. They farmed the land to provide a reliable food supply for themselves and their families. Scenes such as this Chinese rice field show how little some people's lives have changed through the centuries.

Slower Pace

Thanks to television, cheap air travel and the Internet, today we know more about people in other cultures than ever before. New ideas and fashions spread very quickly. However, in the ancient world, travel was slow and often dangerous. Many people lived their whole lives without travelling more than a few miles from their home towns and villages. Communities were isolated and developed their own styles of clothing, houses and tools. Most people probably knew nothing about how people lived in the next village – or even that other countries existed.

Creating a good home has been a priority for people for thousands of years. Humans originally evolved in equatorial Africa, where the weather is warm enough for people to live outside in every season. But even there, people needed to shelter from rain or

ANCIENT FASHIONS
Styles of dress varied from one area to another, and did not change from one year to the next, as ideas were slow to travel. Viking clothes were typically loose-fitting, and made of wool and linen. They were fastened with decorated metal clasps and buckles. Dyes were made from local plants and insects, so fabric colours also varied from place to place.

hot sun in caves or shelters. The remains of the oldest known huts in Africa date back 300,000 years.

When people lived by hunting and gathering wild plants, they built simple homes that could be easily put up, dismantled and moved. This was because they often had to move on in search of new food sources. It was not worth building a permanent house, if they were going to have to leave it behind.

When humans started to farm for a living, people settled down and stayed in one place, probably for the rest of their lives. It became worthwhile to build more solid homes. Farming brought other changes, too. Hunter-gatherers had small families as it was difficult to find enough food. Older or weaker members of the family starved. Ancient farmers, however, had as many children as possible. There were then more hands to work the land. Members of the family could also be spared to care for the very old or very young.

MAKESHIFT HOMES
Hunter-gatherers roamed the land looking for food. They needed homes that could be moved easily. Summer tents were built by Ice Age people in Pincevant, France. They were made from animal skins, held up with wooden poles and secured with stones around the bottom.

FARMING METHODS
Sumerian farmers in the Middle East developed an ox-drawn plough around 4000BC, which replaced the hand-held plough. This meant that they could grow more food using fewer workers. Farming methods developed to suit the local environment in each area.

Widespread Farming

Farming first began about 10,000 years ago in the Middle East (also called the Near East). By 2,000 years ago, most of the world's population were farmers, although even today, the Inuits and some tribal peoples still live by hunting. Each area adapted its own farming methods, crops and domestic animals to the local climate, soil and natural environment.

In hot, dry lands, such as Mesopotamia, crops only grew successfully if irrigation canals carried water from rivers to the fields. In cool, wet areas – such as the Viking lands of northern Europe – crops did not grow well, so farmers relied more on raising domestic animals such as sheep and cattle.

Crafts and Trades

Most people in the ancient world had little choice about what they did to earn a living. Formal education was a privilege (and more often for boys than girls). Many children learned their parents' trade or occupation, and as they grew up, they took on more and more responsibilities.

By the time they reached their early teens, young people were treated as adults and might even marry.

Because most settlements were in isolated rural areas, each family learned how to make tools, cooking pots and clothes,

SEARCHING FOR FISH
Fishing was an important source of food in the ancient world. People who lived near rivers, lakes and coastal areas developed all kinds of fishing methods. The Aztec boy pictured uses a stick and paddles to drive fish into his net, which is woven from cactus fibre. Other peoples used hooks, lines and harpoons to catch fish.

and how to build the family home – in addition to growing crops and tending the farm animals. In larger towns, however, specialist skills and trades evolved. Builders, metalworkers, potters, bakers, brewers, shopkeepers, merchants, weavers, soldiers and administrators could all make a living supplying services and skills.

LEARNING BY DOING
In the ancient world, children often learned their parents' trade or occupation. The budding Native American potter pictured is helping her mother to make a water vessel. By the time she reaches her teens, she will be very accomplished at her craft.

Free Time

It is easy to imagine that people in the ancient world lived a life of constant hard

work. In fact, people often had more leisure time than we do today. Farmers had to work hard in the spring and autumn. In summer and winter, there was plenty of spare time. Even slaves in ancient Greece and Rome were given days off, often when there was a festival or holy day (from which the word holiday comes). People in ancient times liked to dress up for their free time and for festivals, and sometimes wore decorative clothing and jewellery.

SPORTS AND GAMES
Ancient cultures developed many sports that often had religious significance. This discus thrower was an athlete in ancient Greece, where the Olympic Games were first held in 776BC. The Olympic competitions were for men only, but the women held their own games in honour of Hera, the goddess of women.

There was no shortage of entertainment. Music, singing and dancing, storytelling, board games and all types of sport were popular everywhere. Many of the same sports are still played today. Athletic games were introduced by the ancient Greeks.

Some ancient forms of entertainment were very violent by modern standards. The Romans enjoyed gladiator shows, where two men fought each other to the death. The Mesoamericans played a ball game that was something like basketball – but the losing team was sacrificed to the gods.

DRESSING UP
People all over the ancient world developed elaborate costumes for celebrations and religious rituals. Lady Murasaki – who wrote the world's first novel, *The Tale of Genji* – wears the rich, silk robes that were popular at the Japanese court in AD1000. Each layer of clothing and even its colour has a special meaning.

RHYTHM OF THE GODS
Music was an important part of religious celebrations. It was developed in all cultures to honour the gods and goddesses, and to mark special days of the year. The members of this Aztec orchestra play rhythms on instruments, such as conch shells, rattles and drums.

Belief in Many Gods

Religious festivals brought many opportunities for celebration. In ancient Greece, they were marked by plays, music and sports competitions.

The main religions in the world today – including Judaism, Christianity and Islam – are monotheistic, meaning that they worship only one god. This was very unusual in the ancient world, when most religions were polytheistic, with many gods. People believed that different gods watched over different activities, and had the power to help or hinder them.

Some gods, such as those of the Celts and the Aztecs, were believed to demand human sacrifices in return for favours.

Life after Death

Preparing for death was an important part of most ancient religions. Some faiths, such as the Indian Hindu religion, believe in reincarnation (being reborn in a different body). Most believed in an afterlife of the spirit. The next world was often thought to be similar to earthly life. In ancient Egypt, people were buried with furniture, tools, weapons and personal belongings that would be useful on their journey. For many in the ancient world, everyday life was something that they expected to continue even after they died.

BEYOND DEATH
The Egyptians preserved the bodies of their dead by a process called mummification. They buried them in richly decorated tombs. The deceased person was then surrounded with furniture, tools, jewellery and clothes that would be useful in the afterlife.

Home, Family & Everyday Life

Discover how people of the first civilizations built their homes and organized their daily lives

From Shelters to Homes

Everyone needs somewhere to live. All over the world, people from different civilizations have built many kinds of homes. From the simplest prehistoric cave-shelters, to the most splendid palaces in Mughal India, a home serves many purposes that are common in all cultures. They provided protection from cold and damp, shade from the hot sun, and comfortable refuge for sleeping, preparing food, raising a family, and entertaining guests.

The layout and construction of houses varied widely. Homes were designed to provide maximum comfort in the local climate, and to withstand local environmental hazards, such as storms, floods, earthquakes, and heavy snow. In northern Europe, the Vikings built houses with thick thatched roofs for insulation from the cold. In Japan, an earthquake zone, lightweight paper screens were used as inner walls in the construction of houses. If these collapsed, they

Round, early farming huts, such as this one, whose remains were found in Banpo in China, date from 6000 B.C. They had wooden frames, plastered walls, and a hole to let out smoke.

Longhouses were alternatives to the round house. These were often found in Europe, and north and south America. Thatch made from reeds from a nearby river lasted longer than straw.

TIMELINE 10,000–200 B.C.

10,000 B.C. People around the world live as nomads, moving from place to place, hunting animals and gathering wild foods. They shelter in strong, solid houses, made of wood, stone, or snow in winter, but travel around, living in tents in summer. Seminomadic lifestyle continues until the 1900s in places such as arctic Russia.

Inside an igloo home of the Arctic Inuit people

10,000 B.C. People living in north and south America develop homes according to the local environment. Some are simple shelters of branches and leaves; others include earth lodges, longhouses made of woven saplings, buffalo-skin tipis, and mud-brick pueblo apartments.

8000–7000 B.C. The world's first settled farming villages are built in the Middle East.

4500 B.C. European farmers build villages of longhouses.

3100–30 B.C. The peak of ancient Egyptian civilization. Egyptians live in houses made of sun-dried mud brick.

European longhouse village

800 B.C.–A.D. 100 The Celts in central and northwestern Europe live as

10,000 B.C.　　　　　　　　　4500 B.C.　　　　　　　　　3000 B

would not harm people and cause much damage.

The materials used to construct a house also shaped its design. Most homes were built using local resources that were easily available. In many countries, including Aztec Mexico and ancient Egypt, mud and clay were shaped into bricks and dried in the sun. Elsewhere, homes were made from wood, stone, and dried grass. Fine stone and timber were rare, and it was difficult to carry them long distances, so they were expensive. The materials used and the size of homes depended on the wealth of the owner. Houses of the wealthy were large and luxurious, with many spacious rooms. Among the poor, all family members might share a simple room that combined as sleeping and living space.

Houses were built on stilts in the marshy regions of Japan, where rice was cultivated in wet paddy fields.

Tipis made of animal skins were held up with wooden poles, and they served as a short-term shelter for Native American peoples.

Most homes were built as permanent shelters, but in some environments, they were designed to fulfill temporary needs. Nomads were people who moved from place to place, hunting animals and gathering wild plants for food. They built homes that were designed to be easily packed away and moved several times a year. Native American hunters on the Great Plains of North America made tipis of buffalo skin. Inuit hunters in the Arctic built shelters from blocks of snow, called igloos,

farmers, building large roundhouses of wattle-and-daub, thatched with straw. They also build fortified towns as centers of trade.

600 B.C. Wealthy families in India build houses of brick and stone. They are painted different colors, according to caste (social status).

600–200 B.C. Ancient Greek families live in houses made of stone or mud bricks. They have separate, private quarters for women, and a dining room for entertaining, used only by men of the family.

c.300 B.C.–A.D. 300 Wealthy Roman families build splendid houses. Town houses were often built around a small enclosed garden, or a courtyard called an atrium. Country houses had elegant rooms for entertaining, plus barracks where slaves and farmworkers could sleep.

300 B.C. In Central America, the Maya build new cities surrounded by fields and farms. Mayan families live in simple homes, with wood or mud walls and thatched roofs.

A wealthy Roman family home.

to live in during the long winter months.

For many people, homes were also places of work. From the time when humans first began to live together in families, women worked at home, caring for babies and young children. In most cultures, women did the cooking and produced household textiles, such as blankets and clothes, for their families. Archaeologists have found children's toys, cooking pots, and the remains of weaving looms in family homes from places as diverse as India and Incan Peru. Men, who made their living as farmers and craftspeople, also worked at home, with other family members helping them. Teamwork was essential for survival. Children worked alongside their parents, learning the skills they would need in adult life. School was only provided for children from wealthy families, as in China and imperial Rome.

Backstrap looms started to be used as early as 2500 B.C. by the people who lived in the Andes mountains of Peru.

All these family and working needs were reflected in house designs. Craft workshops, rooms to display finished goods, and shelters for farm animals often formed part of the family home. Cultural values also influenced housing. In ancient Greece, homes had private rooms where women lived, out of the sight of

Homelife in early Middle Eastern farming villages was a cluster of activity. People often shared their house with the animals. Everyone in the family had a role to play.

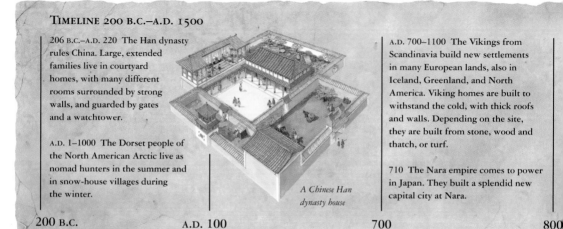

TIMELINE 200 B.C.–A.D. 1500

206 B.C.–A.D. 220 The Han dynasty rules China. Large, extended families live in courtyard homes, with many different rooms surrounded by strong walls, and guarded by gates and a watchtower.

A.D. 1–1000 The Dorset people of the North American Arctic live as nomad hunters in the summer and in snow-house villages during the winter.

A Chinese Han dynasty house

A.D. 700–1100 The Vikings from Scandinavia build new settlements in many European lands, also in Iceland, Greenland, and North America. Viking homes are built to withstand the cold, with thick roofs and walls. Depending on the site, they are built from stone, wood and thatch, or turf.

710 The Nara empire comes to power in Japan. They built a splendid new capital city at Nara.

200 B.C.   **A.D. 100**   **700**   **800**

non-family men. Almost everywhere, people liked to decorate their houses, sometimes in bright colours and patterns, and to furnish them with comfortable bedding, seating and floor-coverings. Some of these decorations had a meaning, with the aim of protecting a house or watching over those

In every Chinese kitchen, a new paper picture of the kitchen god and his wife was put up on New Year's Day.

who lived there. Chinese families often displayed a picture of the Kitchen God, who oversaw their behaviour. Some Native Americans put up tall totem poles outside their homes, carved with images of ancestor spirits to guard the families.

This section charts the development of domestic history in various cultures in turn. It focuses on aspects of everyday life that are common to major civilizations, such as family, childhood, education, housing and food. You will be able to see how these themes evolved and compare how people's lives varied with local environments around the world.

A well-off Aztec couple sit by the fire, while their meal is being cooked. Their colourful clothes and braided hair indicate that they are people of rank.

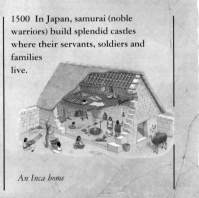

Wooden totem poles outside Native American homes kept a record of the family histories of the people living inside.

1000–1325 The Aztec people of central America leave their homeland in the north of Mexico, and travel south in search of a better place to live. They settle in the central valley of Mexico, and build a new capital city there. It soon grows into one of the largest cities in the world.

1000–1600 The Thule people of the North American Arctic live in huts made of stone and turf.

Inca man and woman gather straw for thatch

*c.*1300–1536 The Inca Empire is powerful in Peru. The Incas are expert builders of stone temples, palaces and city walls, without using metal tools. Ordinary families live in small stone houses, thatched with straw.

1500 In Japan, samurai (noble warriors) build splendid castles where their servants, soldiers and families live.

An Inca home

1000   **1300**   **1500**

Neolithic Villages

WHEN PEOPLE took up farming as a way of life, it meant that they had to stay in the same place for a long time. In some areas, farmers practised slash and burn. This means they cleared land, but moved on after a few years, when their crops had exhausted the soil. Elsewhere, early farming settlements grew into villages five to ten times bigger than earlier hunter-gatherer camps. At first, the farmers still hunted wild animals and foraged for food, but soon their herds and crops supplied most of their needs. They lived in villages of rectangular or circular one-storey houses of stone, mud-brick, or timber and thatch. The houses were joined by narrow lanes or courtyards. Most villages lay on low ground, near well-watered, easily worked land. By using irrigation and crop rotation, later farmers were able to stay in one place for a long time.

INSIDE A LONG HOUSE
The inside of a long house was a place of work as well as providing shelter for the family and their animals. Around the hearth of this reconstructed house are baskets woven from reeds and skins laid out on the floor. Around the walls, tools are stored.

A LONG HOUSE
This is a reconstruction of a typical long house in an early farming village in Europe. The village dates from around 4500BC.

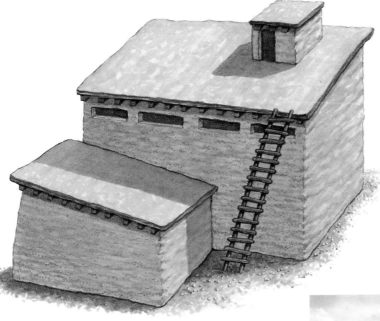

A TOWN HOUSE

This picture shows how a house at Çatal Hüyük in Turkey may have looked. The walls were made of mud-brick, with poles covered with reeds and mud as the roof. All the houses were joined together, with no streets in between. People went about by climbing over the rooftops, entering their homes by a ladder through the roof.

The main room of each house had raised areas for sitting and sleeping on. More than a thousand houses were packed together like this at Çatal Hüyük.

THE OVEN

Many houses contained ovens or kilns, used for baking bread and firing pottery. A kiln allowed higher temperatures to be reached than an open hearth, and therefore produced better pottery. Each village probably made its own pottery.

STONE WALLS

These are the remains of the walls of a house in an early farming village in Jordan. It was built around 7000BC. The walls are made of stone collected from the local area.

The first farming towns and villages appeared in the Near East. Most were built of mud-brick and, over hundreds of years, such settlements were often rebuilt many times on the same site.

Family Life

L IFE WAS HARD for ordinary families in Mesopotamia. Many babies and young children died from disease or because of poor maternity care. Boys from poorer families did not go to school but worked with their fathers, who taught them their trades. Girls stayed at home with their mothers and learned how to keep house and look after the younger children. Some of the details of family life are described in ancient clay tablets. In one tablet, a boy rudely tells his mother to hurry up and make his lunch. In another one, a boy is scared of what his father will say when he sees his bad school report.

In some ways, Mesopotamian society was quite modern. The law said that women could own property and get a divorce. However, if a woman was unable to have a baby, she had to agree to her husband taking a second wife. The second wife and her children had rights too. They remained part of the household even if the first wife had a child after all.

MOTHERHOOD
Having lots of healthy children, especially sons, was very important because families needed children to grow up and work for them. Most women stayed at home to look after their families. Women did not usually go out to work, but some had jobs as priestesses. Some priestesses were single but others were married women.

HOUSEHOLD GOODS
Pottery was used in Mesopotamian homes from the time of the first villages. At first it was hand-made, but later a potter's wheel was used. This pottery jug may have been modelled on a jug made of metal. Tools and utensils were made of stone or metal. There was not much furniture in a Mesopotamian house, just mud-brick benches for sitting or sleeping on. There may have been rugs and cushions to make the homes more homely and comfortable, but none have survived.

MODEL HOUSE
From models such as this one, we know that homes in Mesopotamia were similar to village houses in modern Iraq. They were built of mud-brick and were usually rectangular, with rooms around a central courtyard. Doors and windows were small to keep the house warm in the cold winters, and cool during the hot summers. Flat roofs, reached by stairs from the central court, could be used as an extra room in summer.

MESOPOTAMIAN FASHIONS

A statue of a worshipper found in a temple shows the dress of a Sumerian woman. Dresses were of sheepskin, sometimes with a sheepskin shawl as well, or of woollen cloth. One shoulder was left bare. Some women, who may have been priestesses, wore tall, elaborate hats like this one. Later fashions included long, fringed garments. Sumerian men wore sheepskin kilts, but men in the Assyrian and Babylonian Empires wore long, woollen tunics. Both sexes wore jewellery.

EARNING A LIVING

Most families in ancient Mesopotamia depended on agriculture for a living, just as many people in the Middle East do today. Farmers rented their land from bigger landowners, such as important officials, kings or temples, and had to pay part of what they produced in taxes. Many townspeople had jobs in local government or worked in the textile and metalwork industries.

BUILD IT UP

Mud-bricks are made from a mixture of clayey mud and straw mixed with water. The straw stops the bricks from cracking. The mixture is put in square or oblong moulds and left to dry in the sun for several weeks. The bricks are usually made in the summer after the harvest, when there is plenty of straw available and it is less likely to rain (which would damage the bricks).

straw

clay

GONE FISHING

There were lots of fish in the rivers and fishponds of ancient Iraq, and fish seem to have been an important part of people's diet. Fishbones were found at Eridu, in the south of Sumer, in the oldest level of the temple. Perhaps fish were offered to the water god Enki as an offering. (He is the god with streams of water containing fish springing out of his shoulders.) Some of the carved reliefs from the Assyrian palaces give us rare glimpses into everyday life and include little scenes of men going fishing.

Towns, Homes and Gardens

THE GREAT CITIES of ancient Egypt, such as Memphis and Thebes, were built along the banks of the river Nile. Small towns grew up haphazardly around them. Special workmen's towns such as Deir el-Medina were also set up around major burial sites and temples to help with building work.

Egyptian towns were defended by thick walls and the streets were planned on a grid pattern. The straight dirt roads had a stone drainage channel, or gutter, running down the middle. Parts of the town housed important officials, while other parts were home to craft workers and poor labourers.

Only temples were built to last. They were made of stone. Mud brick was used to construct all other buildings from royal palaces to workers' dwellings. Most Egyptian homes had roofs supported with palm logs and floors made of packed earth. In the homes of wealthier Egyptians, walls were sometimes plastered and painted. The rooms of their houses included bedrooms, living rooms, kitchens in thatched courtyards and workshops. Homes were furnished with beds, chairs, stools and benches. In the cool of the evenings people would sit on the flat roofs or walk and talk in cool, shady gardens.

THE GARDEN OF NAKHT
The royal scribe Nakht and his wife Tjiui take an evening stroll through their garden. Trees and shrubs surround a peaceful pool. Egyptian gardens included date palms, pomegranates, grape vines, scarlet poppies and blue and pink lotus flowers. Artists in ancient Egypt showed objects in the same picture from different angles, so the trees around Nakht's pool are flattened out.

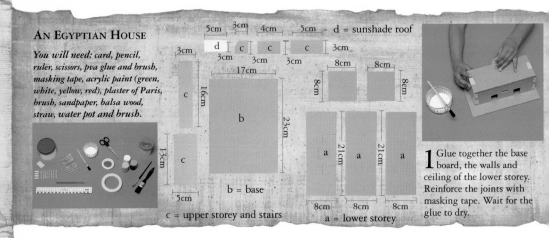

AN EGYPTIAN HOUSE

You will need: card, pencil, ruler, scissors, pva glue and brush, masking tape, acrylic paint (green, white, yellow, red), plaster of Paris, brush, sandpaper, balsa wood, straw, water pot and brush.

d = sunshade roof

b = base

c = upper storey and stairs

a = lower storey

1 Glue together the base board, the walls and ceiling of the lower storey. Reinforce the joints with masking tape. Wait for the glue to dry.

ABOVE THE FLOODS

The homes of wealthy people were often built on platforms to stop damp passing through the mud brick walls. This also raised it above the level of any possible flood damage.

SOUL HOUSES

Pottery models give us a good idea of how the homes of poorer Egyptians looked. During the Middle Kingdom, these soul houses were left as tomb offerings. The Egyptians placed food in the courtyard of the house to feed the person's soul after death.

MUD BRICK

The Egyptians made mud bricks from the thick clay soil left behind by the Nile floods. The clay was taken to the brickyard and mixed with water, pebbles and chopped straw. Mud brick is still used as a building material for houses in Egypt today and is made in the same way.

straw

mud

BRICK MAKING

A group of labourers make bricks. First mud was collected in leather buckets and taken to the building site. There, it was mixed with straw and pebbles. Finally the mixture was put into a mould. At this stage, bricks were sometimes stamped with the name of the pharaoh or the building for which they were made. They were then left to dry in the hot sunshine for several days, before being carried away in a sling.

Egyptian houses had a large main room that opened directly onto the street. In many homes, stairs led up to the roof. People would often sleep there during very hot weather.

2 Now glue together the top storey and stairs. Again, use masking tape to reinforce the joints. When the top storey is dry, glue it to the lower storey.

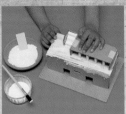

3 Glue the balsa pillars into the front of the top storey. When the house is dry, cover it in wet paste of plaster of Paris. Paint the pillars red or a colour of your choice.

4 Paint the whole building a dried mud colour. Next paint a green strip along the side. Use masking tape to ensure straight edges. Sand any rough edges.

5 Now make a shelter for the rooftop. Use four balsa struts as supports. The roof can be made of card glued with straw. Glue the shelter into place.

Food and Banquets

WORKING PEOPLE in Egypt were often paid in food. They ate bread, onions and salted fish, washed down with a sweet, grainy beer. Flour was often gritty and the teeth of many mummies show signs of severe wear and tear. Dough was kneaded with the feet or by hand, and pastry cooks produced all kinds of cakes and loaves.

BEAUTIFUL BOWLS
Dishes and bowls were often made of faience, a glassy pottery. The usual colour for this attractive tableware was blue-green or turquoise.

A big banquet for a pharaoh was a grand affair, with guests dressed in their finest clothes. A royal menu might include roast goose or stewed beef, kidneys, wild duck or tender gazelle. Lamb was not eaten for religious reasons, and in some regions certain types of fish were also forbidden. Vegetables such as leeks were stewed with milk and cheese. Egyptian cooks were experts at stewing, roasting and baking.

Red and white wines were served at banquets. They were stored in pottery jars marked with their year and their vineyard, just like the labels on modern wine bottles.

A FEAST FIT FOR A KING
New Kingdom noblewomen exchange gossip at a dinner party. They show off their jewellery and best clothes. The Egyptians loved wining and dining. They would be entertained by musicians, dancers and acrobats during the feast.

MAKE A CAKE

You will need: 200g stoneground flour, ¹/₂ tsp salt, 1tsp baking powder, 75g butter, 60g honey, 3tbsp milk, caraway seeds, bowl, wooden spoon, floured surface, baking tray.

1 Begin by mixing together the flour, salt and baking powder in the bowl. Next, chop up the butter and add it to the mixture.

2 Using your fingers, rub the butter into the mixture, as shown. Your mixture should look like fine breadcrumbs when you have finished.

3 Now add 40g of your honey. Combine it with your mixture. This will sweeten your cakes. The ancient Egyptians did not have sugar.

WOMAN MAKING BEER

This wooden tomb model of a woman making beer dates back to 2400BC. Beer was made by mashing barley bread in water. When the mixture fermented, becoming alcoholic, the liquid was strained off into a wooden tub. There were various types of beer, but all were very popular. It was said that the god Osiris had brought beer to the land of Egypt.

DRINKING VESSEL

This beautiful faience cup could have been used to drink wine, water or beer. It is decorated with a pattern of lotus flowers.

DESERT DESSERTS

An Egyptian meal could be finished off with nuts such as almonds or sweet fruits – juicy figs, dates, grapes, pomegranates or melons. Sugar was still unknown so honey was used to sweeten cakes and pastries.

pomegranates

dates

PALACE BAKERY

Whole teams of model cooks and bakers were left in some tombs. This was so that a pharaoh could order them to put on a good banquet to entertain his guests in the other world. Models are shown sifting, mixing and kneading flour, and making pastries. Most of our knowledge about Egyptian food and cooking comes from the food boxes and offerings left in tombs.

Egyptian pastries were often shaped in spirals like these. Other popular shapes were rings like doughnuts, and pyramids. Some were shaped like crocodiles!

4 Add the milk and stir the mixture until it forms a dough. Make your dough into a ball and place it on a floured board or surface. Divide the dough into three.

5 Roll the dough into long strips, as shown. Take the strips and coil them into a spiral to make one cake. Make the other cakes in the same way.

6 Now sprinkle each cake with caraway seeds and place them on a greased baking tray. Finish off by glazing the cakes carefully with a little extra honey.

7 Ask an adult to bake them in an oven at 180°C/Gas Mark 4 for 20 minutes. When they are ready, take them out and leave on a baking rack to cool.

Homes of Rich and Poor

Houses in India differed according to social class. Poor people made their homes out of mud, clay and thatch. Materials such as these do not last long, so few of these houses have survived. By about 600BC, wealthier people were building homes made of brick and stone. It is thought that people's caste determined not only the part of a town or city that they lived in, but also what colour they painted their homes. The Brahmins of Jodhpur in Rajasthan, for example, painted their houses blue.

A wealthy man's house of about AD400 had a courtyard and an outer room where guests were entertained. Behind this were the inner rooms where the women of the house stayed and where food was cooked. Beyond the house itself there were often gardens and fountains surrounded by an outside wall. Homes like this stayed much the same in design over many centuries.

Royal palaces were more elaborate. They had many courtyards and enclosures surrounded by numerous walls. These were to protect the king from beggars and servants who might make a nuisance of themselves. Unlike ordinary homes, palaces changed in design with each new wave of rulers.

DECORATED DOORSTEP
Pictures in chalk and rice powder were drawn on the doorsteps of houses. Over time, they came to signify prosperity and good luck. Making such drawings was one of 64 forms of art that a cultured person was expected to be able to do.

birdcage

mango leaves hung for good luck

water trough

courtyard

MOUNTAIN HOMES
These modern mountain homes made from mud and thatch continue a tradition that is thousands of years old. Unlike valley homes, they have to be well insulated for protection against the colder climate.

THE GOOD LIFE
Life in a rich man's household was divided between the inner area, where he slept and ate, and the outer regions, dominated by a courtyard where he entertained friends, read, listened to music and strolled in the garden. Here, salons (groups) of men would meet to discuss life and politics.

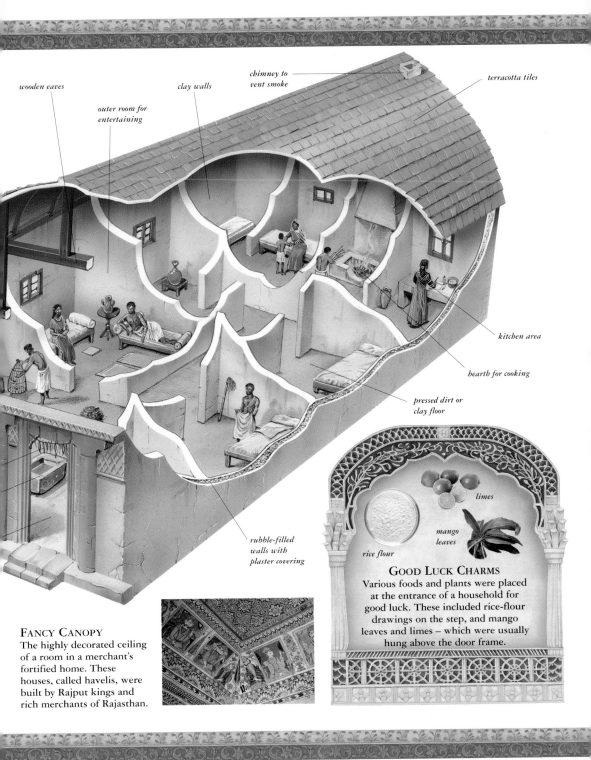

wooden eaves

outer room for
entertaining

clay walls

chimney to
vent smoke

terracotta tiles

kitchen area

hearth for cooking

pressed dirt or
clay floor

rubble-filled
walls with
plaster covering

FANCY CANOPY
The highly decorated ceiling
of a room in a merchant's
fortified home. These
houses, called havelis, were
built by Rajput kings and
rich merchants of Rajasthan.

limes

mango
leaves

rice flour

GOOD LUCK CHARMS
Various foods and plants were placed
at the entrance of a household for
good luck. These included rice-flour
drawings on the step, and mango
leaves and limes – which were usually
hung above the door frame.

Food and Drink

PEOPLE'S STAPLE (BASIC) FOOD depended on what they could grow. In the wetter areas of eastern, western, southern and central India, rice was the staple diet. In the drier areas of the north and north-west, people grew wheat and made it into different kinds of breads.

Apart from these staple foods, people's diets depended on their religion. Buddhists thought that killing animals was wrong, so they were vegetarians. Most Hindus, particularly the upper castes, became vegetarian too. Because they believed the cow was holy, eating beef became taboo (forbidden). When Islam arrived, it brought with it a new set of rules. Muslims are forbidden to eat pork, although they do eat other meat.

The Indians used a lot of spices in cooking, in order to add flavour and to disguise the taste of rotten meat. Ginger, garlic, turmeric, cinnamon and cumin were used from early times. Chillis were only introduced from the Americas after the 1500s.

CELESTIAL FRUITS
A heavenly damsel offers fruits in this stucco painting from Sri Lanka. From earliest times, Indians ate with their hands rather than with implements. Even so, there were rules to be followed. Generally, they could only eat with the right hand, taking care use just their fingers.

EVENING DELIGHTS
A princess enjoys an evening party in the garden. She listens to music by candlelight, and is served drinks, sweets and other foods.

MAKE A CHICKPEA CURRY

You will need: knife, small onion, 30ml vegetable oil, wok or frying pan, wooden spoon, 4cm piece fresh ginger root, 2 cloves garlic, ¼tsp turmeric, 450g tomatoes, 225g cooked chickpeas, salt and pepper, 2tbsp finely chopped fresh coriander, plus coriander leaves to garnish, 2tsp garam masala, a lime.

1 Chop the onion finely. Heat the vegetable oil in a wok. Fry the onion in the oil for two to three minutes, until it is soft. Ask an adult to help you.

2 Chop the ginger finely and add to the pan. Chop the garlic cloves and add them, along with the turmeric. Cook gently for another half a minute.

A RICH BANQUET
Babur, the founder of the Mughal Empire in India, enjoys a banquet of exotic fruits. Under the Mughals, a cuisine known as Mughlai developed. It became famous for its rich and sophisticated flavours.

turmeric

black mustard seeds   *cardamon*

THREE ESSENTIAL SPICES
Turmeric is ground from a root to give food an earthy flavour and yellow colour. Black mustard seed has a smoky, bitter taste. Cardamon – a favourite in northern India – gives a musky, sugary flavour suitable for both sweet and savoury dishes.

LEAF PLATE
In south India, banana leaves were (and are still) used as plates for serving and eating food. South Indian food uses more coconut than the north, and rice-flour is used in several dishes.

DAILY BREAD
Indians eat a variety of baked, griddled or fried breads, such as these parathas. In much of northern and western India, the staple food is wheat, served in the form of unleavened (flat) breads.

Chickpeas are a popular ingredient in Indian cooking. They have been grown in India for thousands of years.

3 Peel the tomatoes, cut them in half and remove the seeds. Then chop them roughly and add them to the onion, garlic and spice mixture.

4 Add the chickpeas. Bring the mixture to the boil, then simmer gently for 10-15 minutes, until the tomatoes have reduced to a thick paste.

5 Taste the curry and then add salt and pepper as seasoning, if it is needed. The curry should taste spicy, but not so hot that it burns your mouth.

6 Add the chopped fresh coriander to the curry, along with the garam masala. Garnish with fresh coriander leaves and serve with slices of lime.

Houses and Gardens

ALL BUILDINGS IN Chinese cities were designed to be in harmony with each other and with nature. The direction they faced, their layout and their proportions were all matters of great spiritual importance. Even the number of steps leading up to the entrance of the house was considered to be significant. House design in imperial China varied over time and between regions. In the hot and rainy south, courtyards tended to be covered for shade and shelter. In the drier climate of the north, courtyards were mostly open to the elements. Poor people in the countryside lived in simple, thatched huts. These were made from timber frames covered in mud plaster. They were often noisy, draughty and overcrowded. In contrast, the spacious homes of the wealthy were large, peaceful and well constructed. Many had beautiful gardens, filled with peonies, bamboo and wisteria. Some of these gardens also contained orchards, ponds and pavilions.

living quarters for owner's immediate family

reception

watch tower

main courtyard

INSIDE A HAN HOUSE

A wealthy family go about their daily lives in a Han dynasty (206BC–AD220) home. The house is built around several courtyards, with a garden at the side and a gatehouse leading out into the streets. A watchtower gives a view of the world outside. The main family building at the rear is two storeys high, but some homes had three or more floors.

MAKE A HOUSE

You will need: thick card, corrugated card, ruler, felt tip pen, scissors, glue and brush, 2.5cm x 0.5cm dowel (x2), masking tape, paint (white, grey, pink), thick and thin paintbrushes, water pot.

Base — 28cm, 24cm

Roof Piece A (x4) — 18cm, 7.5cm

Gate — 7cm, 4cm, 0.5cm

Roof Piece B (x2) — 18cm, 8cm

Wall A — 2cm, 3cm, 9cm, 14.5cm, 25.5cm

Wall C — 3cm, 1.5cm, 2cm, 3cm, 12.5cm, 11.5cm, 13.5cm

Wall E (x2) — 8.5cm, 16cm

Wall B (x2) — 3cm, 3cm, 25.5cm, 13.5cm, 17cm, 10.5cm

Wall D (x2) — 13.5cm, 8.5cm, 11cm, 8.5cm

Wall F (x2) — 9.5cm, 7cm, 9cm

Stairs — 4cm, 2cm, 5.5cm, 6.5cm

Floor (x2) — 15cm, 7.5cm

Roof Bracket (x 6) — 7.5cm, 4cm, 10.5cm

Bend wall F here

1 Cut out card pieces. Glue walls A, E and F (bend F first) to base. Add floor and stairs. Glue dowel under floor. Glue corrugated card to stairs.

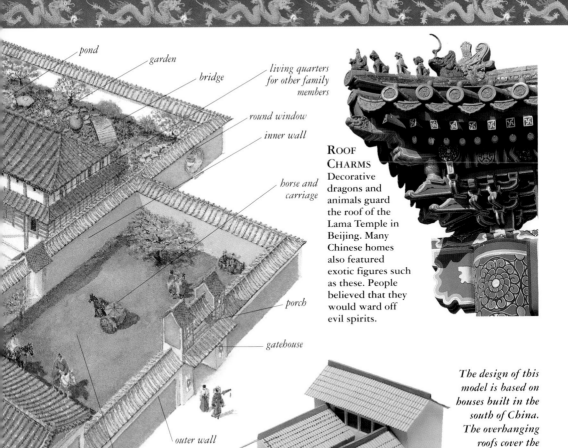

pond

garden

bridge

living quarters
for other family
members

round window

inner wall

horse and
carriage

porch

gatehouse

outer wall

outer courtyard

ROOF CHARMS

Decorative dragons and animals guard the roof of the Lama Temple in Beijing. Many Chinese homes also featured exotic figures such as these. People believed that they would ward off evil spirits.

The design of this model is based on houses built in the south of China. The overhanging roofs cover the courtyard. This helps to keep out rain and to provide shelter from the sun.

2 To assemble second side, repeat method described in step 1. If necessary, hold pieces together with masking tape while the glue dries.

3 Glue B walls to the sides of the base, C wall to the back and D walls to the front. Hold with tape while glue dries. Glue gate between D walls.

4 Assemble A roofs (x2) and B roof (x1). Fix brackets underneath. Glue corrugated card (cut to same size as roof pieces) to top side of roofs.

5 Fix a small piece of card over the gate to make a porch. Paint house, as shown. Use a thin brush to create a tile effect on the removable roofs.

Family Life

KONG FUZI (CONFUCIUS) taught that just as the emperor was head of the state, the oldest man was head of the household and should be obeyed by his family. In reality, his wife ran the home and often controlled the daily lives of the other women in the household.

During the Han dynasty (206BC–AD220) noblewomen were kept apart from the outside world. They could only gaze at the streets from the watchtowers of their homes. It was not until the Song dynasty (AD960–1279) that they gained more freedom. In poor households women worked all day, spending long, tiring hours farming, cooking, sweeping and washing.

For the children of poorer families, education meant learning to do the work their parents did. This involved carrying goods to market, or helping with the threshing or planting. The children of wealthier parents had private tutors at home. Boys hoping to become scholars or civil servants learned to read and write Chinese characters. They also studied maths and the works of Kong Fuzi.

CHINESE MARRIAGE
A wedding ceremony takes place in the late 1800s. In imperial China, weddings were arranged by the parents of the bride and groom, rather than by the couples themselves. It was expected that the couple would respect their parents' wishes, even if they didn't like each other!

LESSONS FOR THE BOYS
A group of Chinese boys take their school lessons. In imperial China, boys generally received a more academic education than girls. Girls were mainly taught music, handicrafts, painting and social skills. Some girls were taught academic subjects, but they were not allowed to sit the civil service examinations.

FOOT BINDING
This foot looks elegant in its beautiful slipper, but it's a different story when the slipper is removed. Just when life was improving for Chinese women, the cruel new custom of footbinding was introduced. Dancers had bound their feet for some years in the belief that it made them look dainty. In the Song dynasty the custom spread to wealthy and noble families. Little girls of five or so had their feet bound up so tightly that they became terribly deformed.

TAKING IT EASY

A noblewoman living during the Qing dynasty relaxes on a garden terrace with her children (c.1840). She is very fortunate as she has little else to do but enjoy the pleasant surroundings of her home. In rich families like hers, servants did most of the hard work, such as cooking, cleaning and washing. Wealthy Chinese families kept many servants, who usually lived in quarters inside their employer's home. Servants accounted for a large number of the workforce in imperial China. During the Ming dynasty (1368–1644), some 9,000 maidservants were employed at the imperial palace in Beijing alone!

RESPECT AND HONOUR

Children in the 1100s bow respectfully to their parents. Confucius taught that people should value and honour their families, including their ancestors. He believed that this helped to create a more orderly and virtuous society.

THE EMPEROR AND HIS MANY WIVES

Sui dynasty emperor Yangdi (AD581–618) rides out with his many womenfolk. Like many emperors, Yangdi was surrounded by women. An emperor married one woman, who would then become his empress, but he would still enjoy the company of concubines (secondary wives).

Fine Food

Chinese cooks today are among the best in the world, with skills gained over thousands of years. Rice was the basis of most meals in ancient China, especially in the south where it was grown. Northerners used wheat flour to make noodles and buns. Food varied greatly between the regions. The north was famous for pancakes, dumplings, lamb and duck dishes. In the west, Sichuan was renowned for its hot chilli peppers. Mushrooms and bamboo shoots were popular along the lower Chang Jiang (Yangzi River).

For many people, meat was a rare treat. It included chicken, pork and many kinds of fish, and was often spiced with garlic and ginger. Dishes featured meat that people from other parts of the world might find strange, such as turtle, dog, monkey and bear. Food was stewed, steamed or fried. The use of chopsticks and bowls dates back to the Shang dynasty (c.1600–1122BC).

THE KITCHEN GOD
In every kitchen hung a paper picture of the kitchen god and his wife. Each year, on the 24th day of the 12th month, sweets were put out as offerings. Then the picture was taken down and burned. A new one was put in its place on New Year's Day.

A TANG BANQUET
These elegant ladies of the Tang court are sitting down to a feast. They are accompanied by music and singing, but there are no men present – women and men usually ate separately. This painting dates from the AD900s, when raised tables came into fashion in China. Guests at banquets would wear their finest clothes. The most honoured guest would sit to the east of the host, who sat facing the south. The greatest honour of all was to be invited to dine with the emperor.

MAKE RED BEAN SOUP

You will need: measuring jug, scales, measuring spoon, 225g aduki beans, 3 tsp ground nuts, 4 tsp short-grain rice, cold water, tangerine, saucepan and lid, wooden spoon, 175g sugar, liquidizer, sieve, bowls.

1 Use the scales to weigh out the aduki beans. Add the ground nuts and the short-grain rice. Measure out 1 litre of cold water in the jug.

2 Wash and drain the beans and rice. Put them in a bowl. Add the cold water. Leave overnight to soak. Do not drain off the water.

3 Wash and dry the tangerine. Then carefully take off the peel in a continuous strip. Leave the peel overnight, until it is hard and dry.

THAT SPECIAL TASTE
Garlic has been used to flavour Chinese dishes and sauces for thousands of years. It may be chopped, crushed, pickled or served whole. Root ginger is another crucial Chinese taste. Fresh chilli peppers are used to make fiery dishes, while sesame provides flavouring in the form of paste, oil and seeds.

sesame   *root ginger*

SHANG BRONZEWARE FIT FOR A FEAST
This three-legged bronze cooking pot dates from the Shang dynasty (*c.*1600BC–1122BC). Its green appearance is caused by the reaction of the metal to air over the 3,500 years since it was made. During Shang rule, metalworkers made many vessels out of bronze, including cooking pots and wine jars. They were used in all sorts of ceremonies, and at feasts people held in honour of their dead ancestors.

BUTCHERS AT WORK
The stone carving *(shown right)* shows farmers butchering cattle in about AD50. In early China, cooks would cut up meat with square-shaped cleavers. It was then flavoured with wines and spices, and simmered in big pots over open fires until tender.

Most peasant farmers lived on a simple diet. Red bean soup with rice was a typical daily meal. Herbs and spices were often added to make the food taste more interesting.

4 Put the soaked beans and rice (plus the soaking liquid) into a large saucepan. Add the dried tangerine peel and 500ml of cold water.

5 Bring the mixture to the boil. Reduce the heat, cover the saucepan and simmer for 2 hours. Stir occasionally. If the liquid boils off, add more water.

6 Weigh out the sugar. When the beans are just covered by water, add the sugar. Simmer until the sugar has completely dissolved.

7 Remove and discard the tangerine peel. Leave soup to cool, uncovered. Liquidize the mixture. Strain any lumps with a sieve. Pour into bowls.

Family Life

FAMILIES IN ANCIENT JAPAN survived by working together in the family business or on the family land. Japanese people believed that the family group was more important than any one individual. Family members were supposed to consider the well-being of the whole family first, before thinking about their own needs and plans. Sometimes, this led to quarrels or disappointments. For example, younger brothers in poor families were often not allowed to marry so that the family land could be handed on, undivided, to the eldest son.

Daughters would leave home to marry if a suitable husband could be found. If not, they also remained single, in their parents' house.

Family responsibility passed down the generations, from father to eldest son. Japanese families respected age and experience because they believed it brought wisdom.

LOOKING AFTER BABY
It was women's work to care for young children. This painting shows an elegant young mother from a rich family dressing her son in a *kimono* (a robe with wide sleeves). The family maid holds the belt for the boy's *kimono*, while a pet cat watches nearby.

WORK
A little boy uses a simple machine to help winnow rice. (Winnowing separates the edible grains of rice from the outer husks.) Boys and girls from farming families were expected to help with work around the house and farmyard, and in the fields.

CARP STREAMER
You will need: pencil, 2 sheets of A1 paper, felt-tip pen, scissors, paints, paintbrush, water pot, glue, wire, masking tape, string, cane.

1 Take the pencil and one piece of paper. Draw a large carp fish shape on to the paper. When you are happy with the shape, go over it in felt-tip pen.

2 Put the second piece of paper over the first. Draw around the fish shape. Next, draw a border around the second fish and add tabs, as shown.

3 Add scales, eyes, fins and other details to both of the fishes, as shown above. Cut them both out, remembering to snip into the tabs. Paint both fishes.

PLAYTIME

These young boys have started two tops spinning close to one another. They are waiting to see what will happen when the tops touch. Japanese children had many different toys with which to play. As well as the spinning top, another great favourite was the kite.

TRADITIONAL MEDICINE

Kuzu and ginger are ingredients that have been used for centuries as treatments in traditional Japanese medicine. Most traditional drugs are made from vegetables. The *kuzu* and ginger are mixed together in different ways depending on the symptoms of the patient. For example, there are 20 different mixtures for treating colds. Ginger is generally used when there is no fever.

kuzu　　*ginger*

HONOURING ANCESTORS

A mother, father and child make offerings and say their prayers at a small family altar in their house. The lighted candle and paper lantern help guide the spirits to their home. Families honoured their dead ancestors at special festivals. At the festival of Obon, in summer, they greeted family spirits who had returned to earth.

4 Put the two fish shapes together, with the painted sides out. Turn the tabs in and glue the edges of the fish together, except for the tail and the mouth.

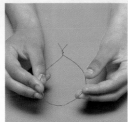

5 Use picture or garden wire to make a ring the size of the mouth. Twist the ends together, as shown Then bend them back. Bind the ends with masking tape.

6 Place the ring in the fish's mouth. Glue the ends of the mouth over the ring. Tie one end of some string on to the mouth ring and the other end to a garden cane.

Families fly carp streamers on Boy's Day (the fifth day of the fifth month) every year. One carp is flown for each son. Carp are symbols of perseverence and strength.

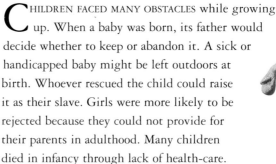

Growing Up

Children faced many obstacles while growing up. When a baby was born, its father would decide whether to keep or abandon it. A sick or handicapped baby might be left outdoors at birth. Whoever rescued the child could raise it as their slave. Girls were more likely to be rejected because they could not provide for their parents in adulthood. Many children died in infancy through lack of health-care.

Education was considered to be important for boys. Even so, it was usually only sons of rich families who received a complete schooling. They were taught a variety of subjects, including reading, music and gymnastics. Boys from poorer families often learnt their father's trade. Education in domestic skills was essential for most girls. A notable exception was in Sparta, where girls joined boys in hard physical training.

Bringing Up Baby
This baby is waving a rattle while sitting in a high chair. The chair also served as a potty. It might have had wheels on it to help the baby learn how to walk.

Bully Off
These two boys are playing a game similar to hockey. On the whole, team sports were ignored in favour of sporting activities where an individual could excel. Wrestling and athletics are two such examples. They were encouraged as training for war.

You are It
Two girls play a kind of t game in which the loser has to carry the winner. Girls had less free time than boys did. They were supposed to stay close to home and help their mothers with housework cooking and looking after the younger children.

Make a Scroll
You will need: 2 x 30cm rods of balsa wood, 5cm in diameter, 4 doorknobs, double-sided sticky tape, sheet of paper 30cm x 30cm, 1 x 7cm rod of balsa wood, 2cm in diameter, craft knife, paintbrush, PVA glue, ink powder.

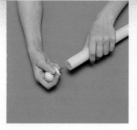

1 Carefully screw a door knob into either end of each 30cm rod of balsa wood, or ask an adult to do it for you. These are the end pieces of the scroll.

2 Cut two pieces of double-sided sticky tape 30cm long. Stick one piece of tape along the top of the paper and another along the bottom.

3 Wrap the top of the paper once around one of the pieces of balsa wood. Repeat this step again for the second piece at the bottom of the paper.

ACTION DOLL

The arms and legs on this terracotta figure are attached with cord so that the shoulders and knees can be moved. A doll such as this was a luxury item, which only a wealthy family could afford to buy for its children. Other popular toys were rattles and hoops.

THE ALPHABET

The first two of the Greek alphabet's 24 letters are called alpha and beta – these names give us the English word "alphabet".

ΑΒΓΔΕΖΗΘΙ

A BG D E Z e TH I

ΚΛΜΝΞΟΠΡΣ

K L M N X O P R S

ΤΥΦΧΨΩ

T U PH KH PS o

LIGHT OF LEARNING

This lamp takes the form of a teacher holding a scroll. Education involved learning poems and famous speeches from scrolls by heart. This was thought to help boys make effective speeches in court or public meetings. Good orators were always well thought of and could wield much influence.

A SECOND MOTHER

Greeks often hired wet nurses (on the left) to breastfeed their babies. Some nurses were forbidden to drink wine in case it affected their milk or made them so drunk that they might harm the baby.

Scrolls in ancient Greece were usually made from animal skin.

ΑΧΙΛΛΕΥΣ

4 Ask an adult to help you with this step. Take the 7cm piece of balsa wood, and use your craft knife to sharpen the end of it into a point.

5 Paint the nib of your pen with glue. This will stop the wood from soaking up the ink. Add water to the ink powder to make ink.

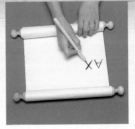

6 In the fact box above is a translation of the ancient Greek alphabet. Use the alphabet as a guide to write a word or some letters on the scroll.

7 The name of the god "Achilles" is written in ancient Greek on the scroll above. Ask a friend to translate it using the alphabet in the fact box.

House and Garden

garden

ONLY WEALTHY ROMANS could afford to live in a private house. A typical town house was designed to look inwards, with the rooms arranged round a central courtyard and a walled garden. Outside walls had few windows and these were small and shuttered. The front door opened on to a short passage leading into an airy courtyard called an *atrium*. Front rooms on either side of the passage were usually used as bedrooms. Sometimes they were used as workshops or shops, having shutters that opened out to the street.

The centre of the atrium was open to the sky. Below this opening was a pool, set into the floor, to collect rainwater. Around the atrium were more bedrooms and the kitchen. If you were a guest or had important business you would be shown into the *tablinium*. The dining room, or *triclinium*, was often the grandest room of all. The very rich sometimes also had a summer dining room, which looked on to the garden.

Houses were made of locally available building materials. These might include stone, mud bricks, cement and timber. Roofs were made of clay tiles.

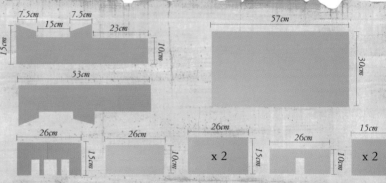

bedroom

*tablinium
(living room
and office)*

LOCKS AND KEYS
This was the key to the door of a Roman house. Pushed in through a keyhole, the prongs at the end of the key fitted into holes in the bolt in the lock. The key could then be used to slide the bolt along and unlock the door.

INSIDE A ROMAN HOME
The outside of a wealthy Roman's town house was usually quite plain, but inside it was highly decorated with elaborate wall paintings and intricate mosaics. The rooms were sparsely furnished, with couches or beds, small side tables, benches and folding stools. There were few windows, but high ceilings and wide doors made the most of the light from the open atrium and the garden.

MAKE A ROMAN HOME
You will need: pencil, ruler, thick card, scissors, PVA glue, paintbrushes, masking tape, corrugated cardboard, thin card, water pot, acrylic paints.

7.5cm 15cm 7.5cm 23cm 57cm

15cm 10mm 30cm

53cm

26cm 26cm 26cm 26cm 15cm

15cm 10cm x 2 15cm 10cm x 2

Cut out pieces of card following the measurements shown.

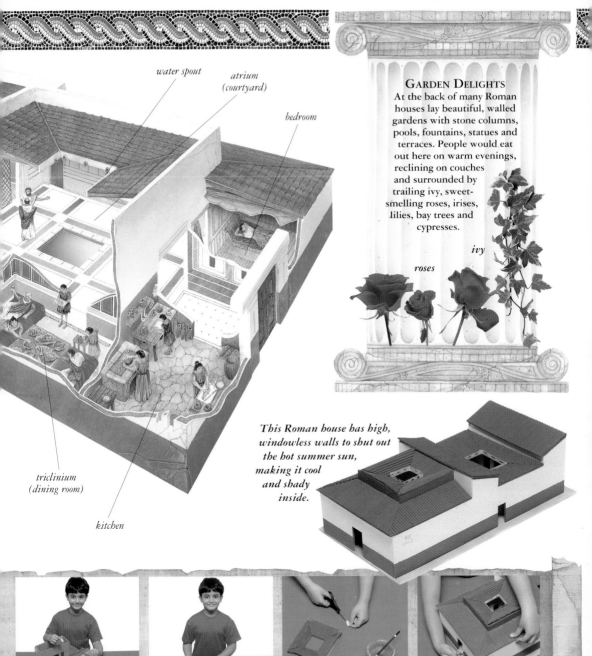

water spout

atrium
(courtyard)

bedroom

triclinium
(dining room)

kitchen

GARDEN DELIGHTS

At the back of many Roman houses lay beautiful, walled gardens with stone columns, pools, fountains, statues and terraces. People would eat out here on warm evenings, reclining on couches and surrounded by trailing ivy, sweet-smelling roses, irises, lilies, bay trees and cypresses.

ivy

roses

This Roman house has high, windowless walls to shut out the hot summer sun, making it cool and shady inside.

1 Cut out the pieces of thick card. Edge each piece with glue. Press the pieces together and reinforce with masking tape, as shown. You have now made the walls of your house.

2 Measure your model and cut out pieces of corrugated cardboard for the roofs. Stick them together with glue, as shown above. Paint the roofs red.

3 Rainwater running down the sloped atrium roof was directed into a pool below by gutters and water spouts. Make gutters from strips of thin card, with holes as spouts.

4 Paint the house walls as shown, using masking tape to get a straight line. Glue on the roofs. Why not finish off your Roman house with some authentic graffiti!

Family Occasions

THE FAMILY was very important to Romans. The father was the all-powerful head of the family, which included everyone in the household – wife, children, slaves, and even close relatives. In the early days of Rome, a father had the power of life and death over his children! However, Roman fathers were rarely harsh and children were much loved by both parents.

Childhood was fairly short. Parents would arrange for a girl to be betrothed at the age of 12, and a boy at 14. Marriages took place a few years later. Brides usually wore a white dress and a yellow cloak, with an orange veil and a wreath of sweetly-scented flowers. A sacrifice would be made to the gods, and everyone would wish the couple well. That evening, a procession with flaming torches and flute music would lead the newly-weds to their home.

Funerals were also marked with music and processions. By Roman law, burials and cremations had to take place outside the city walls.

HAPPY FAMILIES
This Roman tombstone from Germany shows a family gathered together for a meal. From the Latin inscription on it, we know that it was put up by a soldier of the legions, in memory of his dead wife. He lovingly describes her as the "sweetest and purest" of women.

MOTHER AND BABY
A mother tenderly places her baby in the cradle. When children were born, they were laid at the feet of their father. If he accepted the child into the family, he would pick it up. In wealthy families, a birth was a great joy, but for poorer families it just meant another mouth to feed. Romans named a girl on the 8th day after the birth, and a boy on the 9th day. The child was given a *bulla*, a charm to ward off evil spirits.

TOGETHERNESS
When a couple were engaged, they would exchange gifts as a symbol of their devotion to each other. A ring like this one might have been given by a man to his future bride. The clasped hands symbolize marriage. Gold pendants with similar patterns were also popular.

MOURNING THE DEAD

A wealthy Roman has died and his family have gone into mourning. Laments are played on flutes as they prepare his body for the funeral procession. The Romans believed that the dead went to Hades, the Underworld, which lay beyond the river of the dead. A coin was placed in the corpse's mouth, to pay the ferryman. Food and drink for the journey was buried with the body.

TILL DEATH US DO PART

A Roman marriage ceremony was rather like a present-day Christian wedding. The couple would exchange vows and clasp hands to symbolize their union. Here, the groom is holding the marriage contract, which would have been drawn up before the ceremony. Not everyone found happiness, however, and divorce was quite common.

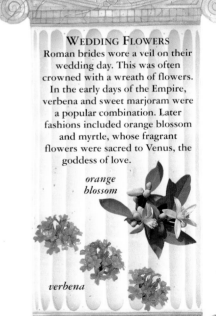

WEDDING FLOWERS

Roman brides wore a veil on their wedding day. This was often crowned with a wreath of flowers. In the early days of the Empire, verbena and sweet marjoram were a popular combination. Later fashions included orange blossom and myrtle, whose fragrant flowers were sacred to Venus, the goddess of love.

orange blossom

verbena

Lessons and Learning

OST CHILDREN in the Roman Empire never went to school. They learned a trade from their parents or found out about sums by trading on a market stall. Boys might be trained to fight with swords or to ride horses, in preparation for joining the army. Girls would be taught how to run the home, in preparation for marriage.

Wealthy families did provide an education for their sons and sometimes for their daughters, too. They were usually taught at home by a private tutor, but there were also small schools. Tutors and schoolmasters would teach children arithmetic, and how to read and write in both Latin and Greek. Clever pupils might also learn public speaking skills, poetry and history. Girls often had music lessons at home, on a harp-like instrument called a lyre.

INKPOTS AND PENS
Pen and ink were used to write on scrolls made from papyrus (a kind of reed) or thin sheets of wood. Ink was often made from soot or lamp-black, mixed with water. It was kept in inkpots such as these. Inkpots were made from glass, pottery or metal. Pens were made from bone, reeds or bronze.

WRITING IN WAX
This painting shows a couple from Pompeii. The man holds a parchment scroll. His wife is probably going through their household accounts. She holds a wax-covered writing tablet and a stylus to scratch words into the wax. A stylus had a pointed end for writing and a flat end for rubbing out.

A WRITING TABLET
You will need: sheets and sticks of balsa wood, craft knife, ruler, PVA glue, paintbrush, brown acrylic paint, water pot, modelling clay, work board, rolling pin, modelling tool, skewer, purple thread, pencil (to be used as a stylus), gold paint.

1 Use the craft knife to cut the balsa sheet into two rectangles 10cm x 22cm. The sticks of balsa should be cut into four lengths 22cm long and four lengths 10cm long.

2 Glue the sticks around the edges of each sheet as shown. These form a shallow hollow into which you can press the 'wax'. Paint the two frames a rich brown colour.

3 Roll out the modelling clay on a board and place a balsa frame on top. Use the modelling tool to cut around the outside of the frame. Repeat this step.

TEACHER AND PUPILS

This stone sculpture from Roman Germany shows a teacher seated between two of his pupils. They are reading their lessons from papyrus scrolls. Children had to learn poetry and other writings by heart. Any bad behaviour or mistakes were punished with a beating.

WRITING IT DOWN

Various materials were used for writing. Melted beeswax was poured into wooden trays to make writing tablets. Letters were scratched into the wax, which could be used again and again. Powdered soot was mixed with water and other ingredients to make ink for writing on papyrus, parchment or wood.

soot

melted beeswax

Roman numerals on papyrus

I	II	III	IV	V
1	2	3	4	5

VI	VII	VIII	IX	X
6	7	8	9	10

LETTERS IN STONE

Temples, monuments and public buildings were covered in Latin inscriptions, such as this one. Each letter was beautifully chiselled by a stonemason. These words are carved in marble. The inscription marked the 14th birthday of Lucius Caesar, the grandson of the Emperor Augustus.

4 Cut off about 1cm all around the edge of each modelling clay rectangle. This helps to make sure that the modelling clay will fit inside the balsa wood frame.

5 Carefully press the clay into each side – this represents the wax. Use the skewer to poke two holes through the inside edge of each frame, as shown.

6 Join the two frames together by threading purple thread through each pair of holes and tying it securely together. You have now made your tablet.

Paint the pencil gold to make it look as if it is made of metal. Use it like a stylus to scratch words on your tablet. Why not try writing in Latin? You could write CIVIS ROMANVS SVM, which means "I am a Roman citizen".

Life on the Farm

MEN, WOMEN AND CHILDREN were all expected to play their parts in running a Celtic farm. It seems likely that both men and women worked in the fields. Men usually did the ploughing, but the women probably carried out tasks such as weeding the crops. Everyone helped at harvest time because it was vital to gather the grain as soon as it was ripe. There were countless other jobs that needed doing to keep the farm running smoothly, such as combing sheep, caring for sick animals, milking cows, collecting eggs, repairing thatched roofs, and fetching water. Along with all the other tasks around the farm, parents had to teach their children the skills they would need in adult life. Many Celtic parents sent their sons and daughters to live in other households until they were grown up. This was a way of making close bonds of friendship between families and tribes and also taught the children extra skills.

WRAPPED AND WARM
This carved stone statue of a baby wrapped in a blanket was made in Celtic France. Compared with today, it must have been difficult for mothers and grandmothers to keep young children clean, warm, dry and out of danger on a busy farm.

LOCKED UP
Keys like these were used to lock wooden chests containing valuable goods, such as the family's marriage wealth. This was the bride's dowry (money or treasure given by her father) plus an equal amount given by the husband on their wedding day. In some Celtic lands, wives had the right to inherit this if they outlived their husbands.

MAKE A POT

You will need: paper, bowl, PVA glue, water, balloon, petroleum jelly, card, pair of compasses, pencil, ruler, scissors, masking tape, cardboard core from roll of adhesive tape, pin, red and black paint, paintbrushes.

1 To make papier-mâché, tear paper or newspaper up into small strips. Fill a bowl with 1 part PVA glue to 3 parts water. Add the paper pieces and soak.

2 Blow up the balloon and cover in petroleum jelly. Cover the balloon in a layer of papier-mâché mixture. Leave to dry, then slowly build up more layers.

3 On the card draw a circle 20 cm in diameter. Draw a second circle inside it 9 cm in diameter. Mark off a quarter of both circles. Cut the large circle out.

DYED IN THE WOOL

The Romans reported that the Celts liked patterned, brightly coloured clothes. Sheep's wool was often dyed before being woven into cloth. Dyes were made from flowers, bark, berries, leaves or lichen boiled together with salt, crushed rock or stale urine. The wool was soaked in this mixture then boiled again, or left to soak for several hours.

sheep's wool   lichen

HAND-WOVEN

Many Celtic women made clothes and blankets from sheep's wool from their own farms. First, they cleaned and sorted the wool, then they spun it into thread. The thread was woven on an upright loom. Heavy weights kept the warp (vertical) threads straight while the weft (horizontal) thread was passed in-between.

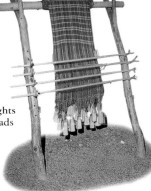

PEDESTAL POTS

Celtic women made simple pottery bowls and dishes for use at home. Wealthy Celtic people could also afford elegant vases and jugs like these pedestal pots (pots with feet), made by expert craftworkers in towns.

BUTTER BUCKET

Wooden buckets such as this were used on many Celtic farms, but few have survived. This one was found buried in a bog in northern Scotland. It contained butter. The damp, airless conditions in the bog had stopped the wood rotting.

Decorate your pedestal pot with a swirling pattern in typical Celtic style. The Celts liked bright colours – the pot that inspired this model was originally bright red.

4 Cut a quarter of the outer circle and all of the inner circle out, as shown. The outer circle will be the pot base. Stick the ends together with tape.

5 Use the cardboard inner from a roll of adhesive tape to make the stem of the pot. Attach it to the card base with masking tape.

6 Burst the balloon with a pin. Cut the top end of the pot off evenly. Attach the base and stem to the bottom of the pot with masking tape.

7 Paint the whole pot with red paint, including the stem and neck. Then add the Celtic pattern, as shown above, in black paint.

Food and Drink

FOOD WAS VERY IMPORTANT TO THE CELTS. They enjoyed eating and drinking, and were not ashamed of getting drunk, or of rowdy behaviour. They did not, however, approve of people getting too fat. Roman writers reported that Celtic warriors were ordered not to let out their belts, but to lose weight, when clothes around their waists became too tight! The Celts produced most of their own food on their farms. They needed to buy only items such as salt (used to preserve meat and fish), and luxury goods such as wine. They also hunted and fished for many wild creatures, and gathered wild fruits, nuts, herbs and mushrooms from meadows and forests. Celtic families were famous throughout Europe for their hospitality to strangers. It was their custom to offer food and drink to any visitor, and not to ask who they were or where they were from until the end of the meal.

HANGING CAULDRON
Meals for large numbers of people were cooked in a big cauldron. This bronze cauldron, iron chain and hook were made around 300BC in Switzerland. A cauldron could also be used for boiling water, heating milk to make cheese, or brewing mead.

CELTIC CASSEROLE
Meat, beans, grains and herbs were stewed in a covered clay pot. The pot could be placed directly on glowing embers or (as shown here) balanced on a hearthstone. This stone hearth, with a hollow pit for the fire, was found at an oppidum (Celtic town) in France.

MAKE SOME OATCAKES
You will need: 225 g oatmeal, 75 g plain flour, salt, baking soda, 50 g butter, water, bowl, sieve, wooden spoon, small saucepan, heat-resistant glass, board, rolling pin, baking tray, wire tray.

1 Preheat the oven to 220°C/425°F/Gas 7. Put 225 g of oatmeal into a large bowl. Add 75 g of plain flour. Sieve the flour into the bowl.

2 Next add 1 teaspoon of salt to the oatmeal and flour mixture. Mix all the ingredients in the bowl together well using a wooden spoon.

3 Add a quarter teaspoon of bicarbonate of soda (baking soda) to the oatmeal and flour mixture. Mix it in well and then put the bowl to one side.

GRINDING GRAIN

All kinds of grain were ground into flour using hand-powered querns (mills) like this one. The grains were poured through a hole in the top stone. This stone was then turned round and round. The grains became trapped and were crushed between the top and bottom stones, spilling out of the quern sides as flour.

FRUITS FROM THE FOREST

The Celts liked eating many of the same fruits and nuts that we enjoy today. However, they had to go and find them growing on bushes and trees. We know that the Celts ate fruit because archaeologists have found many seeds and pips on rubbish heaps and in lavatory pits at Celtic sites.

wild cherries

apples

hazelnuts

blackberries

OUT HUNTING

Celtic men went hunting and fishing for sport, and also as a way of finding food. This stone carving, showing a huntsman and his dogs chasing deer, was made around AD800 in Scotland. By then, Celtic power had declined, but many Celtic traditions persisted.

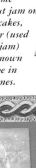

Enjoy your oatcakes plain, like the Celts did, or eat them with butter, cheese or honey. All these were favourite Celtic foods. Today, some people put jam on their oatcakes, but sugar (used to make jam) was unknown in Europe in Celtic times.

4 Next, melt the butter in a small saucepan over a low heat. Make sure that it does not burn. Add the melted fat to the oat and flour mixture.

5 Boil some water. Place a little of the water in a mug or heat-resistant glass. Gradually add the boiled water to the mixture until you have a firm dough.

6 Turn the dough out on to a board sprinkled with a little oatmeal and flour. Roll the dough until it is about 1 cm thick. Cut the dough into 24 circles.

7 Place the circles of dough on a greased baking tray. Bake in the oven for 15 minutes. Allow the oatcakes to cool on a wire tray before serving.

Family Life

EVEN IN MODERN ICELAND, everybody seems to know who is related to whom and where they live. In Viking times too, a large number of relatives played their part in the family, including grandparents, aunts and uncles. They were all very aware of family links, and loyalty was fierce. If one member of a family was harmed, then the other members of the family would seek revenge. This led to feuds – quarrels between one family and another that simmered on from one generation to the next. Feuds led to fights, theft and sometimes even as far as murder.

The father of the household had great power over other members of the family. If he thought a newborn baby was a weakling, he could leave it to die. When a Viking farmer died, his eldest son inherited the farm. The rest of the family would have to move away, and the younger sons

HELPING OUT
This reconstruction of a market stall in Jorvik shows a young lad helping his parents during a day's trading. Children often followed in the same trade as their parents. This boy would have learnt how to haggle over prices. He would also know how to weigh silver.

would have to find new land of their own to farm. Mothers were often strong, determined women who had great influence in the family. There was little schooling. Learning how to fight with a sword or use an axe was more important than reading and writing. As children grew up, they were expected to work hard and to help around the house. They were sometimes fostered out to families on other farms and had to work in return for their keep.

FAMILY MEMORIALS
The Vikings often put up memorial stones to honour relatives and friends when they died. This stone from Sweden was put up by Tjagan and Gunnar in loving memory of their brother Vader.

LIVING IN FEAR

Old tales tell how Vikings fought each other mercilessly during long, bitter feuds between families. Murderous bands might turn up at a longhouse by night, threatening to burn down the roof and kill everybody inside. Viking households also risked attack from local peoples or other raiders wherever they settled.

WANTING CHILDREN

A woman who wanted to make a good marriage and have children would pray to Frey, the god of love and fertility. On these gold foil charms from Sweden, Frey is shown with his beautiful wife Gerda. She was the daughter of a giant called Gymir.

GROWING UP

Children were expected to work hard in Viking times. Boys were taught farming, rowing and sailing. Girls were taught how to spin and weave, milk cows and prepare food. When all the daily tasks had been done, boys probably played games or went fishing. Viking girls may have spent some of their free time gathering berries and mushrooms.

BURIAL GRAVE

This skeleton belongs to a Viking woman from Iceland. Archaeologists have been able to tell how women lived in the Viking age by examining the goods placed in their graves. These were possessions for them to use in the next world.

Viking Women

VIKING WOMEN could not speak at the assembly, yet they had more independence than many European women of their day. They could choose their own husband, own property and be granted a divorce. At a wedding, both the bride and groom had to make their marriage vows before witnesses. Memorial stones show that many husbands loved their wives and treated them with respect.

Women certainly needed to be tough in the harsh landscapes and cold climates of countries such as Iceland or Greenland. It was their job to make woollen or linen clothes for the family, to prepare and cook food and to clean the home.

It was the women who usually had to manage the farm and its workers while their men were off raiding or trading. They never knew if their husbands, brothers and sons would return from the wars in the British Isles or be lost in a storm at sea.

WELCOME HOME
A woman in typical Viking dress welcomes a warrior returning from the wars. She has long hair tied back by a scarf and is wearing a pleated dress. The woman is a valkyrie, one of Odin's maidens in Valholl. This charm comes from Öland in Sweden.

A DAY'S WORK
In this reconstruction from Jorvik (York), a Viking woman goes out to fetch water from the well. Hissing geese beat their wings and scatter in her path. Women's work lasted from dawn till nightfall, with clothes to darn, poultry to look after, meals to cook and children to scold! Most women also spent several hours a day spinning and weaving wool into cloth to make clothes.

PRACTICAL BUT PRETTY

Viking women wore long tunics fastened by a pair of brooches. This Viking brooch was found in Denmark. It is over 1,000 years old and is made of gold. Women wore clothing that was both practical and comfortable.

GETTING READY

Before a wedding or a visit to the fair, a Viking woman may have smoothed or pleated her dress on a board like this one. A glass ball would have been used instead of an iron. This whalebone board comes from Norway.

WEAVING AT HOME

Viking looms were like this one. The warps, or upright threads, hang from a crossbar. The weft, or cross threads, pass between them to make cloth. Weaving was done by women in every Viking home.

THE NEW QUEEN

This picture shows Queen Aelfgyfu alongside her husband King Cnut, in England. Aelfgyfu was Cnut's second wife. They are placing a cross on an altar. Queens were the most powerful women in Scandinavian society.

BELOVED WIFE

This stone was put up by King Gorm as a monument to his wife. The inscription reads 'King Gorm made this memorial to his wife Thyri, adornment of Denmark'. The messages written on such stones show the qualities that Vikings admired most in women.

Native American Homes

During the winter months, the Inuit of the far north built their dome-shaped homes out of blocks of ice or with hard soil, wood and whale bones. Houses had to be adapted to their surroundings. Where wood was plentiful in the east, a variety of homes was built. The wikiup, or wigwam, was dome-shaped and made out of thatch, bark or hide, tightly woven across an arch of bent branches. Basic, rectangular thatched houses were built from a construction of chopped twigs covered with a mixture of clay and straw, or mud. Near the east coast, massive longhouses, up to 45m long, with a barrel-shaped roof, were made from local trees. Some tribes lived in different kinds of shelters depending on the season. The Plains Indians mostly lived in tipis (tents made of hide) or sometimes in earth lodges. The nearest to modern buildings were the homes of the Pueblos in the Southwest. These were terraced villages built of bricks made of mud. The Pueblo Indians also built round underground ceremonial chambers with a hidden entrance in the roof.

At Home
A Mandan chief relaxes with his family and dogs inside his lodge. Notice how a hole is cut in the roof to let out smoke from the fire and let fresh air in. Earth lodges were popular with Mandan and Hidatsa people on the Upper Missouri. The layout followed strict customs. The family would sleep on the south side, guests slept on the north. Stores and weapons were stored at the back. The owner of this home has his horse inside to prevent it from being stolen while the family is asleep.

Totem Pole
Totem poles were usually found in the far northwest of the United States. They were carved out of wood, often from the mighty thuja (red cedar) trees. Tall totem poles were erected outside the long plank houses of the Haida people. These homes were shared by several families. The poles were carved and painted to keep a record of the family histories of the people inside. They were also sometimes made to honour a great chief.

Homes on the Plains
The hides of around 12 buffaloes were used to cover a family tipi belonging to a Plains Indian. Tipi comes from a Siouan word meaning to dwell. Hides were sewn together and stretched over wooden poles about 8m high. When it became too hot inside, the tipi sides were rolled up. In winter, a fire was lit in the centre.

EARTH LODGES

Mandan Indians perform the Buffalo Dance in front of their lodges. These were built by using logs to create a dome frame, which was then covered over with tightly packed earth.

SMOOTH FINISH

Pueblo Indians of the Southwest built their homes from mud and/or stone. The buildings were then covered with adobe, which is made from a mixture of clay and straw. This was spread all over the walls like plaster. It dried hard and smooth.

clay

straw

LAYERS OF BRICK

This ruin was once part of a complex of buildings belonging to Pueblo Indians. Pueblo homes were often multi-storeyed with flat roofs. The floors were reached by ladders. Circular brick chambers were built underground. These were the kivas used for religious and ceremonial rites.

holes in the roof to let out smoke

THE LONGHOUSE

Iroquois people of the Woodlands built long wooden houses. The frame was made of poles hewn from tree trunks with cladding made from sheets of thick bark. Homes were communal. Many families lived in one longhouse, each with their own section built around an open fire.

sleeping platform

higher platform for storing food

Groups of longhouses were built together, sometimes inside a protective fence.

Family Life

ROLES WITHIN THE FAMILY were well-defined. The men were the hunters, protectors and tribal leaders. Women tended crops, made clothes, cared for the home and the sick, and prepared the food. The children's early days were carefree, but they quickly learned to respect their elders. From an early age young girls were taught the skills of craftwork and homemaking by their mothers, while the boys learnt to use weapons and hunt from the men. Girls as young as 12 years old could be married. Boys had to exchange presents with their future in-laws before the marriage was allowed to take place. At birth most children were named by a grandparent. Later, as adults, they could choose another name of their own.

BONES FOR DINNER
This spoon was carved from animal bone. For the early family there were no metal utensils. Many items were made from bone, tusks, antlers or horns. Bone was also used to make bowls.

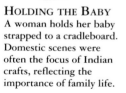

HOLDING THE BABY
A woman holds her baby strapped to a cradleboard. Domestic scenes were often the focus of Indian crafts, reflecting the importance of family life.

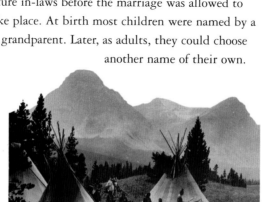

A DAY'S HUNTING
Blackfoot girls look on as men leave camp on a hunting trip. They are in search of bison. If the hunt is successful, the women will help skin the animals then stretch out the hide to dry. Buffalo skins were used to make tipi covers. Softer buckskin, from deer, was used for clothing.

MAKE A KATCHINA DOLL
You will need: cardboard roll, ruler, scissors, compasses, pencil, thick card, PVA glue, brush for glue, masking tape, paints in cream/yellow, green/blue red and black, paintbrush, water pot, red paper.

1 Take the cardboard roll and cut a section of about 4cm (or a third) off the top. This will form the head piece. The larger end will form the body.

2 Use the compass (or end of the cardboard roll) to draw four circles of 2cm radius on card. Then draw a smaller circle 1.5cm radius. Cut them all out.

3 Glue the larger circles to either end of both of the cardboard roll tubes. Leave to dry. Glue the smaller circle of card on top of one end of the longer roll.

ROLE PLAY

Children love to copy their elders, and this little Sioux girl is wearing an adult's large headdress. She is holding a favourite doll to pose for the picture. Playing with dolls taught girls about their future role as a carer. Boys enjoyed learning how to ride, shoot arrows and hunt.

FAMILY GATHERING

A Cree family in Canada enjoys a quiet evening around the fire. American Indian families were usually small as no more than two or three children survived the harsh life. However, a lodge was often home to an extended family. There could be two or three sisters, their families and grandparents under one roof.

Katchina dolls were made by the Hopi people to represent different spirits. This is the Corn katchina. Some parents gave the dolls to their children to help them learn about tribal customs.

BABY CARRIER

For the first year of its life, a baby would spend its time strapped to a cradleboard, such as this one influenced by the eastern Woodland tribes. It was also used by eastern Sioux, Iowa, Pawnee and Osage parents. A baby could sleep or be carried in safety while laced in its cradle, leaving the mother free to work. The board was strapped to the mother's back.

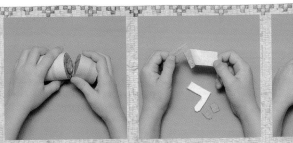

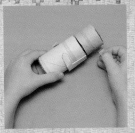

4 The smaller cardboard circle forms the doll's neck. Fix the small cardboard roll (the head) on top of the larger cardboard roll (the body) with glue.

5 Cut two small L-shapes from card to form the arms. Then cut two small ear shapes from the card. Cover these shapes with masking tape.

6 Glue the arms on to the body and the ears on to the sides of the head, so that they stick out at right angles. Paint the doll the colours shown above.

7 While the paint is drying, cut two small feather shapes from red paper. Glue these on to the top of the doll's head, so that they stick into the air.

Settlements and Homes

MOST ANCIENT ARCTIC GROUPS lived in small villages containing a few families at most. The villages were spread out over a wide area, so each group had a large territory in which to hunt. In winter, the Inuit, Saami and other groups lived in sturdy houses built partly underground to protect them from the freezing conditions above. In summer, or when travelling from place to place, they lived in tents or temporary shelters.

In Siberia and parts of Scandinavia, groups such as the Nenets did not settle in one place. Their homes were lightweight tents, called chums in Siberia, made up of a framework of wooden poles and covered with animal skins. These chums could withstand severe Arctic blizzards and kept everyone warm inside when temperatures were icy.

TENT LIFE
A Nenet herder loads up a sledge outside his family's chum in preparation for another day's travel across Siberia. Chums were convenient, light and easy to assemble and dismantle. Some Nenets still live in chums, as their ancestors have done for generations.

BUILDING MATERIALS
A deserted building made from stone and whale bone stands on a cliff in Siberia. Building materials were scarce in the Arctic. In coastal regions, people built houses with whale bones and driftwood gathered from the beach. Inland, houses were mainly built with rocks and turf.

ARCTIC DWELLING
This illustration shows a house in the Alaskan subarctic with a portion cut away to show how it is made. Houses such as this one were buried under the ground. People entered by ladder through the roof.

MAKE A NENET TENT
You will need: 3 blankets (two at 2 x 1.5 m and one at 1.2 x 1.2 m), tape measure, string, scissors, 10 bamboo sticks (nine 180 cm long and one 30 cm long), black marker, black thread, a log or stone.

1 Cut small holes 10 cm apart along the shorter sides of the two large blankets. Thread a piece of string through the holes and tie the string together.

2 Cut a 60-cm length of string. Tie the 30-cm-long stick and a black marker 55 cm apart. Use the marker to draw a circle on the smaller blanket.

3 Tie four bamboo sticks together at one end. Open out the sticks onto the base blanket. Place the sticks on the edge of the circle so they stand up.

BONY BUNKER

Whale bone rafters arch over the remains of a home in Siberia. Part of the house was often built underground. First, the builders dug a pit to make the floor. Then they built low walls of rocks and turf. Long bones or driftwood laid on top of the walls formed sturdy rafters that supported a roof made from turf and stones.

MAKING WINDOWS

An old stone and turf house stands in Arctic Greenland. Ancient peoples made windows by stretching a dried seal bladder over a hole in the wall. The bladder was thin enough to allow light through.

A tent covered with several layers of animal skins made an extremely warm Arctic home, even in the bitterly cold winter. The wooden poles were lashed together with rope.

4 Lean the five extra bamboo sticks against the main frame, placing the ends around the base circle. Leave a gap at the front for the entrance.

5 Tie the middle of the edge of the two larger blankets to the back of the frame, at the top. Make two tight knots to secure the blankets.

6 Bring each blanket round to the entrance. Tie them at the top with string. Roll the blankets down to the base so they lie flat on the frame.

7 Tie five one-metre lengths of thread along the front edge of the blanket. Pull these tight and tie to a log or stone to weigh down the base of the tent.

Seasonal Camps

CHEERFUL GLOW
An igloo near Thule in Greenland is lit up by the glow of a primus stove. The light inside reveals the spiralling shape of the blocks of ice used to make the igloo. Snow crystals in the walls scatter the light so the whole room is bathed in the glow. In the Inuit language, *iglu* was actually a word to describe any type of house. A shelter such as this one was called an *igluigaq*.

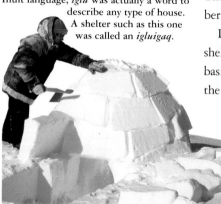

SUMMER is a busy time for Arctic animals and plants. The rising temperature melts the sea ice, and the oceans teem with tiny organisms called plankton. On land, the tundra bursts into flower. Insects hatch out and burrowing creatures, such as lemmings, leave their tunnels in search of food. Wild reindeer, whales and many types of birds migrate to the Arctic to feast on the plentiful supply of food.

The lives of Arctic peoples changed with the seasons too. In Canada, Alaska and Greenland, the Inuit left their winter villages and travelled to the summer hunting grounds. They hunted fish and sea mammals and gathered fruits and berries, taking advantage of the long, bright summer days.

During winter hunting trips, the Inuit built temporary shelters made of snow blocks, commonly called igloos. The basic igloo design was developed hundreds of years ago. It kept the hunters warm even in the harshest Arctic storm.

BUILDING AN IGLOO
An Inuk builds an igloo, using a long ice knife to cut large blocks of tightly packed snow. First, he lays a ring of ice blocks to make a circle up to 3 metres in diameter. Then, some of the blocks are cut to make them slope. As new blocks are added, the walls of the igloo begin to lean inwards, forming the familiar dome-shaped igloo. This method is exactly the same as the one used by his ancestors centuries ago.

MAKE A MODEL IGLOO
You will need: self-drying clay, rolling pin, cutting board, ruler, modelling tool, scissors, thick card (20 x 20 cm), pencil, water bowl, white paint, paint brush.

1 Roll out the self-drying clay. It should be around 8 mm thick. Cut out 30 blocks of clay; 24 must be 2 x 4 cm and the other 6 blocks must be 1 x 2 cm.

2 Cut out some card to make an irregular shape. Roll out more clay (8 mm thick). Put the template on the clay and cut around it to make the base of the igloo.

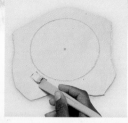

3 Mark out a circle with a diameter of 12 cm. Cut out a small rectangle on the edge of the circle (2 x 4 cm) to make the entrance to the igloo.

IGLOO VILLAGE

This engraving, made in 1871, shows a large Inuit village in the Canadian Arctic. Most Inuit igloos were simple, dome-like structures. The Inuit built these temporary shelters during the winter hunting trips.

THE FINAL BLOCK

An Inuit hunter carefully places the final block of ice onto the roof of his igloo. Ancient hunters used sharp ice knives to shape the blocks so that they fitted together exactly. Any gaps were sealed with snow to prevent the icy winds from entering the shelter.

A SNUG HOME

An Inuit hunter shelters inside his igloo. A small entrance tunnel prevents cold winds from entering the shelter and traps warm air inside. Outside, the temperature may be as low as −70°C. Inside, heat from the stove, candles and the warmth of the hunter's body keeps the air at around 5°C.

Inuit hunters built temporary shelters by fitting ice blocks together to form a spiralling dome structure called an igloo. Only firmly packed snow was used to make the building blocks.

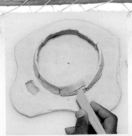

4 Stick nine large blocks around the edge of the circle. Use water to make the clay stick to the base. Cut across two rectangular blocks as shown above.

5 Using your modelling tool, carefully cut a small piece of clay from the corner of each of the remaining blocks as shown above.

6 Starting from the two blocks cut earlier, build up the walls, slanting each block in as you go. Use the six small blocks at the top. Leave a hole at the top.

7 Use the modelling tool to form a small entrance to the igloo behind the rectangle already cut into the base. When the clay has dried, paint the igloo white.

Arctic Children

MODEL IGLOO

An Inuit toddler plays with a model igloo at a nursery in the Canadian Arctic. The blocks of wood spiral upwards in the same way as the blocks of ice do in a real igloo, so the toy helps modern children to learn the ancient art of building igloos.

CHILDREN were at the centre of most Arctic societies. Inuit babies and younger children spent most of their time riding on their mother's back, nestled in a snug pouch called an *amaut*. The babies of many Arctic groups were named for a respected member of the community and their birth was celebrated with a huge feast. As children grew older, other members of the family helped the mother to bring up her child.

Today, most Arctic children go to school when they are young. However, the children of past generations travelled with their parents as the group moved to fresh reindeer pastures or new hunting grounds. Very young boys and girls were treated equally. As they grew up, however, children helped with different tasks and learned the skills that they would need later on in life. Boys learned how to hunt and look after animals. Girls learned to sew and cook and to work with animal skins.

BIRTHDAY FEAST

Traditional food is prepared at the birthday celebration of the young boy sitting at the table. Parents often named their newborn babies after people who had been respected in the community, such as a great hunter. The baby was thought to inherit that person's skills and personality.

FEEDING BIRDS TOY

You will need: self-drying clay, rolling pin, ruler, modelling tool, board, two toothpicks, white and brown paint, water pot, paint brush.

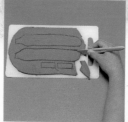

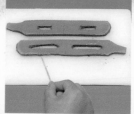

1 Roll out some of the clay into a 22 x 14 cm rectangle with a thickness of around 1 cm. Cut out two large paddles (18 x 3 cm) and two stalks (4 x 2 cm).

2 Cut two slots on paddle 1 (5 cm x 8 mm) and two on paddle 2 (2.5 cm x 8 mm). Use a toothpick to pierce a hole in the side of paddle 1 through these slots.

3 Roll out two egg shapes, each about 5 x 3.5 cm, in the palm of your hands. Make two bird heads and stick them to the egg-shaped bodies.

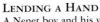

RIDING HIGH
One of the children in this old illustration is being carried in a special hood, called an *amaut*, high on the back of his mother's jacket. The second child is tucked inside her mother's sealskin boots. However, it was less common for a child to be carried in this way.

LENDING A HAND
A Nenet boy and his younger brother help to feed a reindeer calf that has lost its mother. Fathers taught their sons to handle animals from a very early age. Children were encouraged to look after the family's tame deer and dogs.

PLAYING WITH DOLLS
A doll dressed in a soft fleecy coat rests on a Nenet sledge in Arctic Russia. Many Arctic girls like to play with dolls, as children do around the world. Traditionally, the dolls' heads were carved from ivory. The doll in the picture, however, is made of modern plastic.

Some Arctic children had toys with moving parts, such as this model of two birds. Traditionally, the animals would have been carved from bone or ivory. The child pulled the paddles to make the birds bob up and down.

4 Stick the stalks you made earlier to the base of each bird's body. Using the toothpick, pierce a small hole through the stalk, close to the body.

5 Leave the clay bird to dry on its side. You will need to support the stalk with a small piece of clay to hold the bird upright as it dries.

6 Place the stalk of each bird in the slots in the paddles. Push a toothpick into the holes in the edge of paddle 1, through the stalks and out the other side.

7 Add two small pieces of clay to the bottom of each stalk to keep the birds in place. You can paint the toy once the clay has dried.

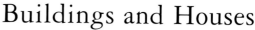

Buildings and Houses

PEOPLE LIVING in Mesoamerica used local materials for building. They had no wheeled transport, so carrying building materials long distances was quite difficult. Stone was the most expensive and longest-lasting building material. It was used for religious buildings, rulers' palaces and tombs. The homes of ordinary people were built more quickly and easily of cheaper materials, such as Sun-dried mud bricks, called adobe, or mud smeared over a framework of wooden poles. For strength, the walls might have stone foundations.

All Mesoamerican homes were very simply furnished. There were no chairs or tables, curtains or carpets – just some jars and baskets for storage and a few reed mats. Everyone, from rulers to slaves, sat and slept on mats on the floor. Most ordinary Aztec homes were L-shaped or built around a courtyard, with a separate bathroom for washing and a small shrine to the gods in the main room.

FAMILY HOME
This present-day Maya family home is built in traditional style, with red-painted mud-and-timber walls. It has one door and no windows. The floor is made of pounded earth. The roof, thatched with dried grass, is steeply sloped so the rain runs off it.

BURIED UNDERGROUND
Archaeologists have discovered these remains of houses at the Maya city of Copan. The roofs, walls and doors have rotted away, but we can still see the stone foundations. The houses are small and tightly packed together.

MAKE A MAYA HOUSE

You will need: thick card, pencil, ruler, scissors, glue, masking tape, terracotta plaster paste (or thin plaster coloured with paint), balsa wood strips, water pot, wide gummed paper tape, brush, short lengths of straw.

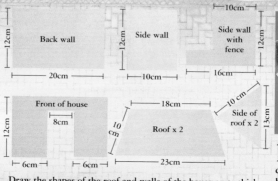

Back wall — 12cm, 20cm

Side wall — 12cm, 10cm

Side wall with fence — 10cm, 12cm, 16cm

Front of house — 12cm, 8cm, 6cm, 6cm

Roof x 2 — 10 cm, 18cm, 23cm

Side of roof x 2 — 10 cm, 13cm

Draw the shapes of the roof and walls of the house on to thick card, using the measurements shown. (Please note that the templates are not shown to scale.) Cut the pieces out.

1 Cut out a rectangle 25cm x 15cm from thick card for the base. Stick the house walls and base together with glue. Use masking tape for support.

STONEMASONS AT WORK
Mesoamerican masons constructed massive buildings using very simple equipment. Their wedges were made from wood, and their mallets and hammers were shaped from hard volcanic stone. Until around AD900 metal tools were unknown. Fine details were added by polishing stonework with wet sand.

PLASTER
Big stone buildings, such as temples, were often covered with a kind of plaster called stucco. This was then painted with ornate designs. Plaster was made by burning limestone and mixing it with water and coloured earth. By the 1400s, there was so much new building in Tenochtitlan that the surrounding lake became polluted with chemicals from the plaster making.

plaster

limestone

SKILFUL STONEWORK
This carved stone panel from the Maya city of Chichen-Itza is decorated with a pattern of crosses. It was used to provide a fine facing to thick walls made of rubble and rough stone. This wall decorates a palace building.

A Maya house provided a cool shelter from the very hot Mexican Sun, as well as keeping out rain.

2 Paint the walls and base with plaster paste. This will make them look like Sun-dried mud. You could also decorate the doorway with balsa wood strips.

3 Put the house on one side to dry. Take your roof pieces and stick them together with glue. Use masking tape to support the roof, as shown.

4 Moisten the wide paper tape and use it to cover the joins between the roof pieces. There should be no gaps. Then cover the whole roof with glue.

5 Press lengths of straw into the glue on the roof. Work in layers, starting at the bottom. Overlap the layers. Fix the roof to the house using glue.

Family Life

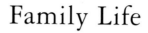

FAMILIES WERE very important in Maya and Aztec times. By working together, family members provided themselves with food, jobs, companionship and a home. Each member of a family had special responsibilities. Men produced food or earned money to buy it. Women cared for babies and the home. From the age of about five or six, children were expected to do their share of the family's work by helping their parents. Because family life was so important, marriages were often arranged by a young couple's parents, or by a matchmaker. The role of matchmaker would be played by an old woman who knew both families well. Boys and girls got married when they were between 16 and 20 years old. The young couple usually lived in the boy's parents' home.

Aztec families belonged to local clan-groups, known as *calpulli*. Each *calpulli* chose its own leader, collected its own taxes and built its own temple. It offered help to needy families, but also kept a close eye on how members behaved. If someone broke the law, the whole clan might be punished for that person's actions.

MOTHER AND SON
These Maya clay figures may show a mother and her son. Boys from noble families went to school at about 15. They learned reading, writing, maths, astronomy and religion.

PAINFUL PUNISHMENT
This codex painting shows a father holding his son over a fire of burning chillies as a punishment. Aztec parents used severe punishments in an attempt to make their children honest and obedient members of society.

SPICE
Hot, spicy chilli peppers were an essential part of many Maya and Aztec meals. In fact, the Aztecs said that if a meal lacked chillies, it was a fast, not a feast! Chillies were used in stews and in spicy sauces, and they were used in medicine too. They were crushed and rubbed on aching muscles or mixed with salt to ease toothache.

red chillies

dried chillies, preserved for winter use

green chillies

IXTILTON
This Aztec mask is made of a black volcanic stone called obsidian. It shows the god Ixtilton, helper of Huitzilopochtli, the Aztecs' special tribal god. Aztec legends told how Ixtilton could bring darkness and peaceful sleep to tired children.

HUSBAND AND WIFE
The bride and groom in this codex picture of an Aztec wedding have their clothes tied together. This shows that their lives are now joined. Aztec weddings were celebrated with presents and feasting. Guests carried bunches of flowers, and the bride wore special make-up with her cheeks painted yellow or red. During the ceremony, the bride and groom sat side by side on a mat in front of the fire.

GUARDIAN GODDESS
The goddess Tlazolteotl is shown in this codex picture. She was the goddess of lust and sin. Tlazolteotl was also said to watch over mothers and young children. Childbirth was the most dangerous time in a woman's life, and women who died in childbirth were honoured like brave soldiers.

LEARNING FOR LIFE
A mother teaches her young daughter to cook in this picture from an Aztec codex. The girl is making tortillas, which are flat maize pancakes. You can see her grinding the corn in a *metate* (grinding stone) using a *mano* (stone used with the metate). Aztec mothers and fathers trained their children in all the skills they would need to survive in adult life. Children from the families of expert craftworkers learned their parents' special skills.

An Inca House

A TYPICAL HOUSE in an Inca town such as Machu Picchu was built from blocks of stone. White granite was the best, being very hard and strong. The roof of each house was pitched at quite a steep angle, so that heavy mountain rains could drain off quickly. Timber roof beams were lashed to stone pegs on the gables, and supported a wooden frame. This was thatched with a tough grass called *ichu*.

Most houses had just one storey, but a few had two or three, joined by rope ladders inside the house or by stone blocks set into the outside wall. Most had a single doorway hung with cloth or hide, and some had an open window on the gable end.

Each building was home to a single family and formed part of a compound. As many as half a dozen houses would be grouped around a shared courtyard. All the buildings belonged to families who were members of the same *ayllu*, or clan.

MUD AND THATCH
Various types of houses were to be seen in different parts of the Inca Empire. Many were built in old-fashioned or in regional styles. These round and rectangular houses in Bolivia are made of mud bricks (adobe). The houses are thatched with *ichu* grass.

upper storey

inside hearth

courtyard

FLOATING HOMES
These houses are built by the Uru people, who fish in Lake Titicaca and hunt in the surrounding marshes. They live on the lake shore and also on floating islands made of matted *totora* reeds. Their houses are made of *totora* and *ichu* grass. Both these materials would have been used in the Titicaca area in Inca times. The reeds are collected from the shallows and piled on to the floor of the lake. New reeds are constantly added.

PICTURES AND POTTERY

Houses with pitched roofs and windows appear as part of the decoration on this pottery from Pacheco, Nazca. To find out about houses in ancient Peru, historians look at surviving towns and ruins, at housing styles still in use today and at old pictures and designs on objects.

SQUARE STONE, ROUND PEG

Squared-off blocks of stone are called ashlars. These white granite ashlars make up a wall in the Inca town of Pisaq. They are topped by a round stone peg. Pegs like these were probably used to support roof beams or other structures, such as ladders from one storey to another.

gable

roofbeam

roof peg

wall niche

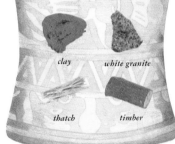

BUILDING MATERIALS

The materials used to build an Inca house depended on local supplies. Rock was the favourite material. White granite, dark basalt and limestone were used when possible. Away from the mountains, clay was made into bricks and dried hard in the sun to make adobe. Roof beams were formed from timber poles. Thatch was made of grass or reed.

clay

white granite

thatch

timber

BUILDING TO LAST

The Incas built simple, but solid, dwellings in the mountains. The massive boulders used for temples and fortresses are here replaced by smaller, neatly cut stones. See how the roof beams are lashed to the gables to support the thatch. Stone roofs were very rare, even on the grandest houses. Timber joists provide an upper storey. The courtyard is used just as much as the inside of the house for everyday living.

Married Life

WEDDINGS WERE SOME of the happiest occasions in an Inca village. They offered a chance for the whole community to take time off work. The day was celebrated with dancing, music and feasting. The groom would probably be 25 years of age, at which point he was regarded as an adult citizen, and his bride would be rather younger – about 20.

For the first year of the marriage, a couple did not have to pay any tax either in goods or labour. However, most of their lives would be spent working hard. When they were elderly, they would still be expected to help with household chores. Later still, when they became too old or sick to look after themselves, they received free food and clothes from the State warehouse. They would then be cared for by their clan or family group.

Not everyone was expected to get married. The *mamakuna* (virgins of the Sun) lived rather like nuns, in a special convent in Cuzco. They wove fine cloth and carried out religious duties. No men were allowed to enter the *mamakuna's* building.

WEDDING CLOTHES
An Inca nobleman would get married in a very fine tunic. This one is from the southern coast of Peru. Commoners had to wear simpler clothes, but couples were presented with free new clothes from the State warehouses when they married.

REAL PEOPLE
This jar from the Moche period is over 1,300 years old. Unlike the portraits on many jars, it seems to show a real person sitting down and thinking about life. It reminds us that ancient empires were made up of individuals who fell in love, raised children and grew old, just as people do today.

MARRIAGE PROSPECTS
Two Inca noble women are painted on the side of this *kero* (wooden beaker). Women of all social classes were only allowed to marry with the approval of their parents and of State officials. They were expected to remain married for life and divorce was forbidden. If either the husband or wife was unfaithful, he or she could face trial and might even be put to death.

A ROYAL MARRIAGE

A prince of the emperor's family marries in Cuzco. The scene is imagined by an artist of the 1800s. An emperor had many secondary wives in addition to his sister-empress. Between them they produced very many princes and princesses. Inca royal familes were divided by jealousy and by complicated relations, which often broke out in open warfare. The emperor ordered his officials to keep tight control over who married whom. His own security on the throne depended on it.

A HOME OF THEIR OWN

When a couple married, they left their parents' houses and moved into their own home, like this one at Machu Picchu. The couple now took official control of the fields they would work. These had been allocated to the husband when he was born. Most couples stayed in the area occupied by their own clan, so their relatives would remain nearby.

HIS AND HERS

The everyday lives of most married couples in the Inca Empire were taken up by hard work. Men and women were expected to do different jobs. Women made the *chicha* beer and did the cooking, weaving and some field work. Men did field work and fulfilled the *mit'a* labour tax in service to the Inca State. They might build irrigation channels or repair roads.

Work, Trade & Farming

Find out about the development of
money, crafts, farming methods, and
trading networks around the world

From Survival to Specialization

Our ancestors, the first humans, survived by hunting animals and gathering wild food for almost half a million years. They lived mostly as nomads, moving from place to place according to the season. They followed herds of animals or shoals of fish, and gathered nuts, berries and other wild plants. Their job was to survive – to find food, make tools and build shelters. They traded with other travelling people they encountered by exchanging useful goods they had for food, weapons or jewellery that they wanted or needed.

Around 12,000BC, the lifestyles of some hunter-gatherer communities began to change. They started to build permanent settlements close to reliable water supplies, to plant and harvest crops, and to domesticate (tame and use) animals. This change happened in different ways and at different times, from one part of the world to the other, depending on climate change and the local environment. By around 5000BC, there were farmers in almost every inhabited continent.

The development of farming

For early farmers, farming was difficult, back-breaking work. There were only stone and wood tools to work the soil. Seeds were scattered by hand.

The wild auroch was the ancestor of early farm cattle. Bones found by archaeologists show that early domesticated cattle were smaller than their wild relatives.

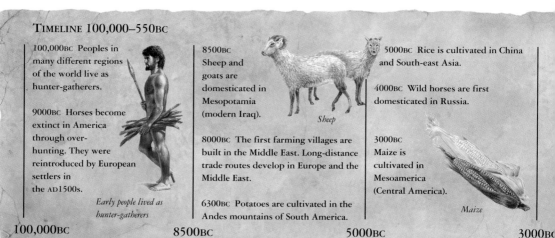

servants, scribes, stonemasons, soldiers, lawyers and officials. As towns grew bigger and more complex, so did people's needs. They needed comfortable homes, public buildings and good roads. They wanted doctors, teachers and priests to look after their physical, mental and spiritual wellbeing. Over the centuries, craftworkers, entertainers and artists also came to live and work alongside merchants and craftworkers in towns. The large numbers of people living there meant that they would find willing audiences and rich patrons to support them.

As towns grew into trading centres, rulers became responsible for governing the people and providing safe passage for merchants. Mesopotamian kings were often surrounded by other nobles who helped with running their empire or to celebrate a successful bull hunt!

In this section, you can compare how different working activities, from farming and building to textile production and craftwork, developed in different civilizations through time. You will be able to see which regions became known for particular industries and how trading links were first established between the Americas, Europe, the Middle East and South-east Asia.

Mesoamerican featherworkers wove feathers to make shields, headdresses, cloaks and fans. Mesoamerican craft goods were known for their beautiful designs.

surround it with chinampas (market-gardens) – where they grow fruit, vegetables and flowers.

1475 The Aztecs conquer the trading city of Tlatelolco, and make it the greatest market in Central America.

1540 The first European traders and missionaries arrive in Japan. European traders hope to find spices and rich silks. Missionaries want to spread the Christian faith throughout Japan.

1603 A long period of peace in Japan. Trade and towns expand, and new forms of art and entertainment, such as kabuki plays, develop.

1700–1900 European whaling expeditions and trading companies introduce great changes to traditional life for many people in the Arctic.

Portuguese sailor

Whale hunting in the Arctic

1475   1600   1700   1900

The First Crops

IN ABOUT 8000BC, people in the Near East began growing their own food for the first time. Instead of simply gathering the seeds of wild grasses, such as wheat and barley, they saved some of it. Then, the following year, they planted it to produce a crop. As they began to control their food sources, the first farmers found that a small area of land could now feed a much larger population. People began living in permanent settlements in order to tend their crops and guard their harvest. Over the next 5000 years, farming spread from the Near East to western Asia, Europe and Africa. Farming also developed separately in other parts of Asia around 6500BC and in America by about 7000BC.

The first farms were in hill country where wheat and barley grew naturally and there was enough rain for crops to grow. As populations increased, villages began to appear along river valleys, where farmers could water their crops at dry times of the year.

STONE TOOLS
This chipped flint is the blade of a hoe. It was used in North America between about AD900 and AD1200, but it is very similar to the hoes used by the first farmers to break up the soil. Rakes made of deer antlers were used to cover over the seeds. Ripe corn was harvested with sharp flint sickle blades.

SICKLE BLADE
This flint sickle blade has been hafted, or inserted, into a modern wooden handle. Ears of ripe corn would either have been plucked by hand or harvested with sickles such as this.

WILD RICE
Rice is a type of grass that grows in hot, damp areas, such as swamps. It was a good food source for early hunter-gatherers along rivers and coasts in southern Asia. The seeds were collected when ripe and stored for use when little other food was available. The grain could be kept for many months.

WORLD CROPS

The first plants to be domesticated, or farmed, were those that grew naturally in an area. Wheat and barley grew wild in the Near East. In India, China and southeast Asia, rice was domesticated by 5000BC and soon became the main food crop. Around 3000BC in Mexico, farmers grew maize, beans and squash. Farther south in the Andes mountains, the chief crops were potatoes, sweet potatoes and maize.

maize   *butternut squash*

GRINDING GRAIN

This stone quern, or hand-mill, is 6000 years old. It was used to grind grain into a coarse flour for making porridge or bread. The grain was placed on the flat stone and ground into flour with the smooth, heavy rubbing stone. Flour made in this way often contained quite a lot of grit. To make bread, water was added to the flour. The mixture was then shaped into flat loaves, which were baked in a clay oven.

STRAIGHT TRACK

Several tracks were built across marshes between 4000 and 2000BC in southern England. In some cases these were to link settlements to nearby fields of crops. The long, thin rods used to build the track above tell us a lot about the surrounding woodlands. The trees were coppiced, which means that thin shoots growing from cut hazel trees were harvested every few years.

A STEP UP

These terraced hillsides are in the Andes mountains of Peru. In mountainous areas where rainfall was high, some early farmers began cutting terraces, or steps, into the steep hillsides. The terraces meant that every scrap of soil could be used for planting. They prevented soil from eroding, or washing away. Farmers also used terracing to control the irrigation, or watering, of their crops. One of the first crops to be cultivated in Peru was the potato, which can be successfully grown high above sea level.

Taming Animals

ABOUT THE SAME time that people began to grow crops, they also started to domesticate (tame) wild animals. Wild sheep, goats, pigs and cattle had been hunted for thousands of years before people started to round them up into pens. Hunters may have done this to make the animals easier to catch. These animals gradually got used to people and became tamer. The first animals to be kept like this were probably sheep and goats around 8500BC in the Near East.

Herders soon noticed that larger animals often had larger young. They began to allow only the finest animals to breed, so that domestic animals gradually became much stronger and larger than wild ones. As well as four-legged livestock, chickens were domesticated for their eggs and meat. In South America, the llama was kept for its meat and wool, along with ducks and guinea pigs. In southeast Asia, pigs were the most important domestic animals.

WILD CATTLE
This bull is an aurochs, or wild ox. The aurochs was the ancestor of today's domestic cattle. Taming these huge, fierce animals was much harder than keeping sheep and goats. Wild cattle were probably not tamed until about 7000BC. The aurochs became extinct in AD1627. In the 1930s, a German biologist re-created the animal by crossing domesticated breeds such as Friesians and Highland cattle.

WILD HORSES
Horses were a favourite food for prehistoric hunter-gatherers. This sculpture of a wild horse was found in Germany. It was made around 4000BC. Horses also often appear in cave art. They were probably first domesticated in Russia around 4400BC. In America, horses had become extinct through over-hunting by 9000BC. They were reintroduced by European explorers in the AD1500s.

DINGOES AND DOGS

The dingo is the wild dog of Australia. It is the descendant of tame dogs that were brought to the country more than 10,000 years ago by Aboriginal Australians. Dogs were probably the first animals to be domesticated. Their wolf ancestors were tamed to help with hunting and, later, with herding and guarding. In North America, dogs were used as pack animals and dragged a *travois* (sled) behind them.

DESERT HERDERS

Small herds of wild cattle were probably first domesticated in the Sahara and the Near East. This rock painting comes from the Tassili n'Ajjer area of the Sahara Desert. It was painted in about 6000BC at a time when much of the Sahara was covered by grassland and shallow lakes. The painting shows a group of herders with their cattle outside a plan of their house.

LLAMAS

The llama was domesticated in central Peru by at least 3500BC. It was kept first for its meat and wool, but later it was also used for carrying food and goods long distances. A relative of the llama, the alpaca, was also domesticated for its wool.

GOATS AND SHEEP

Rock paintings in the Sahara show goats and sheep, among the first animals to be domesticated. They were kept for their meat, milk, hides and wool, and are still some of the most common farmed animals.

Trade and Distribution

STONE AGE PEOPLE did not use banknotes and coins for money, as we do. Instead they bartered, or exchanged, things. When one person wanted a bowl, for example, he or she had to offer something in exchange to the owner of the bowl – perhaps a tool or ornament. Towards the end of the Stone Age, however, people began to use shells or stone rings as a kind of currency.

Even isolated hunter-gatherer groups came into contact with each other and exchanged things, such as seashells, for tools or hides. With the beginning of farming around 8000BC in the Near East, however, long-distance exchange and a more organized trading system began. New activities, such as farming, pottery and weaving, needed specialized tools, so a high value was put on suitable rocks. In western Europe, flint mines and stone quarries produced axe blades that were prized and traded over great distances. Sometimes goods were traded thousands of kilometres from where they were made.

COWRIE SHELLS
Small, highly polished cowrie shells were popular as decoration for clothes and jewellery in prehistoric times. The shells have been found scattered around skeletons in burial sites, many of which are hundreds of kilometres from the coast. Later, cowrie shells were used as money in Africa and parts of Asia.

AXES
A good strong axe was a valuable commodity. It was particularly important for early farmers, who used it to chop down trees and clear land for crops. Axe heads made of special stone were traded over wide distances.

BURIED WITH WEALTH
This communal burial on the Solomon Islands in the Pacific Ocean shows the deceased accompanied by shells and ornaments. Shells have been used for money for thousands of years – in fact, for longer and over a wider area than any currency including coins. One hoard of shells, found in Iraq, was dated before 18,000BC.

STONE TRADE

During the neolithic period there was a widespread trade in stone for axes. At Graig in Clwyd, Wales (*left*), stone was quarried from the scree slopes and taken all over Britain. The blades were roughed out on site, then transported to other parts of the country, where they were ground and polished into axe heads. Rough, unfinished axes have been found lying on the ground at Graig.

FUR TRAPPER

A modern Cree trapper from the Canadian Arctic is surrounded by his catch of pine marten pelts. Furs were almost certainly a valuable commodity for prehistoric people, especially for hunter-gatherers trading with more settled farmers. They could be traded for food or precious items such as amber or tools.

SKINS AND PELTS

White Arctic fox skins are left to dry in the cold air. In winter, Arctic foxes grow a thick white coat so that they are well camouflaged against the snow. Furs like this have traditionally been particularly valuable to Arctic people, both for the clothing that makes Arctic life possible and for trading.

Banking and Trade

THE PEOPLE OF MESOPOTAMIA were very enterprising and expert business people. They travelled long distances to obtain goods they needed, importing timber, metal and semi-precious stones.

Around 2000BC, the Assyrians had a widespread, long-distance trading network in Anatolia (modern Turkey). The headquarters were in the northern Mesopotamian city of Ashur and the trade was controlled by the city government and by large family firms.

The head of a firm usually stayed in Ashur but trusted members of the family were based in Anatolian cities such as Kanesh. From here they conducted business on the firm's behalf, going on business trips around Anatolia, and collecting any debts or interest on loans. Deals were made on a credit basis, for the Assyrian families acted as money-lenders and bankers as well. On delivery, goods and transportation (the donkeys) were exchanged for silver, which was then sent back to Ashur. In about 2000BC, one Kanesh businessman failed to send back the silver, and the firm threatened to send for the police.

TROPHIES AND TAX
Carved ivory furniture, like this panel, and bronze bowls were often carried off after successful battles. There is little evidence of trade in Mesopotamia from 900 to 600BC. The Assyrian kings took anything they wanted from the people they defeated. They collected as tax whatever was needed, such as straw and food for horses.

TRADE TO KANESH
Donkeys or mules are still used to transport goods from one village to another in modern Iraq. When trade with ancient Turkey was at its peak, donkey caravans (lines) took large amounts of tin and textiles through the mountain passes to Kanesh. A typical load for one donkey would usually consist of 130 minas (about 65kg) of tin (which was specially packed and sealed by the city authorities), and ten pieces of woollen cloth.

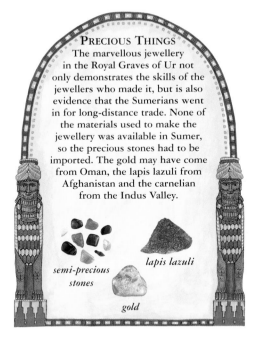

PRECIOUS THINGS
The marvellous jewellery in the Royal Graves of Ur not only demonstrates the skills of the jewellers who made it, but is also evidence that the Sumerians went in for long-distance trade. None of the materials used to make the jewellery was available in Sumer, so the precious stones had to be imported. The gold may have come from Oman, the lapis lazuli from Afghanistan and the carnelian from the Indus Valley.

semi-precious stones

lapis lazuli

gold

STRIKING A DEAL
Two merchants make a contract. One is agreeing to supply goods for a certain amount of silver, and the other is promising to pay by a certain date. The details of a deal were written on a clay tablet and impressed with the cylinder seals of the two men. Often a copy was made and put in a clay envelope. If there was a dispute about the deal later, the envelope would be broken and the agreement checked.

LETTERS FROM KANESH
The site of the trading settlement of Kanesh, where the Assyrians did an enormous amount of business, has been excavated. A great many clay tablets were found, many of them business letters. From these letters, it is clear that the Anatolian princes had the first pick of the goods brought by Assyrian merchants. They charged the merchants taxes on their donkey caravans. In return, the princes protected the roads and provided insurance against robbers.

CASH AND CARRY
There was no money in Mesopotamia, so goods were usually paid for in silver. Silver was measured in shekels and each shekel weighed about 8g. It was carefully weighed to make sure that the person paying gave an amount equal to the value of the goods bought.

Workers and Slaves

PLOUGHING WITH OXEN
This model figure from a tomb is ploughing the soil with oxen. The Egyptian farm workers' daily toil was hard. Unskilled peasant labourers did not own land and were paid little.

THE PHARAOHS may have believed that it was their links with the gods that kept Egypt going, but really it was the hard work of the ordinary people. It was they who dug the soil, worked in the mines and quarries, sailed the boats on the river Nile, marched with the army into Syria or Nubia, cooked food and raised children.

Slavery was not very important in ancient Egypt, but it did exist. Most of the slaves were prisoners who had been captured during the many wars that Egypt fought with their neighbours in the Near East. Slaves were usually treated well and were allowed to own property.

Many Egyptian workers were serfs. This meant that their freedom was limited. They could be bought and sold along with the estates where they worked. Farmers had to be registered with the government. They had to sell crops at a fixed price and pay taxes in the form of produce. During the season of the Nile floods, when the fields lay under water, many workers were recruited into public building projects. Punishment for those who ran away was harsh.

TRANSPORTING A STATUE
These workers are moving a huge stone statue on a wooden sled hauled by ropes. Many farm workers had to labour on large public building works, building dams or pyramids, each summer and autumn. Their food and lodging were provided, but they were not paid wages. Only the official classes were exempt from this service, but anyone rich enough could pay someone else to do the work for them. Slaves were used for really hard labour, such as mining and quarrying.

COUNTING GEESE

A farmer's flock of geese is counted out in this wall painting. Every other year, government officials visited each farm. They would count the animals to see how much tax had to be paid to the pharaoh. Taxes were paid in produce rather than money. The scribe on the left is recording this information. Scribes were members of the official classes and therefore had a higher position than other workers.

CARRYING BREAD

A woman carries a tray of loaves on her head. Most of the cooking in large houses and palaces was done by male servants, but baking bread was the job of the women. Baking was one of the few public jobs open to women.

GRINDING CORN

This model from 2325BC shows a female servant grinding wheat or barley grains into flour. She is using a stone hand-mill called a quern.

GIVE THAT MAN A BEATING

This tomb painting shows an official overseeing work in the fields. Unskilled peasant farmers were attached to an estate belonging to the pharaoh, a temple, or a rich landowner. Farmers who could not or would not give a large percentage of their harvest in rent and taxes to the pharaoh were punished harshly. They might be beaten, and their tools or their house could be seized as payment. There were law courts, judges and local magistrates in place to punish tax collectors who took bribes.

Farmers and Crops

HARVEST FESTIVAL
A priestess makes an offering of harvest produce in the tomb of Nakht. The picture shows some of the delicious fruits grown in Egypt. These included figs, grapes and pomegranates.

FARMING TOOLS
Hoes were used to break up soil that had been too heavy for the ploughs. They were also used for digging soil. The sharp sickle was used to cut grain.

sickle   *hoes*

THE ANCIENT EGYPTIANS called the banks of the Nile the Black Land because of the mud that was washed downstream each year from Central Africa. The Nile flooded in June, depositing this rich, fertile mud in Egypt. The land remained underwater until autumn.

By November the ground was ready for ploughing and then sowing. Seeds were scattered over the soil and trampled in by the hooves of sheep or goats. During the drier periods of the year, farmers dug channels and canals to bring water to irrigate their land. In the New Kingdom, a lifting system called the *shaduf* was introduced to raise water from the river. The success of this farming cycle was vital. Years of low flood or drought could spell disaster. If the crops failed, people went hungry.

Farm animals included ducks, geese, pigs, sheep and goats. Cows grazed the fringes of the desert or the greener lands of the delta region. Oxen were used for hauling ploughs and donkeys were widely used to carry goods.

TOILING IN THE FIELDS
Grain crops were usually harvested in March or April, before the great heat began. The ears of wheat or barley were cut off with a sickle made of wood and sharpened flint. In some well-irrigated areas there was a second harvest later in the summer.

MAKE A SHADUF
You will need: card, pencil, ruler, scissors, pva glue, masking tape, acrylic paint (blue, green, brown), water pot and brush, balsa wood strips, small stones, twig, clay, hessian, string .
Note: mix green paint with dried herbs for the grass mixture.

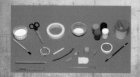

c = water tank

15cm   2.5 cm   3cm

5cm   5cm   9cm   c   9cm   9cm

23cm   23cm   *a*   23cm   3.5cm   2.5 cm

7cm   3.5 cm

4cm

16cm   *b*   23cm

5cm   5cm   23cm

15cm   8cm

a = irrigation channel & river bank   3.5cm   4cm

Cut out the cardboard shapes (a), (b) and (c) as shown.   7cm

b = river

1 Glue the edges of boxes (a), (b) and (c), as shown. Bind them with masking tape until they are dry. Paint the river (b) and the water tank (c) blue and leave to dry.

HERDING THE OXEN

This New Kingdom wall painting shows oxen being herded in front of a government inspector. Cattle were already being bred along the banks of the Nile in the days before the pharaohs. They provided milk, meat and leather. They hauled wooden ploughs and were killed as sacrifices to the gods in the temples.

NILE CROPS

The chief crops were barley and wheat, used for making beer and bread. Beans and lentils were grown alongside leeks, onions, cabbages, radishes, lettuces and cucumbers. Juicy melons, dates and figs could be grown in desert oases. Grapes were grown in vineyards.

leeks   onions

WATERING MACHINE

The *shaduf* has a bucket on one end of a pole and a heavy weight at the other. First the weight is pushed up, lowering the bucket into the river. As the weight is lowered, it raises up the full bucket.

The mechanical lifting system called the shaduf *was invented in the Middle East. It was brought into Egypt about 3,500 years ago.*

2 Paint the river bank with the green grass mixture on top, brown on the sides and the irrigation channel blue. Next, get the balsa strips for the frame of the shaduf.

3 Glue the strips together, supporting them with masking tape and a piece of card. When dry, paint the frame brown. Glue the stones onto the water tank.

4 Use a twig for the shaduf pole. Make a weight from clay wrapped in hessian. Tie it to one end of the pole. Make a bucket from clay, leaving two holes for the string.

5 Thread the string through the bucket and tie to the pole. Tie the pole, with its weight and bucket, to the shaduf frame. Finally, glue the frame to the bank.

Skilled Workers

In ancient Egypt, skilled workers formed a middle class between the poor labourers and the rich officials and nobles. Wall paintings and models show us craft workers carving stone or wood, making pottery, or working precious metals. There were boat builders and chariot makers, too.

Artists and craft workers could be well rewarded for their skills, and some became famous for their work. The house and workshops of a sculptor called Thutmose was excavated in el-Amarna in 1912. He was very successful in his career and was a favourite of the royal family.

Craft workers often lived in their own part of town. A special village was built at Deir el-Medina, near Thebes, for the builders of the magnificent, but secret, royal tombs. Among the 100 or so houses there, archaeologists found delivery notes for goods, sketches and plans drawn on broken pottery. Working conditions cannot always have been very good, for records show that the workers once went on strike. They may well have helped to rob the tombs that they themselves had built.

GLASS IN GOLD
This pendant shows the skill of Egyptian craft workers. It is in the form of Nekhbet the vulture, goddess of Upper Egypt. Glass of many colours has been set in solid gold using a technique called cloisonné. Like many other such beautiful objects, it was found in the tomb of Tutankhamun.

JEWELLERS AT WORK
Jewellers are shown at their work benches in this wall painting from 1395BC. One is making an ornamental collar while the others are working with precious stones or beads. The bow strings are being used to power metal drill bits.

A HIVE OF INDUSTRY

Skilled craftsmen are hard at work in this bustling workshop. Carpenters are sawing and drilling wood, potters are painting pottery jars, and masons are chiselling stone. A foreman would inspect the quality of each finished item.

DEIR EL-MEDINA

The stone foundations of the village of Deir el-Medina may still be seen on the west bank of the Nile. They are about 3,500 years old. In its day, Deir el-Medina housed the skilled workers who built and decorated the royal tombs in the Valley of the Kings. The men worked for eight days out of ten. The village existed for four centuries and was large and prosperous. Nevertheless, the workmen's village did not have its own water supply, so water had to be carried to the site and stored in a guarded tank.

SURVEYING THE LAND

Officials stretch a cord across a field to calculate its area. These men have been employed to survey an estate for government records.

bow drill

bradawl

smoothing stone

chisel

oil flask

drill

adze

axe

saw

pull saw

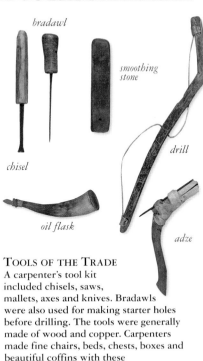

TOOLS OF THE TRADE

A carpenter's tool kit included chisels, saws, mallets, axes and knives. Bradawls were also used for making starter holes before drilling. The tools were generally made of wood and copper. Carpenters made fine chairs, beds, chests, boxes and beautiful coffins with these sophisticated tools.

Trade and Conquest

A T ITS HEIGHT, the Egyptian empire stretched all the way from Nubia to Syria. The peoples of the Near East who were defeated by the pharaohs had to pay tribute in the form of valuable goods such as gold or ostrich feathers. However, the Egyptians were more interested in protecting their own land from invasion than in establishing a huge empire. They preferred to conquer by influence rather than by war.

Egyptian trading influence spread far and wide as official missions set out to find luxury goods for the pharaoh and his court – timber, precious stones or spices. Beautiful pottery was imported from the Minoan kingdom of Crete. Traders employed by the government were called *shwty*. The ancient Egyptians did not have coins, and so goods were exchanged in a system of bartering.

Expeditions also set out to the land of Punt, probably a part of east Africa. The traders brought back pet apes, greyhounds, gold, ivory, ebony and myrrh. Queen Hatshepsut particularly encouraged these trading expeditions. The walls of her mortuary temple record details of them and also show a picture of Eti, the Queen of Punt.

WOODS FROM FARAWAY FORESTS
Few trees grew in Egypt, so timber for making fine furniture had to be imported. Cedarwood came from Lebanon and hardwoods such as ebony from Africa.

ALL THE RICHES OF PUNT
Sailors load a wooden sailing boat with storage jars, plants, spices and apes from the land of Punt. Goods would have been exchanged in Punt for these items. Egyptian trading expeditions travelled to many distant lands and brought back precious goods to the pharaoh. This drawing is copied from the walls of Hatshepsut's temple at Deir el-Bahri.

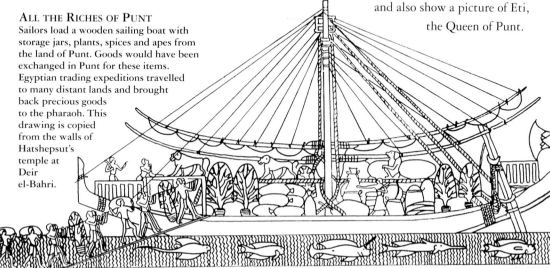

SYRIAN ENVOYS

Foreign rulers from Asia and the Mediterranean lands would send splendid gifts to the pharaoh, and he would send them gifts in return. These Syrians have been sent as representatives of their ruler, or envoys. They have brought perfume containers made of gold, ivory and a beautiful stone called lapis lazuli. The vases are decorated with gold and lotus flower designs. The pharaoh would pass on some of the luxurious foreign gifts to his favourite courtiers.

NUBIANS BRINGING TRIBUTE

Nubians bring goods to the pharaoh Thutmose IV – gold rings, apes and leopard skins. Nubia was the land above the Nile cataracts (rapids), now known as northern Sudan. The Egyptians acquired much of their wealth from Nubia through military campaigns. During times of peace, however, they also traded with the princes of Nubia for minerals and exotic animals.

EXOTIC GOODS

Egyptian craftsmen had to import many of their most valuable materials from abroad. These included gold, elephant tusks (for ivory), hardwoods such as ebony and softwoods such as cedar of Lebanon. Copper was mined in Nubia and bronze (a mixture of copper and tin) was imported from Syria.

ivory

ebony

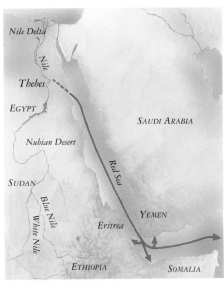

A WORLD OF TRADE

The Egyptians travelled over the Red Sea to the mysterious land of Punt. This modern map shows the voyage the traders would have made. No one is sure of the exact location of Punt, but it was probably present-day Somalia, Eritrea, Yemen or southern Sudan.

Chinese Society

THE RIVER VALLEYS AND COASTS of China have always been among the most crowded places on Earth. Confucius, with his love of social order, had taught that this vast society could be divided into four main groups. At the top were the nobles, the scholars and the landowners. Next came the farmers, including even the poorest peasants. These people were valued because they worked for the good of the whole nation, providing the vast amounts of food necessary to feed an ever-increasing population. In third place were skilled workers and craftsmen. In the lowest place of all were the merchants, because Confucius believed they worked for their own profit rather than for the good of the people as a whole. However, the way in which Chinese society rewarded these groups in practice did not fit the theory at all. Merchants ended up becoming the richest citizens, lending money to the upper classes. In contrast, the highly valued peasants often led a wretched life, losing their homes to floods and earthquakes or starving in years of famine.

TOP BRASS
This is what important government officials would have looked like in the early 1600s. The government employed several thousand high-ranking officials. The civil service was regarded as the most honourable and best rewarded profession. The entry examinations were open to all men. Even the poor could rise to ruling class if they passed the examinations.

THE IDEAL ORDER?
A government official tours the fields, where respectful peasants are happily at work. This painting shows an idealized view of the society proposed by Confucius. The district prospers and flourishes because everybody knows their place in society. The reality was very different – while Chinese officials led comfortable lives, most people were very poor and suffered great hardship. They toiled in the fields for little reward. Officials provided aid for the victims of famine or flood, but they never tackled the injustice of the social order. Peasant uprisings were common through much of Chinese history.

Working in the Claypits

The manufacture of pottery was one of imperial China's most important industries. There were state-owned factories as well as many smaller private workshops. The industry employed some very highly skilled workers, and also thousands of unskilled labourers whose job was to dig out the precious clay. They had to work very hard for little pay. Sometimes there were serious riots to demand better working conditions.

Dragon-backbone Machine

Peasants enlist the aid of machinery to help work the rice fields. The life of a peasant was mostly made up of back-breaking toil. The relentless work was made slightly easier by some clever, labour-saving inventions. The square-pallet chain pump (*shown above*) was invented in about AD100. It was known as the dragon-backbone machine and was used to raise water to the flooded terraces where rice was grown. Men and women worked from dawn to dusk to supply food for the population.

Life Behind a Desk

Country magistrates try to remember the works of Confucius during a tough public examination. A pass would provide them with a path to wealth and social success. A failure would mean disgrace. The Chinese civil service was founded in about 900BC. This painting dates from the Qing dynasty (1644–1912). There were exams for all ranks of officials and they were very hard. The classic writings had to be remembered by heart. Not surprisingly, candidates sometimes cheated!

Tokens of Wealth

Merchants may have had low social status, but they had riches beyond the dreams of peasants. They amassed wealth through money-lending and by exporting luxury goods, such as silk, spices and tea. The influence of the merchant class is reflected in the first bronze Chinese coins (*c.*250BC), which were shaped to look like knives, hoes and spades. Merchants commonly traded or bartered in these tools.

knife

hoe

Farming and Crops

EIGHT THOUSAND YEARS AGO most Chinese people were already living by farming. The best soil lay beside the great rivers in central and eastern China, where floods left behind rich, fertile mud. As today, wheat and millet were grown in the north. This region was mostly farmed by peasants with small plots of land. Rice was cultivated in the warm, wet south, where wealthy city-dwellers owned large estates. Pears and oranges were grown in orchards.

Tea, later to become one of China's most famous exports, was first cultivated about 1,700 years ago. Hemp was also grown for its fibres. During the 500s BC, cotton was introduced. Farmers raised pigs, ducks, chickens and geese, while oxen and water buffalo were used as labouring animals on the farm.

Most peasants used basic tools, such as stone hoes and wooden rakes. Ploughs with iron blades were used from about 600BC. Other inventions to help farmers were developed in the next few hundred years, including the wheelbarrow, a pedal hammer for husking grain and a rotary winnowing fan.

PIGS ARE FARM FAVOURITES
This pottery model of pigs in their sty dates back about 2,000 years. Pigs were popular farm animals, as they are easy to feed and most parts of a pig can be eaten. They were kept in the city as well as in rural country areas.

FEEDING THE MANY
Rice has been grown in the wetter regions of China since ancient times. Wheat and millet are grown in the drier regions. Sprouts of the Indian mung bean add important vitamins to many dishes.

mung beans

millet

rice

wheat

CHINESE TEAS
Delicate leaves of tea are picked from the bushes and gathered in large baskets on this estate in the 1800s. The Chinese cultivated tea in ancient times, but it became much more popular during the Tang dynasty (AD618–906). The leaves were picked, laid out in the sun, rolled by hand and then dried over charcoal fires.

WORKING THE LAND

A farmer uses a pair of strong oxen to help him plough his land. This wall painting found in Jiayuguan dates back to about 100BC. Oxen saved farmers a lot of time and effort. The Chinese first used oxen in farming in about 1122BC.

KEEPING WARM

This model of a Chinese farmer's lambing shed dates from about 100BC, during the Han dynasty. Sheepskins were worn for warmth, but wool never became an important textile for clothes or blankets in China.

HARVESTING RICE – CHINA'S MAIN FOOD

Chinese peasants pull up rice plants for threshing and winnowing in the 1600s. Farming methods were passed on by word of mouth and in handbooks from the earliest times. They advised farmers on everything from fertilizing the soil to controlling pests.

A TIMELESS SCENE

Peasants bend over to plant out rows of rice seedlings in the flooded paddy fields of Yunnan province, in southwest China. This modern photograph is a typical scene of agricultural life in China's warm and wet southwest region. Little has changed in hundreds of years of farming.

The Secret of Silk

For YEARS, THE CHINESE tried to stop outsiders finding out how they made their most popular export – *si*, or silk. The shimmering colours and smooth textures of Chinese silk made it the wonder of the ancient world. Other countries such as India discovered the secret of silk making, but China remained the producer of the world's best silk.

Silk production probably dates back to late Stone Age times (8000BC–2500BC) in China. Legend says that the process was invented by the empress Lei Zu in about 2640BC. Silkworms (the caterpillars of a type of moth) are kept on trays and fed on the leaves of white mulberry trees. The silkworms spin a cocoon (casing) of fine but very strong filaments. The cocoons are plunged into boiling water to separate the filaments, which are then carefully wound on to reels.

A filament of silk can be up to 1,200 metres long. Several filaments are spun together to make up thread, which is then woven into cloth on a loom. The Chinese used silk to make all kinds of beautiful products. They learned to weave flimsy gauzes and rich brocades, and they then wove elaborate coloured patterns into the cloth in a style known as *ke si*, or cut silk.

PREPARING THE THREAD
A young woman winds silk thread on to bobbins in the late 1700s. Up to 30 filaments of silk could be twisted together to make silk thread for weaving. The Chinese made ingenious equipment for spinning silk into thread. They also built looms for weaving thread into large rolls of fabric. By the 1600s, the city of Nanjing alone had an estimated 50,000 looms.

LOAD THOSE BALES!
Workers at a Chinese silk factory of the 1840s carry large bales of woven silk down to the jetty. From there the woven cloth would be shipped to the city. It might be used to make a costume for a lady of the court, or else exported abroad. The Chinese silk industry reached its peak of prosperity in the mid-1800s.

THE DRAGON ON THE EMPEROR'S BACK

A scaly red dragon writhes across a sea of yellow silk. The dragon was embroidered on to a robe for an emperor of the Qing dynasty. The exquisite clothes made for the Chinese imperial court at this time are considered to be great works of art.

WINDING SILK

Silk is being prepared at this workshop of the 1600s. The workers are taking filaments (threads) from the cocoons and winding them on to a reel. Traditionally, the chief areas of silk production in imperial China were in the east coast provinces of Zhejiang and Jiangsu. Silk was also produced in large quantities in Sichuan, in the west.

MAKING SILK

Raising silkworms is called sericulture. It can be a complicated business. The caterpillars have to be kept at a controlled temperature for a month before they begin spinning their silk cocoons.

adult silkmoth and cocoons

silkmoth larva

MAGIC MULBERRIES

These Han dynasty workers are collecting mulberry leaves in big baskets, over 2,000 years ago. These would have been used to feed the silkworms. Silkworms are actually the larva (caterpillars) of a kind of moth. Like most caterpillars, silkworms are fussy feeders and will only eat certain kinds of plant before they spin cocoons.

Markets and Trade

T HE EARLIEST CHINESE TRADERS used to barter (exchange) goods, but by 1600BC people were finding it easier to use tokens such as shells for buying and selling. The first metal coins date from about 750BC and were shaped like knives and spades. It was Qin Shi Huangdi, the first emperor, who introduced round coins. These had holes in the middle so that they could be threaded on to a cord for safe-keeping. The world's first paper money appeared in China in about AD900.

There were busy markets in every Chinese town, selling fruit, vegetables, rice, flour, eggs and poultry as well as cloth, medicine, pots and pans. In the Tang dynasty capital Chang'an (Xian), trading was limited to two large areas – the West Market and the East Market. This was so that government officials could control prices and trading standards.

CHINESE TRADING
Goods from China changed hands many times on the Silk Road to Europe. Trade moved in both directions. Porcelain, tea and silk were carried westwards. Silver, gold and precious stones were transported back into China from central and southern Asia.

raw silk   *Chinese tea*

CASH CROPS
Tea is trampled into chests in this European view of tea production in China. The work looks hard and the conditions cramped. For years China had traded with India and Arabia. In the 1500s it began a continuous trading relationship with Europe. By the early 1800s, China supplied 90 per cent of all the world's tea.

MAKE A PELLET DRUM
You will need: large roll of masking tape, pencil, thin cream card, thick card, scissors, glue and brush, 2.5cm x 30cm thin grey card, thread, ruler, needle, bamboo stick, paint (red, green and black), water pot, paintbrush, 2 coloured beads.

1 Use the outside of the tape roll to draw 2 circles on thin cream card. Use the inside to draw 2 smaller circles on thick card. Cut out, as shown.

2 Glue grey strip around one of smaller circles. Make 2 small holes each side of strip. Cut two 20cm threads. Pass through holes and knot.

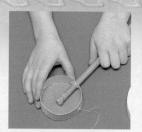

3 Use the scissors to make a hole in the side of the strip for the bamboo stick. Push the stick through, as shown. Tape the stick to the hole.

THE SILK ROAD

The trading route known as the Silk Road developed during the Han dynasty. The road ran for 11,000 kilometres from Chang'an (modern Xian), through Yumen and Kasghar, to Persia and the shores of the Mediterranean Sea. Merchants carried tea, silk and other goods from one trading post to the next.

FROM DISTANT LANDS

A foreign trader rides on his camel during the Tang dynasty. At this time, China's international trade began to grow rapidly. Most trade was still handled by foreign merchants, among them Armenians, Jews and Persians. They traded their wares along the Silk Road, bringing goods to the court at the Tang dynasty capital, Chang'an.

BUYERS AND SELLERS

This picture shows a typical Chinese market in about 1100. It appears on a Song dynasty scroll and is thought to show the market in the capital, Kaifeng, at the time of the New Year festival.

Twist the drum handle to make the little balls rattle. In the hubbub of a street market, a merchant could shake a pellet drum to gain the attention of passers by. He would literally drum up trade!

4 Tape the stick handle down securely at the top of the drum. Take the second small circle and glue it firmly into place. This seals the drum.

5 Draw matching designs of your choice on the 2 thin cream card circles. Cut out a decorative edge. Paint in the designs and leave them to dry.

6 Paint the bamboo stick handle red and leave to dry. When the stick is dry, glue the 2 decorated circles into position on top of the 2 smaller circles.

7 Thread on the 2 beads. Make sure the thread is long enough to allow the beads to hit the centre of the drum. Tie as shown. Cut off any excess.

Money and Trade

TRADE WITH DISTANT COUNTRIES has been important for India as far back as the ancient civilization of the Indus Valley. Later, trade routes became established up and down the length of India as well as with faraway places. Luxurious and precious goods such as spices, jewels, ebony, ivory and teak, were the main trade objects.

One highly prized import was silk from China.

The first coins in India, which had very simple designs, date from about 500BC. They were probably introduced from Persia (modern Iran). By about 100BC, coins were widely used to pay for goods and services in city markets and courts, but were less common in villages, where people simply exchanged goods, a practice called bartering. Bartering remained the normal way of trading for villagers until Mughal times.

Many different types of coins were produced, including square ones. Some had portraits of kings and gods on them, and were often inscribed with the name of the ruling king. They were made of gold, silver, copper and alloys (mixes of metals). Silver seems to have been frequently used for the best coins, but it sometimes ran short when it was in demand for making statues and ornaments instead.

HEADS OR TAILS

A king of the Gupta dynasty with a stringed instrument is shown on a gold coin dating from around AD350. Portraits of ancient Hindu royalty were most often to be found on coins. Few other likenesses, such as sculptures or carvings, exist of ancient Hindu kings.

SHELLING OUT

Cowrie shells were used as currency (money) in coastal areas. They were also used inland when precious metals were scarce. Cowries were the lowest form of coinage. In one court poem, it is said that King Ramapala of Bengal paid his army in cowrie shells.

TRADE ROAD FOR SILK

The Silk Road stretched for more than 7,000 km from China to Anatolia (modern Turkey) and beyond. It was a trade route for items such as silk, jewels and spices. Travellers along the Silk Road also brought new ideas. China and Central Asia were introduced to Buddhism, and many Chinese pilgrims came to India via the Silk Road.

TRADING IN SPICE

Saffron is an aromatic spice grown in north India. Sandalwood is a musky-smelling wood, produced mainly in the south. Both were rare and valuable, and were among India's most prized trading items. They were exported to the Middle East and to China.

saffron

ARAB TRADING VESSEL

This painting shows an Arab trading ship. The Indian Ocean became an important trading zone after the rise of Islam in the AD600s. The ocean linked the powerful empires of Arabia to eastern lands, including India, South-east Asia and China. Muslim merchants ruled the seas from the AD700s until the coming of the Europeans in the 1500s.

TRADERS TRAVELLING TOGETHER

A wall mural from Rajasthan shows a caravan (a group of merchants travelling together). Camels were ideal for travel in western Rajasthan, which is mostly desert. From Mughal times, Rajasthani merchants were famous throughout India for being good at making money,

COIN MEDALLION

A gold coin of the Mughal emperor Jahangir (1605-1627) has a portrait on one side and a Persian inscription on the other. This coin was probably not used in trade but was instead worn as a sign of the emperor's favour. Using coins as decorations – especially if the coins were made of gold – dates back to the AD100s. At that time Roman coins were made into jewellery in southern India.

Textiles and Printing

MAKING TEXTILES HAS ALWAYS BEEN an important activity in India. There are records of ancient Romans buying Indian cloth, so the textile trade must have been well established by then. As fabric does not last very well, there are few examples from before AD900, but sculptures show us the kinds of cotton cloth that were made. In Buddhist and Hindu sculptures, clothing is generally light and draws attention to the shape of the body.

India's textiles show a lot of different influences. Silk originally came from China, but from about AD100 it was produced in India and became an important Indian export. From about AD1100, Turkish and then Persian invaders introduced floral designs. Fine carpets also began to be made following Persian traditions and styles. Some places began to specialize in the production or sale of textiles. In Mughal times, silks and muslin (fine cotton fabric) were produced at Ahmedabad, Surat and Dhaka, while Kanchipuram, near Madras, became known for its fine silk saris. The Coromandel coast, Gujarat and Bengal all became textile export centres.

DRAPED GARMENT
A red sandstone figure from Jamalpur dates from about AD400, and shows the Buddha dressed in a fine muslin garment. Many clothes in ancient India were draped and folded rather than sewn.

SPINNING WHEEL
A woman sits at her spinning wheel. Weavers were important because Indian fabrics were in great demand in Europe.

MAKE A PRINTING BLOCK

You will need: paper, felt-tipped pen, scissors, halved raw potato, blunt knife, 20 x 15 cm piece of beige calico fabric, iron, scrap paper, paints, paintbrush.

1 Copy the pattern shown here on to a sheet of paper. You can invent your own Indian design, if you prefer. Carefully cut out the pattern.

2 Place the cut-out pattern on the cut surface of the halved potato. Draw around the outline of the pattern with a felt-tipped pen.

3 Use the knife to cut away the potato around the pattern. Your pattern should be raised about 5 mm above the rest of the potato half.

PERSIAN-STYLE CARPET

This fine, wool carpet is decorated with floral patterns. In Mughal times, many fine carpets like this one were produced in India. Carpet weaving was a skill learned in the north-west of India from Persian craftworkers.

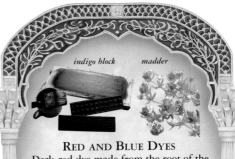

indigo block *madder*

RED AND BLUE DYES

Dark-red dye made from the root of the madder plant, and violet-blue dye made from the leaves of the indigo plant were used to dye textiles during Mughal times. Little is known about the way in which textiles were dyed in earlier times.

PRINTING COTTON CLOTH

A Punjabi man prints a pattern on to a length of cotton with a printing block. Dyes for cotton cloth were usually made from vegetables.

HUNTING COAT

This satin hunting coat has scenes and animals of the hunt embroidered on it in silk. It is typical of the type of dress worn by Mughal nobles.

Printing blocks were used in Mughal times to decorate fabric for festivals and other special occasions.

4 Ask an adult to help you to iron the fabric. Lay the ironed fabric on top of scrap paper. Apply paint to part of your printing block with a paintbrush.

5 Brush a different colour of paint on to your printing block. Give the block an even coat of paint that is not too heavy. Do not drench the block.

6 Press the printing block on to the fabric a few times. When the paint design starts to fade, apply more paint to the block with the paintbrush.

7 When the print design has dried, add some colourful details. Try out different colours on your printing block, or alter the pattern on the fabric.

Country Living

MOST GREEKS LIVED IN the countryside and worked as farmers. The mountainous landscape, poor, stony soil and hot, dry climate restricted what crops they could produce and which animals they could keep. Olive trees and bees flourished in these conditions. Olives provided oil and bees supplied honey (the main sweetener in food) and wax. Grain, such as barley, was difficult to grow, and the land used for its production had to be left fallow every other year to recover its fertility. Country people kept oxen to pull ploughs and drag heavy loads, and they used donkeys to carry goods to market. Rural areas also produced important materials used by city craftworkers. These included timber, flax for linen, horn and bone for glue, and leather.

Country life was hazardous, as droughts, floods, wolves and warfare threatened their livelihoods. Over the centuries, another problem developed. As forests were cut down for timber and fuel, soil erosion increased, leaving even less fertile land. The search for new agricultural land prompted the growth of Greek colonies along the shores of the Mediterranean and the Black Sea.

OLIVE HARVEST
This vase shows men shaking and beating the branches of an olive tree to bring down its fruit. Olives were eaten and also crushed to extract their oil. The oil was used for cooking, cleaning, as a medicine and a fuel for lamps.

FOOD FOR THE POT
Meat was obtained through hunting and the rearing of domesticated animals. Hunting was considered a sport for the rich, but it was a serious business for the poor, who hoped to put extra food on their tables. Simple snares, nets and slings were used to trap lizards and hares and to bring down small birds.

GONE FISHING
Many Greeks lived near water. The sea, rivers and lakes provided fish and shellfish which were their main source of protein. Fish was smoked or salted for future use. Always at the mercy of storms and shipwreck, fishermen prayed to the sea god Poseidon to save them.

PLOUGHING WITH OXEN

This terracotta figure from Thebes shows a farmer ploughing with two oxen. The plough was made of wood, but the part that broke up the earth was tipped with iron. Oxen were stronger and less expensive than horses, making them ideal for heavy work. When oxen died, they yielded hides for leather as well as horn, meat, sinew, which was used as twine, and fat that could be turned into candle tallow.

HARVEST GODDESS

Demeter was the goddess of grain and growth. She looked after plants, children and young people. The first part of her name *deme* is an ancient word for the Earth, the second part, *meter*, means "mother". Farmers believed that their success depended on uncontrollable forces such as the rain, the Sun, and diseases which attacked plants and livestock. Special prayers and sacrifices were made to Demeter to ask for her help in preventing such disasters. Festivals were held in honour of the goddess at crucial times during the harvest, before ploughing, when the corn began to sprout, and after it had been harvested.

SNACKS

Drying food was a good way of preserving it in a warm country like Greece. The Greeks ate raisins and dried apricots as a dessert or used them to sweeten other foods. Olives were another popular snack or appetizer.

raisins

olives

apricots

Travel and Trade

THE MOUNTAINOUS LANDSCAPE of ancient Greece was too rocky for carts or chariots, so most people rode donkeys or walked. Sea travel was simpler – the many islands of the eastern Mediterranean made it possible to sail from one port to another without losing sight of land. Merchant ships were sailed because they were too heavy to be rowed. Greek sailors had no compasses. By day they relied on coastal landmarks and at night they navigated by the stars. However, neither method was reliable. A sudden storm could throw a ship off course or cause it to sink. Merchant ships carried olive oil, wool, wine, silver, fine pottery and slaves. These goods were traded in return for wheat and timber, both of which were scarce in Greece. Other imported products included tin, copper, ivory, gold, silk and cotton.

Coinage
The gold coin above shows Zeus, ruler of the gods, throwing a thunderbolt. Coins were invented in Lydia (in present-day Turkey) around 635BC, and introduced to Greece soon afterwards. Before that, the Greeks had used bars of silver and rods of iron as money. Greek coins were also made of silver, bronze and electrum, a mixture of gold and silver.

Sea God
Poseidon was the god of the sea, horses and earthquakes. Sailors prayed and made sacrifices to him, hoping for protection against storms, fogs and pirates. He is usually pictured holding a trident, the three-pronged spear used by Greek fishermen. At the trading port of Corinth, the Isthmian Games were held every other year in honour of Poseidon.

Hard Currency
The first coins may have been used to pay mercenary soldiers, rather than for trading or collecting taxes. The earliest coins usually bore a religious symbol or the emblem of a city. Only later did they show the head of a ruler. The coin on the right shows the sea god Poseidon with his trident. The coin on the left bears the rose of Rhodes. Many countries that traded with the Greeks copied their idea of using coins for money.

SHIPPING

The ship on the right is a sail-powered merchantman. The criss-cross lines represent a wooden and rope catwalk stretched over the cargo, which was stored in an uncovered hold. Liquids such as wine and olive oil were transported and sold in long narrow pottery jars called amphorae, which could be neatly stacked in the hold. Merchant ships faced many dangers that could cause the loss of their cargo. Pirates and storms were the worst of these.

WEIGHING OUT

Most dry goods were sold loose and had to be weighed out on a balance such as this one. Officials would oversee the proceedings to ensure that they were fair. They stopped merchants and traders from cheating one another. In Athens, these officials were known as *metronomoi*. It was essential for merchants to familiarize themselves with the various systems of weights and measures used in different countries.

MARKET STALLS

The agora or market-place was to be found in the centre of every Greek town. Market stalls sold a wide range of goods including meat, vegetables, eggs, cheese and fish. Fish was laid out on marble slabs to keep it cool and fresh.

clams

 mussels

prawns

RIDING

Mountainous countryside made travelling overland difficult in Greece. The few roads that did exist were in poor condition. For most people, walking was the only way to reach a destination. Horses were usually only used by wealthy people to travel on. Donkeys and mules were used by tradesmen to transport large loads. Longer journeys were made by boat.

Arts and Crafts

THE ARTISTS AND CRAFTWORKERS of ancient Greece were admired for the quality of their work. They produced many objects of art including beautiful pottery, fine jewellery and impressive sculptures. Materials they worked with included stone, gold, silver, glass, gemstones and bronze. They also used wood, leather, bone, ivory and horn.

Most goods were made on a small scale in workshops surrounding the agora (market-place). A craftsman might work on his own or with the help of his family and a slave or two. In the larger workshops of such cities as Athens, slaves laboured to produce bulk orders of popular goods. These might include shields, pottery and metalwork which were traded around the Mediterranean Sea for a large profit.

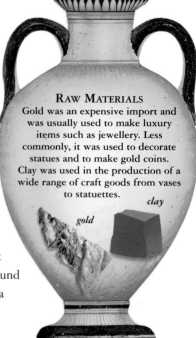

RAW MATERIALS
Gold was an expensive import and was usually used to make luxury items such as jewellery. Less commonly, it was used to decorate statues and to make gold coins. Clay was used in the production of a wide range of craft goods from vases to statuettes.

clay

gold

BULK PRODUCTION
Above is a terracotta mould, and on the right, the casting taken from it. Making a mould was a skilled and time-consuming task. Using a mould made it possible to produce items faster and more cheaply than carving each piece individually.

PANATHENAIC VASE
You will need: balloon, bowl, PVA glue, water, newspaper, two rolls of masking tape, black pen, scissors, sheet of paper 42cm x 30cm, card, pencil, paintbrush, black and cream paint.

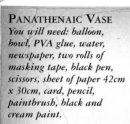

1 Blow up the balloon. Cover it with two layers of papier mâché (paper soaked in one part glue, two parts water). Leave on one side to dry.

2 Using a roll of masking tape as a guide, draw and cut out two holes at the top and bottom of the balloon. Throw away the burst balloon.

3 Roll the sheet of paper into a tube. Make sure that it will fit through the middle of the roll of masking tape. Secure the tube with tape or glue.

VASE PAINTING

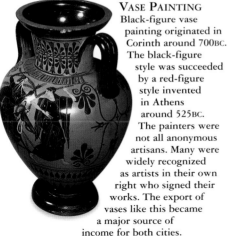

Black-figure vase painting originated in Corinth around 700BC. The black-figure style was succeeded by a red-figure style invented in Athens around 525BC. The painters were not all anonymous artisans. Many were widely recognized as artists in their own right who signed their works. The export of vases like this became a major source of income for both cities.

HOT WORK

In this scene two blacksmiths are forging metal at a brick furnace. Metal goods were expensive to produce. The furnaces themselves were fuelled by charcoal (burnt wood) which was expensive to make because wood was scarce in Greece. In addition, supplies of metal often had to be imported, sometimes from great distances. For example, tin, which was mixed with local copper to make bronze, was brought from southern Spain.

Amphorae like this one were given as prizes at the Panathenaic games. They were decorated with sporting images.

GOLD PECTORAL

This gold pectoral, made on the island of Rhodes in the 7th century BC, was meant to be worn across the breast. Gold was rare in Greece. It was usually imported at great expense from surrounding areas such as Egypt or Asia Minor.

4 Push the tube through the middle of the balloon. Tape into place. Push a roll of masking tape over the bottom of the paper tube and tape.

5 Tape the second roll of masking tape to the top of the tube. Make sure that both rolls are securely attached at either end of the paper tube.

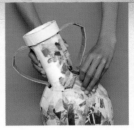

6 Cut two strips of card, 15cm long. Attach them to either side of the vase, as seen above. Cover the entire vase with papier mâché, and leave to dry.

7 Using a pencil, copy the pattern seen on the vase in the picture above on to your vase. Carefully paint in the pattern and leave on one side to dry.

Shopping – Roman Style

IN MOST LARGE TOWNS, shops spread out from the forum and along the main streets. Shops were usually small, family-run businesses. At the start of the working day, shutters or blinds would be taken from the shop front and goods put on display. Noise would soon fill the air as bakers, butchers, fishmongers, fruit and vegetable sellers all began crying out that their produce was the best and cheapest. Joints of meat might be hung from a pole, while ready-cooked food, grains or oils would be sold from pots set into a stone counter. Other shops sold pottery lamps or bronze lanterns, kitchen pots and pans or knives, while some traders repaired shoes or laundered cloth. Hammering and banging coming from the workshops at the back added to the clamour of a busy main street.

ROMAN MONEY
The same currency was used throughout the Roman Empire. Coins were made of gold, silver and bronze. Shoppers kept their money in purses made of cloth or leather or in wooden boxes.

HOW'S BUSINESS?
This carving shows merchants discussing prices and profits while an assistant brings out goods from the stockroom. Most Roman shops were single rooms, with stores or workshops at the back.

GOING TO MARKET
This is a view of Trajan's Market, which was a five-storey group of shops set into a hillside in Rome. Most Roman towns had covered halls or central markets like this, where shops were rented out to traders.

A ROMAN DELICATESSEN

About 1,700 years ago this was the place to buy good food in Ostia, the seaport nearest to Rome. Bars, inns and cafés were fitted with stone counters that were often decorated with coloured marble. At lunchtime, bars like this would be busy with customers enjoying a meal.

A BUTCHER'S SHOP

A Roman butcher uses a cleaver to prepare chops while a customer waits for her order. Butchers' shops have changed very little over the ages – pork, lamb and beef were sold, and sausages were popular, too. On the right hangs a steelyard, a metal bar with a pan like a scale, for weighing the meat.

DISHING IT UP

These are the remains of a shop that sold food. Set into the marble counter are big pottery containers, called *dolia*. These were used for displaying and serving up food, such as beans and lentils. They were also used for keeping jars of wine cool on hot summer days. The containers could be covered with wooden or stone lids to keep out the flies.

Fields and Animals

THE CELTS WERE FARMING PEOPLE. They cleared fields, planted crops, and bred livestock. They also fenced meadowland, and kept out their grazing animals until they had cut and dried the meadow grass to make hay for winter fodder. Celtic farmers used an iron-tipped plough, pulled by oxen, to turn over the soil in their fields and prepare the ground for planting. Seeds of grain were scattered by hand on ploughed land in early spring; the crops were ready to harvest in late summer or autumn. The Celts' most important crops were wheat, oats and barley, which could be cooked to make porridge, or ground into flour.

The most common farm animals were pigs, cattle, sheep and goats. As well as producing meat, animals provided milk (used to make butter and cheese), wool (spun and woven into cloth), and hides (which were tanned to make leather). The Celts also reared ducks and geese, for meat and eggs. Manure from animals and birds was used as a fertilizer on the fields. In some areas, Celtic farmers dug pits for marl (natural lime) to spread on their land. The lime helped to fertilize the soil and make the crops grow.

BULL'S EYE
Cattle were the most important farm animals in many Celtic lands. Oxen were used to pull carts and farm machinery, as well as for food. All cattle were highly prized, and were the main source of wealth for many farmers. Irish myths and legends tell of daring raids, when Celtic warriors galloped off to attack enemy farms and take all their cattle away.

SICKLE AND HOE
As crops grew in the fields, the Celtic farmer used a hoe (right) to keep the weeds down. The crops were harvested with a sharp, curved sickle (above). This hoe and sickle date from the La Tène era (450–50BC). Farming tools such as these were made by blacksmiths out of iron. Grain crops and hay were sometimes cut by an animal-drawn reaping machine, called a *vallus*. It was made of wood, with iron cutting blades.

WILD PAIR
The Celts raised pigs on their farms as well as hunting wild boar in the woods. Farm pigs were much smaller and thinner than European pigs today. They had long legs and stripy, bristly hair. In Celtic art, the boar was a symbol of great strength and power. These two little bronze pigs were probably made as offerings to the gods.

GRACEFUL GOOSE
This stone slab was carved in Scotland, in about AD450. It shows a goose turning round to preen its tail feathers. Geese were kept for their meat, eggs and grease. Goose grease could be rubbed on sore, dry skin, and used to soften and waterproof leather. Although the evidence has not survived, it seems likely that soft goose feathers were used to make warm bedding as well.

RARE BREED
The Soay sheep is an ancient breed that is rare today. It is similar to the sheep kept by Celtic farmers. It is small, nimble and hardy, and has long horns. Soay sheep do not need shearing because their fleece sheds naturally in summer. The wool can then be combed or pulled out by hand.

GOOD GRAINS
The Celts' main food crops were grains such as wheat, barley, oats and rye. These crops were harvested in late summer, heated over firepits to remove moisture, then stored in underground chambers (historians call them souterrains) for winter use.

wheat

barley

RIDGE AND FURROW
This photo shows ancient ridges and furrows in south-west England, created by later medieval farmers using techniques that may have been developed by the Celts. During the Celtic era, farmers began to move away from the light, well-drained soils on hilltops and slopes, clearing new fields on the heavier, wetter but more fertile land in valley bottoms. They invented heavy ploughs, fitted with wheels and pulled by oxen, to help cultivate this land.

Towns and Trade

FOR THOUSANDS OF YEARS, different parts of Europe have been linked by long-distance trade. Well-known trade routes followed great river valleys, such as the Rhine, the Rhône and the Danube, or connected small ports along the coast, from Ireland to Portugal. As early as 600BC, traders from the Mediterranean claimed to have sailed through the Straits of Gibraltar and over the sea to the British Isles. After around 200BC, the Celts began to build fortified settlements as centres of government, craftwork and trade. Some grew up around existing hill forts or villages, others occupied fresh sites. The Romans called them *oppida*, the Latin word for town. Some of the oppida were very large. For example, Manching, in southern Germany, covered about 380 hectares, and its protective walls were 7 kilometres long.

WINE LOVERS
The Celts were very fond of wine, which they imported from Italy. Roman wine merchants transported their wine in tall pottery jars called amphorae. You can see four amphorae at the back of this picture.

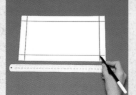

HIGH VALUE
Celts learned how to make coins from the Macedonians, who lived in eastern Europe. The first Celtic coins were made of pure precious metals, such as gold and silver. They were made by stamping a metal disc between two dies (moulds).

SMALL CHANGE
In the second half of the Celtic era, coins were made from alloys (mixed metals) containing only a small amount of silver or gold. These coins were much less valuable than the earlier, pure metal ones. This alloy coin was made around 100BC in western France.

MAKE A WAGON
You will need: white card, ruler, felt-tip pen, scissors, balsa wood, PVA glue, masking tape, sandpaper, pair of compasses, paint and paintbrush, drawing pins, bradawl, leather thong.

1 Take a piece of stiff white card measuring 29 cm x 16 cm. Using a ruler and felt-tip pen, draw lines 2 cm in from the edges of the card.

2 Make cuts in the corners of the card, as shown. Score along the lines and fold the edges up to make a box shape. This is the body of the wagon.

3 Take a piece of card 27 cm x 12 cm. Take two lengths of balsa wood 20 cm long. Stick them across the card, 4 cm in from the two ends.

GREAT BRITAIN

MAITHABY

KEMMELBERG

UXISAME

MOSOMAGUS **STEINSBURG**
CONTIOMAGUS
LUTETIA **RUBIN**
MELUN **HERAPE** **SEGODUNUM**
CENABUM **REINHEIM** **ZAVIST**
MT LASSOIS **HEUNEBERG**
CHASSEY **STUPAVA**

ROANNE **CHATILLON-SUR-GLANE**
LUGDUNUM

MANTUA
ESTE
SPINA
CELTIBERIA **FELSINA**
(SPAIN AND PORTUGAL) **MASSALIA**

KEY

- ⚭ Iron
- ⚬ Tin
- ⚱ Amphorae (wine jars)
- ⚱ Amber
- ⚱ Salt

LONG-DISTANCE TRADE

Celtic merchants and craftworkers in different lands were linked together by a network of trade routes, leading north-south and east-west. Few traders would have travelled the length of any one route. Instead, merchants from different countries met at trading towns. Valuable goods might be bought and sold several times along a trade route before reaching their final owner.

TOWN WALLS

Oppida were surrounded by strong, defensive walls. These ruined ones are from a Celtic town in southern France. Within the walls, houses, streets and craft workshops were laid out in well-planned, orderly rows.

This model wagon is based on the remains of funeral wagons found buried in Celtic graves. The Celts used wagons that were more roughly made but easier to steer for carrying heavy loads.

4 Take two sticks of balsa wood 26 cm and 11 cm long. Sand the end of the long stick to create a slight indent to fit against the short piece. Glue together.

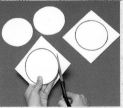

5 Use the pair of compasses to draw four circles, each 10 cm in diameter, out of card. Next, carefully cut the circles out, as shown above.

6 Glue the box on to the piece of card. Attach the wheels to the balsa wood shafts by pressing a drawing pin through the centre of each wheel.

7 Make two holes in the front of the wagon with a bradawl. Thread the leather thong through the holes and attach the steering pole. Paint the wagon silver.

Traders and Merchants

Tʜᴇ Vɪᴋɪɴɢs were second to none as successful merchants. Their home trade was based in towns such as Hedeby in Denmark, Birka in Sweden and Kaupang in Norway. As they settled new lands, their trading routes began to spread far and wide. They traded in countries as far apart as Britain, Iceland and Greenland.

In about 860 Swedish Vikings opened up new routes eastwards through the lands of the Slavs. They rowed and sailed down rivers such as the Volga, Volkhov and Dniepr. Viking sailors hauled their boats around rapids and fought off attacks from local peoples. Their trade turned the cities of Holmgard (Novgorod) and Könugard (Kiev) into powerful states. This marked the birth of Russia as a nation. Merchants crossed the Black Sea and the Caspian Sea. They travelled on to Constantinople (Istanbul), capital of the Byzantine empire, and to the great Arab city of Baghdad.

Viking warehouses were crammed with casks of wine from Germany and bales of woollen cloth from England. There were furs and walrus ivory from the Arctic and timber and iron from Scandinavia. Vikings also traded in wheat from the British Isles and rye from Russia.

COINS
These silver coins were found on the site of the market place in Birka. They were minted in Hedeby in around 800.

MAKING MONEY
This disc is a die – a metal stamp used to punch the design onto the face of a coin. The die is from York, in England. It has a sword design.

AMBER KING
This carved amber king is a piece from a board game. Amber was exported from the lands around the Baltic Sea. It was much prized by traders and by craftworkers, who also made it into jewellery and lucky charms.

MAKE A COIN AND DIE

You will need: self-drying clay and tool, board, rolling pin, scissors, compasses, pencil, paper, PVA glue, brush, paintbrush, bronze and silver paint.

1 Roll out a large cylinder of clay and model a short, thick handle at one end. This is the die. Leave it in a warm place to harden and dry.

2 Cut out a circle from paper. It should be about the same size as the end of the die. Draw a simple shape on the paper circle, with a pencil.

3 Cut the paper circle in half. Cut out the shape as shown. If you find it hard to cut the shape out, you could ask an adult to cut it out with a craft knife.

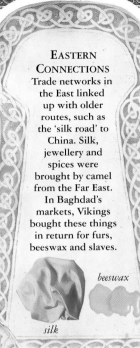

EASTERN CONNECTIONS

Trade networks in the East linked up with older routes, such as the 'silk road' to China. Silk, jewellery and spices were brought by camel from the Far East. In Baghdad's markets, Vikings bought these things in return for furs, beeswax and slaves.

beeswax

silk

walrus ivory — FINLAND
NORWAY — ASIA
SCOTLAND — timber — stones — SWEDEN — furs — slaves
IRELAND — wool — DENMARK — furs
ENGLAND — wheat — amber — slaves — POLAND
pottery — honey — glass — slaves
salt — FRANCE — silver — GERMANY — beeswax — silver
wine — jewellery — TURKEY — jewellery
EUROPE — silk — silk
wine — silk — silver

TRADE MAP

The routes taken by Viking traders fanned out south and east from their homelands. As well as exotic goods from the East, everyday items such as salt, pottery and wool were brought back from western Europe.

scales

weights

The first coins to show Viking kings were minted in England.

FAIR TRADING

Scales and weights were used by merchants wherever they traded. Some could be folded up inside a small case.

scales

4 Glue the cut paper pieces onto the end of the die with PVA glue. You may need to trim the pieces if they are too big to fit on the end.

5 Viking dies would have been made of bronze, or some other metal. Paint your die a bronze colour. Make sure you paint an even coat.

6 Roll out some more clay. Use the die to stamp an impression into the clay. This is your first coin. You can make as many as you like.

7 Use a modelling tool to cut around the edge of the coin. Make more coins from the left-over clay. Let the coins harden and dry and then paint them silver.

Markets and Trade

NORTH AMERICAN INDIANS HAD a long tradition of trading. The Hopewell civilizations of about AD200 brought metals and other materials to their centres around the Ohio valley. The Calusas in southern Florida had a vast trade network both inland and across the sea to the Bahamas and Cuba. Many people would travel long distances to buy and sell goods at a regular meeting place. Although some tribes used wampum (shell money), most swapped their goods. People from settled villages exchanged agricultural products such as corn and tobacco for buffalo hides, baskets or eagle feathers from nomadic tribes. When European traders arrived, in the 1600s, they exchanged furs and hides for horses, guns, cotton cloth and metal tools. Early trading posts such as the Hudson's Bay Company were built by whites. These posts were usually on rivers which could be reached easily by canoe.

WORDS OF A WAMPUM
A Mohawk chief, King Hendrick of the League of Five Nations, was painted on a visit to Queen Anne's court in London in 1710. He holds a wampum belt made from shells. These were made to record historic events such as the formation of the League of Five Nations of the Iroquois.

BASKETS FOR GOODS
Crafts, such as this Salish basket, were sometimes traded (or swapped) between tribes, and later with Europeans. Indians particularly wanted woollen blankets while European traders eagerly sought bison robes.

COLONIAL TRADERS
A native hunter in Canada offers beaver skins to colonial fur traders in 1777. They would probably have been made into beaver hats. Beaver fur was the most important item the Woodlands tribes had to trade, as competition between European nations for animal skins was fierce. This trade was partly to blame for many tribal conflicts. The Iroquois were renowned beaver hunters who ruthlessly guarded their hunting territory.

SHELL SHOW

A Plains Indian is holding up a wampum belt decorated with shells. The belts were usually associated with the Iroquois and Algonquian tribes who used them to trade, as currency, or to record tribal history. Quahog clam shells were strung together to make a long rectangular belt with patterns showing tribal agreements and treaties. Even colonists used them as currency when there were no coins around.

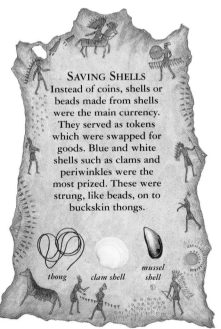

SAVING SHELLS

Instead of coins, shells or beads made from shells were the main currency. They served as tokens which were swapped for goods. Blue and white shells such as clams and periwinkles were the most prized. These were strung, like beads, on to buckskin thongs.

thong   clam shell   mussel shell

TRADING POSTS

North American Indians would gather in the Hudson's Bay trading post. In return for bringing in pelts (animal furs), the Indians would be given European goods. Many would be useful such as iron tools and utensils or coloured cloth. Firearms and liquor traded from around 1650 did the tribes more harm than good. As trade increased, more trappers and hunters frequented the trading posts. Later, some of the fur trade posts became military forts and attracted settlers who built towns around them.

Trappers and Traders

THE WHALING INDUSTRY boomed during the 1700s. By 1800, however, the Europeans had slaughtered so many whales that these great creatures faced extinction, and some Arctic groups lost a valuable source of food. As the whaling industry declined, so the European settlers looked for new ways to profit from the region. Merchants soon realized that the soft, warm fur of Arctic mammals, such as sea otters and Arctic foxes, would fetch a high price in Europe. They began to trade with local hunters for these skins, setting up trading posts across the Arctic. In every region, the fur trade was controlled by the nation that had explored there first. Russia controlled all trade rights in Alaska. A British business called the Hudson Bay Trading Company controlled business in Canada.

Arctic people came to rely on the Europeans for metal tools and weapons. Soon, many Arctic people abandoned their traditional life of hunting. Instead, they trapped mammals for their skins and sold them to the merchants. Arctic people entered troubled times. Diseases previously unknown in the region, such as measles and tuberculosis, killed thousands of men, women and children.

SKINS FOR SALE
The skins of seals and Arctic foxes hang in a store in northwest Greenland. During the 1800s and early 1900s, otter, fox and mink fur became extremely popular in Europe. European merchants made huge profits from the trade but paid Arctic hunters low rates for trapping these valuable animals.

CONVENIENCE FOOD
In 1823 this tin of veal was prepared for Sir William Parry's expedition to the Arctic. European explorers, whalers and traders introduced many foods to the native Arctic peoples. Local trappers exchanged furs for food and other goods. However, the result was that some Arctic people began to rely on the food provided by the traders rather than hunting for their own food.

TRADING POST
This engraving, made around 1900, shows an Inuit hunter loading his sledge with European goods at a trading post in the far north of Canada. By the mid-1800s, fortified posts such as this had sprung up all over Arctic North America. The British Hudson Bay Trading Company, which was set up in the 1820s, became very wealthy exploiting Canada's natural resources.

ADDICTED TO ALCOHOL

Whisky was traded throughout the Arctic in the 1800s and 1900s. As well as goods made from metal, merchants introduced European foods and stimulants, such as tea, coffee, sugar, alcohol and tobacco, to the Arctic. Many Arctic hunters became addicted to spirits, such as whisky. This made them rely even more heavily on traders who could supply them with alcohol.

SCRIMSHAW

During the long Arctic nights or lengthy voyages across the ocean, European explorers, sailors and traders occupied their time carving pictures and patterns on whale bones and walrus tusks. This work was called scrimshaw. First, a design was scratched in the bone or tusk using a knife or needle. Then the artist made the picture visible by rubbing soot into the scratches.

soot

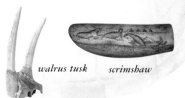

walrus tusk   scrimshaw

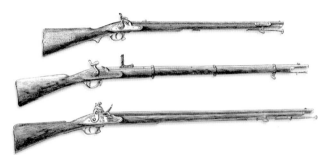

POWERFUL WEAPON

This engraving shows a number of British rifles from the 1840s. During the 1800s and 1900s, European guns and rifles transformed traditional hunting methods in the Arctic. Rifles were much more accurate than the old Arctic weapons, bows and arrows, and could target prey from a much greater distance.

GOODS FOR TRADE

Local hunters trade with Europeans in a local store in this engraving. Hundreds of metal tools and weapons were traded by Europeans in the Arctic, most often for animal skins. European merchants also bartered rifles, saws, knives, drills, axes and needles. The Inuit and other Arctic groups soon came to depend on these valuable tools and weapons.

Farming

PEOPLE LIVING in different regions of Mesoamerica used various methods to cultivate their land. Farmers in the rainforests grew maize, beans and pumpkins in fields they cleared by slashing and burning. They cut down thick, tangled bushes and vines, leaving the tallest trees standing. Then they burned all the chopped-down bushes and planted seeds in the ashes. But the soil was only fertile for a few years. The fields were left to turn back into forest, and new ones were cleared. Maya farmers also grew crops in raised fields. These were plots of land along the edge of rivers and streams, heaped up with rich, fertile silt dug from the riverbed.

Aztec farmers planted maize wherever they could, on steep rocky hillsides and the flat valley floor. But they grew their biggest crops of fruit, flowers and vegetables in gardens called *chinampas*. These were reclaimed from the marshy shallows along the shores of Lake Texcoco and around the island city of Tenochtitlan.

MAIZE GOD
This stone statue shows Yum Caax (Lord of the Forest Bushes), the Maya god of maize. It was found at Copan. All Mesoamerican people honoured maize goddesses or gods, as the crop was so important.

DIGGING STICKS
Mesoamerican farmers had no tractors, horses or heavy ploughs to help them prepare their fields. Instead, a sharp-bladed wooden digging stick, called an *uictli*, was used for planting seeds and hoeing weeds. Some farmers in Mesoamerica today find digging sticks are more efficient than the kind of spade traditionally used in Europe.

FIELD WORK
This painting by Mexican artist Diego Rivera shows Aztecs using digging sticks to hoe fields of maize. You can see how dry the soil is. If the May rains failed, or frosts came early, a whole year's crop would be lost. Mesoamerican farmers made offerings to the rain god between March and October.

Chinampa soil was made even more fertile by using human manure.

Sticky mud was collected from the lake bottom. Along with compost and manure, this mud was poured on top of the chinampas.

The chinampa was held together by stakes, thick water vegetation and the tangled roots of trees.

FLOATING GARDENS

Chinampas were a sort of floating garden. They were made by sinking layers of twigs and branches under the surface of the lake and weighting them with stones. *Chinampas* were so productive that the government passed laws telling farmers when to sow seeds. This ensured there would be a steady supply of vegetables and flowers for sale in the market.

VEGETARIANS

Many ordinary Mesoamerican people survived on a largely vegetarian diet, based on maize and beans. This would be supplemented by other fresh fruits and vegetables in season. Meat and fish were expensive, luxury foods. Only rulers and nobles could afford to eat them every day.

beans

prickly pear

SLASH AND BURN

Mesoamerican farmers used a technique called slash and burn to clear land for farming. Crops grew very quickly in Mesoamerica's warm climate.

FOREST FRUITS

This Aztec codex painting shows men and women gathering cocoa pods from trees. Cocoa was so valuable that it was sent as tribute to Tenochtitlan.

The Mesoamerican Market

THE MARKET PLACE was the heart of many Mesoamerican cities and towns. Traders, craftworkers and farmers met there to exchange their produce. Many market traders were women. They sold cloth or cooking pots, made by themselves or their families, and maize, fruit, flowers and vegetables grown by their husbands. In big cities, such as the trading centre of Tlatelolco, government officials also sold exotic goods that had been sent to the Aztec rulers as tribute (taxes) by conquered city-states. After the Aztecs conquered Tlatelolco in 1473, it soon became the greatest market in Mesoamerica. It was reported that almost 50,000 people came there on the busiest days.

Long-distance trade was carried out by merchants called *pochteca*. Gangs of porters carried their goods. The work was often dangerous, but the rewards were great.

MERCHANT GOD
Yacatecuhtli was the Aztec god of merchants and traders. In the codex picture above, he is shown standing in front of a crossroads marked with footprints. Behind him (*right*), is a tired porter with a load of birds on his back.

MAIZE MARKET
Mesoamerican farmers grew many different varieties of maize, with cobs that were pale cream, bright yellow, or even deep blue. Their wives took the maize to market, as selling was women's work. This modern wall-painting shows Aztec women buying and selling maize in the great market at Tlatelolco. At the market, judges sat in raised booths, keeping a lookout for thieves and cheats.

MAKE A MAYA POT

You will need: self-drying clay, board, rolling pin, masking tape, modelling tool, water bowl, small bowl, petroleum jelly, PVA glue, glue brush, yellow and black paint, paintbrush, water pot.

1 Roll out the clay until it is approximately 5mm thick. Cut out a base for the pot with a modelling tool. Use a roll of masking tape as a guide for size.

2 Roll out some long sausages of clay. Coil them around the base of the pot to build up the sides. Join and smooth the clay with water as you go.

3 Model a lip at the top of the pot. Leave it to dry. Cover a small bowl with petroleum jelly. Make a lid by rolling out some clay. Place the clay over the bowl.

JOURNEY'S END

This modern painting shows merchants and porters arriving at the market city of Tlatelolco. Such travellers made long journeys to bring back valuable goods, such as shells, jade and fig-bark paper. Young men joining the merchants' guild were warned about tiredness, pain and ambushes on their travels.

SKINS

Items such as puma, ocelot and jaguar skins could fetch a high price at market.

BARTER

Mesoamerican people did not have coins. They bought and sold by bartering, exchanging the goods they wanted to sell for other peoples' goods of equal value. Costly items such as gold-dust, quetzal feathers and cocoa beans were exchanged for goods they wanted to buy.

colourful feathers   *cocoa beans*

MARKET PRODUCE

In Mexico today, many markets are still held on the same sites as ancient ones. Many of the same types of foodstuffs are on sale there. In this modern photograph, we see tomatoes, avocados and vegetables that were also grown in Aztec times. Today, as in the past, most market traders and shoppers are women.

Mesoamerican potters made their pots by these coil or slab techniques. The potter's wheel was not used at all in Mesoamerica. The pots were sold at the local market.

4 Turn your pot upside down and place it over the rolled-out clay. Trim away the excess clay with a modelling tool by cutting around the top of the pot.

5 Use balls of clay to make a turtle to go on top of the lid. When both the lid and turtle are dry, use PVA glue to stick the turtle on to the centre of the lid.

6 Roll three small balls of clay of exactly the same size for the pot's feet. When they are dry, glue them to the base of the pot. Make sure they are evenly spaced.

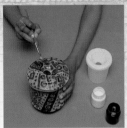

7 Paint the pot with Aztec designs in black and yellow. When you have finished, varnish the pot with a thin coat of PVA glue to make it shiny.

Master Masons

THE ROCKS of the Andes mountains provided high quality granite that was used for impressive public buildings. These included temples, fortresses, palaces, holy shrines and aqueducts (stone channels for carrying water supplies).

The *mit'a* labour system provided the workforce. In the quarries, massive rocks weighing up to 120 tonnes were cracked and shifted with stone hammers and bronze crowbars. They were hauled with ropes on log rollers or sleds. On site, the stones were shaped to fit and rubbed smooth with water and sand. Smaller stone blocks were used for upper walls or lesser buildings.

The expert Inca stonemasons had only basic tools. They used plumblines (weighted cords) to make sure that walls were straight. They used no mortar or cement, but the stones fitted together perfectly. Many remain in place to this day. Most public buildings were on a grand scale, but all were of a simple design.

BUILDING THE TEMPLE
These rectangular stone blocks were part of the holiest site in the Inca Empire, the *Coricancha* (Temple of the Sun). Inca stonework was deliberately designed to withstand the earthquakes that regularly shake the region. The original temple on this site was badly damaged by a tremor in 1650.

BRINGER OF WATER
This beautifully engineered stone water-channel was built across a valley floor by Inca stonemasons. Aqueducts, often covered, were used both for irrigation and for drinking supplies. Irrigation schemes were being built in Peru as early as around 4,500 years ago.

AN INCA GRANARY
You will need: ruler, pencil, beige, dark and cream card, scissors, white pencil, paints, paintbrush, water pot, pair of compasses, masking tape, PVA glue, hay or straw.

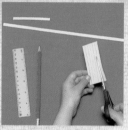

1 Use a ruler and pencil to mark eight strips 8.5cm long and 0.25cm wide, and one strip 36cm long and 0.25cm wide on beige card. Cut them out.

2 On the dark card, draw a curved shape 34cm along the base, 11cm in height and 30cm along the top. Cut it out. Cut out a doorway 6cm high.

3 Paint another piece of card a stone colour. Leave it to dry. Cut it into "blocks" about 2cm high. Glue them one by one on to the building shape.

HISTORY IN STONE

Stone walls and streets, such as these fine examples still standing in Ollantaytambo, survive to tell a story. Archaeology is much more difficult in the rainforests to the east, where timber structures rot rapidly in the hot, moist air. That is one reason we know more about the way people lived in the Andes than in the Amazon region.

INCA DESIGN

A building in Machu Picchu shows an example of typical Inca design. Inca stonemasons learned many of their skills from earlier Peruvian civilizations. Openings that are wider at the bottom than the top are seen only in Inca buildings. They are said to be trapezoid.

A MASSIVE FORTRESS

Llamas still pass before the mighty walls of Sacsahuaman, at Cuzco. This building was a fortress with towers and terraces. It also served as a royal palace and a sacred shrine. Its multi-sided boulders are precisely fitted. It is said to have been built over many years by 30,000 labourers. It was one of many public buildings raised in the reign of Pachakuti Inka Yupanki.

Storehouses were built of neat stone blocks. They kept precious grain dry and secure.

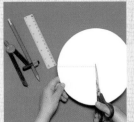

4 Use compasses to draw a circle 18cm across on cream card. Cut it out and cut away one quarter. Tape the straight cut edges together to form a cone.

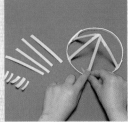

5 Make a circle by joining the ends of the 36cm strip with masking tape. Then fix the eight 8.5cm strips around the edge and in the middle as shown.

6 Glue short lengths of straw or hay all over the cardboard cone to form the thatched roof of the granary. The thatch should all run in the same direction.

7 Join the edges of the walls with masking tape. Fold in the sides of the doorway. Place the rafters on top. The thatched roof fits over the rafters.

Art, Culture & Entertainment

Learn about the development of writing, art, music, sports, leisure, and pleasure in different civilizations

Life, Leisure and Enjoyment

Daily life is more than just working, eating and sleeping. From the time of the earliest organized human societies, over 50,000 years ago, men and women have enjoyed telling stories, listening to music, dancing and playing games. Early humans decorated their clothes, tools, weapons and shelters with patterns and magic symbols. They even created lifelike images of the world around them. The earliest-known paintings of people and animals – discovered in caves in Europe – date from almost 30,000 years ago. The artwork is skilled, which suggests a long tradition of artists working for hundreds of years before, slowly perfecting their techniques. It seems clear that, even though early peoples' lives were often a struggle for survival in a harsh environment, there was time to draw and paint.

Animals were often depicted in cave paintings. They are believed to represent the creatures that Stone Age people hunted for food.

Music has always been a popular form of entertainment in Japan. This woman is playing a *shamisen* – a three-stringed instrument.

Sculpture, ornaments and painting have always been important for many reasons. Most simply, people like things to look

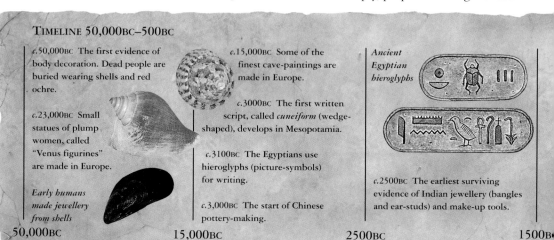

TIMELINE 50,000BC–500BC

*c.*50,000BC The first evidence of body decoration. Dead people are buried wearing shells and red ochre.

*c.*23,000BC Small statues of plump women, called "Venus figurines" are made in Europe.

Early humans made jewellery from shells

*c.*15,000BC Some of the finest cave-paintings are made in Europe.

*c.*3000BC The first written script, called *cuneiform* (wedge-shaped), develops in Mesopotamia.

*c.*3100BC The Egyptians use hieroglyphs (picture-symbols) for writing.

*c.*3,000BC The start of Chinese pottery-making.

Ancient Egyptian hieroglyphs

*c.*2500BC The earliest surviving evidence of Indian jewellery (bangles and ear-studs) and make-up tools.

50,000BC   15,000BC   2500BC   1500B•

Tribal peoples valued the skills that went into creating patterned pots.

good. All around the world, craftworkers made everyday items, such as blankets or food-baskets, as attractive as possible. The type and style of decoration used varied from culture to culture, and over the centuries. The available materials were also important, such as clay for pottery, or coloured pigments for paints and dyes. Wealthy people could afford items made from valuable substances, such as silk or porcelain (both from China), or employ skilled artists to create fine statues, carvings, pottery and mosaics, such as those surviving from ancient Greece and Rome.

People have also always liked to look good. Men and women in ancient Egypt wore make-up and had elaborate hairstyles. In India, traditional clothing was simple, but people wore fancy accessories and jewels. In many civilizations, people have also liked decorating their own bodies, with piercing, body-paint and tattoos.

An Aztec woman is shown wearing bangles, a chunky necklace and earrings. She obviously took a lot of pride in her appearance.

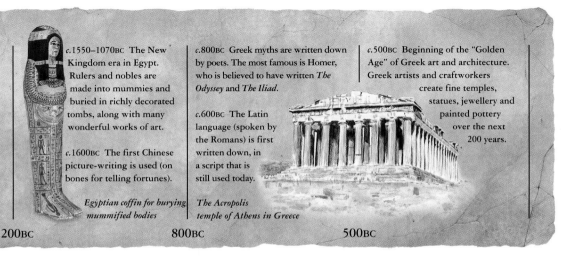

*c.*1550–1070BC The New Kingdom era in Egypt. Rulers and nobles are made into mummies and buried in richly decorated tombs, along with many wonderful works of art.

*c.*1600BC The first Chinese picture-writing is used (on bones for telling fortunes).

Egyptian coffin for burying mummified bodies

*c.*800BC Greek myths are written down by poets. The most famous is Homer, who is believed to have written *The Odyssey* and *The Iliad*.

*c.*600BC The Latin language (spoken by the Romans) is first written down, in a script that is still used today.

The Acropolis temple of Athens in Greece

*c.*500BC Beginning of the "Golden Age" of Greek art and architecture. Greek artists and craftworkers create fine temples, statues, jewellery and painted pottery over the next 200 years.

200BC   800BC   500BC

Patterns, pictures, stories, myths, legends, dancing and music added an extra layer of meaning to people's lives. They helped people to express their beliefs, manage their fears and sometimes (they thought), to make contact with the invisible world of gods, spirits, ghosts and dead ancestors. Some art forms offered magical protection to hunters and children. Others, such as costumes and jewellery were used in ceremonies that marked important stages in peoples' lives, such as birth, marriage or death.

Chinese letters are called characters. They are read down, from right to left.

The arts often provided excellent entertainment. Watching skilled performances – from simple tunes played on prehistoric deer-bone flutes to elegant Japanese court theatre – gave people pleasure. Sometimes, they helped them to understand their feelings, hopes and fears, and the world around them. Singers, poets and storytellers retold ancient myths in words and music. This often became a way of preserving the history of families and tribes. Around 5,000 years ago,

The decorations of North American Indian tribes, such as this rattle, often had spiritual significance.

This Mesopotamian board game may have been played like Ludo. It is made from wood and decorated with a mosaic of shell and coloured stone.

TIMELINE 400BC–AD1700

380BC Servian Wall is built to defend Rome from attack. Over the next 500 years, Roman architects and engineers designed and built many roads, forts, water-systems, and fine public buildings (such as temples and amphitheatres) in the lands ruled by Rome.

292BC The Maya people of Central America begin to write using picture-symbols.

AD300–700 The Moche people of South America are expert goldsmiths.

AD868 First printed book produced using wood-blocks, in China.

AD750–1100 The Viking age. The Vikings are expert metalworkers and they also enjoy music and sagas (dramatic adventure-stories).

AD1040 Chinese invent new form of printing using moveable type.

1300 Start of Noh drama in Japan. Plays performed by male actors only.

1300–1500 Chancay and Inca peoples of Peru create brilliantly coloured clothes decorated with beads and

Chinese calligraphy

400BC   AD300   AD800   1300

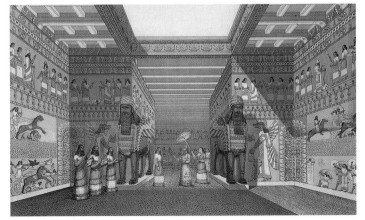

Ancient civilizations in the Near East, such as those of Egypt and Mesopotamia, put great effort into creating visually stunning interiors. This is the internal hall of a Mesopotamian palace.

in the Middle East, artists and craftworkers also began to use picture symbols to record useful information or important events. Picture-writing was also developed in China before 1500BC. From that time on, many people around the world used writing as a new art form. It was another way of passing on traditions, telling ancient stories, myths and legends, or expressing important beliefs and ideas.

In a thematic history such as this, you can follow developments in different aspects of art and culture in turn. You will be able to see how dress, accessories, sport, entertainmnent, ornamental and decorative arts, writing and storytelling evolved through time and varied from culture to culture.

Greek girls were expected to spend their time helping in the home but many still had time to enjoy a game of tag.

Costumes at the Inca August Festival

feathers, many of which they wear to seasonal festivals.

1500 A new garment, a long, loose robe called a *kimono,* becomes fashionable in Japan.

1500s to 1700s Musicians and dancers entertain Mughal rulers at royal courts in India. The Mughals also collect beautiful books, paintings and jewels.

1600 Start of Japanese Kabuki popular drama and bunraku puppet plays.

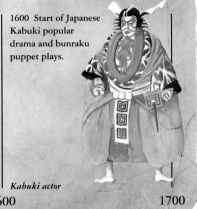

Kabuki actor

1500   1600   1700

Stone Age Jewellery

CEREMONIAL DRESS
The amazing headdress, face painting and jewellery still seen at ceremonies in Papua New Guinea may echo the richness of decoration in Stone Age times.

MEN AND WOMEN WORE JEWELLERY from as early as the Stone Age. Necklaces and pendants were made from all sorts of natural objects. Brightly coloured pebbles, snail shells, fishbones, animal teeth, seashells, eggshells, nuts and seeds were all used. Later, semi-precious amber and jade, fossilized jet and handmade clay beads were also used. The beads were threaded on to thin strips of leather or twine made from plant fibres.

Other jewellery included bracelets made of slices of elephant or mammoth tusk. Strings of shells and teeth were made into beautiful headbands. Women plaited their hair and put it up with combs and pins. People probably decorated their bodies and outlined their eyes with pigments such as red ochre. They may have tattooed and pierced their bodies too.

BODY PAINT
These Australian Aboriginal children have painted their bodies with clay. They have used patterns that are thousands of years old.

BONES AND TEETH
Necklaces were often made from the bones and teeth of a walrus. This one comes from Skara Brae in the Orkney Islands. A hole was made in each bead with a stone tool, or with a wooden stick spun by a bow drill. The beads were then strung on to a strip of leather or twine.

MAKE A NECKLACE
You will need: self-drying clay, rolling pin and board, modelling tool, sandpaper, ivory and black acrylic paint, paintbrush, water pot, ruler, scissors, chamois leather, card, double-sided sticky tape, PVA glue, leather laces.

1 Roll out the clay on a board and cut out four crescent shapes with the modelling tool. Leave them on the board to dry.

2 Rub the crescents lightly with sandpaper and paint them an ivory colour. You could varnish them later to make them shiny.

3 Cut four strips of leather about 9cm x 3cm. Use the edge of a piece of card to make a black criss-cross pattern on the strips.

NATURAL DECORATION

We know about the wide variety of materials used in Stone Age jewellery from cave paintings and ornaments discovered in graves. Shells were highly prized and some were traded over long distances. Other materials included deers' teeth, mammoth and walrus ivory, fish bones and birds' feathers.

a selection of sea shells

A WARRIOR'S HEADDRESS

The headdress of this Yali warrior from Indonesia is made of wild boars' teeth. The necklace is made of shells and bone. Headdresses and necklaces made of animals' teeth may have had a spiritual meaning for Stone Age people. The wearer may have believed that the teeth brought the strength or courage of the animal from which they came.

BANGLES AND EAR STUDS

Jewellery found at Harappa in Pakistan included these items. They date from between 2300BC and 1750BC and are made from shells and coloured pottery. Archaeologists in Harappa have found remains of the shops that sold jewellery.

Stone Age people believed that wearing a leopard claw necklace brought them magical powers.

4 When they are dry, fold back the edges of each strip and hold in place with double-sided sticky tape.

5 Brush the middle of each crescent with glue and wrap the leather around, forming a loop at the top, as shown.

6 Plait together three leather laces to make a thong. Make the thong long enough to go around your neck and be tied.

7 Thread the leopard's claws on to the middle of the thong, arranging them so that there are small spaces between them.

Egyptian Vanity

THE ANCIENT EGYPTIANS were very fond of jewellery. The rich wore pieces finely crafted from precious stones and metals. Cheaper adornments were made from glass and polished stones. Make-up was also important for both men and women. They wore green eyeshadow made from a mineral called malachite and black eyeliner made from galena, a type of lead. Lipsticks and blusher were made from red ochre. The Egyptians liked to tattoo their skin, and they also used perfumes. Most men were clean shaven. Wigs were worn by men and women, even by those who had plenty of hair of their own. Grey hair was dyed and there were various remedies for baldness.

A TIMELESS BEAUTY
This limestone head is of Queen Nefertiti, the wife of the Sun-worshipping pharaoh Akhenaten. She seems to be the ideal of Egyptian beauty. She wears a headdress and a necklace. The stone is painted and so we can see that she is also wearing make-up and lipstick.

LOOKING GOOD
Mirrors were made of polished copper or bronze, with handles of wood or ivory. This bronze mirror is from 1900BC. Mirrors were used by the wealthy for checking hairstyles, applying make-up, or simply for admiring one's own good looks! The poor had to make do with seeing their reflection in water.

MAKE A MIRROR
You will need: mirror card, pencil, scissors, self-drying clay, modelling tool, rolling pin and board, small piece of card or sandpaper, gold paint, pva glue and brush, waterpot and brush.

1 Begin by drawing a mirror shape on the white side of a piece of mirror card, as shown. Carefully cut the mirror shape out. Put the card to one side.

2 Take your clay and roll it into a tube. Then mould it into a handle shape, as shown. Decorate the handle with a lotus or papyrus flower, or other design.

3 Now make a slot in the handle with a square piece of card or sandpaper, as shown. This is where the mirror card will slot into the handle.

BIG WIGS AND WAXY CONES

Many pictures show nobles at banquets wearing cones of perfumed grease on their heads. The scent may have been released as the cones melted in the heat. However, some experts believe that the cones were drawn in by artists to show that the person was wearing a scented wig. False hairpieces and wigs were very popular in Egypt. It was common for people to cut their hair short, but some did have long hair that they dressed in elaborate styles.

COSMETICS

During the early years of the Egyptian Empire, black eye kohl was made from galena, a type of poisonous lead! Later soot was used. Henna was painted on the nails and the soles of the feet to make them red. Popular beauty treatments included pumice stone to smooth rough skin and ash face packs.

face pack   *pumice stone*   *kohl*   *henna*

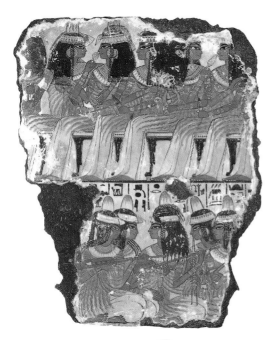

COSMETICS BOWL

Make-up, oils and lotions were prepared and stored in jars and bowls, as well as in hollow reeds or tubes. These containers were made of stone, pottery and glass. Minerals were ground into a powder and then mixed with water in cosmetics bowls to make a paste. Make-up was applied with the fingers or with a special wooden applicator. Two colours of eye make-up were commonly used – green and black. Green was used in the early period, but later the distinctive black eye paint became more popular.

The shape of mirrors and their shining surface reminded Egyptians of the Sun disc, so they became religious symbols. By the New Kingdom, many were decorated with the goddess Hathor or lotus flowers.

4 Place the handle on a wire baking tray and leave it in a warm place to dry. Turn it over after two hours. When it is completely dry, try your mirror for size.

5 It is now time to paint the handle. Paint one side carefully with gold paint and leave it to dry. When it has dried, turn the handle over and paint the other side.

6 Finally, you can assemble your mirror. Cover the base of the mirror card in glue and insert it into the handle slot. Leave it in a warm place to dry.

Clothing and Jewellery in India

BOTH RICH AND POOR PEOPLE IN INDIA have always tended to wear simple clothes dressed up with lots of jewellery, such as earrings, armbands, breastplates, noserings and anklets. They also had elaborate hairstyles decorated with flowers and ornaments.

Religious beliefs influenced how people dressed. Hindu men and women dressed simply in a single piece of fabric that was draped around the hips, drawn up between the legs, then fastened securely again at the waist. For men this was called a *dhoti*. Women wore bodices above the waist but men were often barechested. The female style of dress evolved into the *sari*.

When Islam arrived in India, tailored garments became widespread in the north of the country. People wore sewn cotton trousers called *paijama* or *shalwar*, with a long tunic called a *kamiz* or *kurta*. For men, turbans became popular. Muslim women were expected to dress modestly, so they began to wear veils, a practice that Hindu women also adopted.

SETTING THE TREND
Bangles and ear studs from the Indus Valley are among the earliest ornaments found in India. They are more than 4,000 years old. The styles of these pieces of jewellery, and the designs on them, were used again in later forms of decoration.

BEAUTY AIDS
This mirror, collyrium applicator and hair pin are over 4,000 years old. Large dark eyes were considered a sign of beauty, so women drew attention to their eyes by outlining them with collyrium, a black substance.

ANCIENT DRESS
A painted fragment of a pillar shows a woman wearing a long red skirt and jewellery. The pillar is about 2,000 years old.

MAKE A FLOWER BRACELET

You will need: A5 sheets of thin white card, pencil, scissors, gold paint, paintbrush, A5 sheets of white paper, PVA glue, foil sweet papers, gardening wire, pliers.

1 Draw some simple flower shapes on the white card. They should be about 2 cm in diameter. Give each flower six rounded petals.

2 Carefully cut out each of the flower shapes. Then paint both sides of each flower with gold paint. Leave the flowers to dry.

3 Draw 10 to 12 wedge shapes on the white paper sheets. They should be wider at the bottom than at the top. Cut out the wedge shapes.

COLOURFUL SILK

Silk is a fine, soft thread produced by the larva (grubs) of the silkworm moth when it makes its cocoon. The thread is woven into cloth and dyed. Silk was first brought to India from China along the Silk Road. Indian silk is mostly dyed in bright colours.

silk

HINDU DRESS

In this detail from a painted panel, a Hindu man and woman wear typical dress – a *dhoti* for the man and for the woman, a *sari*. Both men and women liked to wear brightly coloured clothes.

JEWELS FOR ALL

A Rajasthani woman wears traditional jewellery and dress. Nowadays in India, jewellery is still so valued that even the poorer peasants own pieces for special occasions.

Floral designs are common patterns used throughout Indian art.

CLOTHING FOR THE COURT

Courtiers from the Mughal Empire (1526-1857) wore a side-fastening coat called a *jama*. It has a tight body, high waist and flared skirt reaching to below the knees. It is worn over tight-fitting trousers, or *paijama*, gathered at the ankle. A sash, called a *patuka*, is tied to the waist. Courtiers also wore a small turban as a mark of respect.

4 Apply glue to the wedge shapes and roll them up to make beads, leaving a hole through the middle. Paint the beads gold and leave to dry.

5 Carefully cut out tiny circles from the coloured foil paper. Make sure you have enough to stick on to the centre of each flower.

6 Measure gardening wire long enough to go around your wrist. Add 4 cm for a loop. Tape the flowers to the wire and thread on the beads.

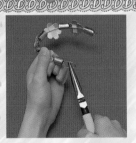

7 To finish the flower bracelet, use a pair of pliers to bend back one end of the wire to form a loop and the other end to form a hook.

Greek Garments

PHYSICAL BEAUTY AND AN ATTRACTIVE appearance were admired in ancient Greece in both men and women. Clothes were simple and practical, and made of wool and linen, which were spun at home. The rich, however, could afford more luxurious garments made from imported cotton or silk. Fabrics were coloured with dyes made from plants, insects and shellfish.

Men and women wore long tunics, draped loosely for comfort in the warm climate, and held in place with decorative pins or brooches. A heavy cloak was added for travelling or in bad weather. The tunics of soldiers and labourers were cut short, so they could move easily. Sandals were usually worn outdoors, though men sometimes wore boots. In hot weather, hats made of straw or wool kept off the sun. A tan was not admired in ancient Greece, because it signified outdoor work as a labourer or a slave. Men cut their hair short, while women coiled long hair in elaborate styles, sometimes with ribbons.

SEE FOR YOURSELF
Glass mirrors were not known to the Greeks. Instead, they used highly polished bronze to see their reflection in. This mirror has a handle in the shaped of a woman. Winged sphinxes sit on her shoulders.

GOLDEN LION
This heavy bracelet dates from around the 4th century BC. It is made of solid gold and decorated with two lion heads. Gold was valuable because there was little of it found in Greece. Most of it was imported from Asia Minor or Egypt.

KEEP IT SIMPLE
The figurine above is wearing a peplos. This was a simple, sleeveless dress worn by Greek women. The only adornment was a belt tied underneath the bust. This statue comes from a Greek colony in southern Italy.

CHITON
You will need: tape measure, rectangle of cloth, scissors, pins, chalk, needle, thread, 12 metal buttons (with loops), cord.

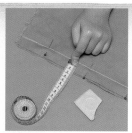

1 Ask a friend to measure your width from wrist to wrist, double this figure. Measure your length from shoulder to ankle. Cut your cloth to these figures.

2 Fold the fabric in half widthways. Pin the two sides together. Draw a chalk line along the fabric, 2cm away from the edge of the fabric.

3 Sew along the chalk line. Then turn the material inside out, so the seam is on the inside. Refold the fabric so the seam is at the back.

TEXTILE TRADE

Clothes in ancient Greece were usually made from wool and linen. The Greeks exported their wool, which was admired for its superior quality. Cotton and silk were imported to make clothes. But only wealthy Greeks could afford clothes made from these materials.

cotton

raw wool

linen

POWDER POT

Greek women used face powder and other cosmetics and kept them in a ceramic pot called a pyxis. This one was made in Athens in about 450BC. The painted decoration shows women spinning and weaving.

spiral band

Clothes were handmade in ancient Greece. Enough material would be woven to fit the person they were being made for exactly, to avoid waste.

BURIAL JEWELLERY

Some pieces of jewellery, like the ones pictured here, were made especially for burial. Very thin sheet gold was beaten into belts and wreaths. Important people like the Kings and Queens of Macedonia were buried in crowns of gold leaves.

wreath

belt

4 Make a gap big enough for your head to fit in, at one of the open ends of the fabric. Mark where the gap is going to be and pin the fabric together there.

5 From the head gap mark a point every 5cm to the end of the fabric. Pin together the front and back along these points. Your arms will fit through here.

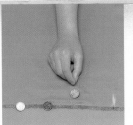

6 At each pin, sew on a button to hold the two sides of material together. To secure the button, sew through the loop several times and knot it.

7 Cut a length of cord, to fit around your waist with a little bit spare to tie. Tie this cord around your waist and bunch the material up, over the cord.

Palace Fashions in Japan

Clothing in early times often depended on how rich you were. In Japan, from around AD600 to 1500, wealthy noble men and women at the emperor's court wore very different clothes from ordinary peasant farmers. Fashions were based on traditional Chinese styles. Both men and women wore long, flowing robes made of many layers of fine, glossy silk, held in place by a sash and cords. Men also wore wide trousers underneath. Women kept their hair loose and long, while men tied their hair into a topknot and wore a tall black hat. Elegance and refinement were the aims of this style.

After about 1500, wealthy samurai families began to wear *kimono* – long, loose robes. *Kimono* also became popular among wealthy artists, actors and craftworkers. The shoguns passed laws to try to stop ordinary people from wearing elaborate *kimono*, but they proved impossible to enforce.

PARASOL
Women protected their delicate complexions with sunshades made of oiled paper. The fashion was for pale skin, often heavily powdered, with dark, soft eyebrows.

GOOD TASTE OR GAUDY?
This woman's outfit dates from the 1700s. Though striking, it would probably have been considered too bold to be in the most refined taste. Men and women took great care in choosing garments that blended well together.

MAKE A FAN

You will need: thick card (38cm x 26cm), pencil, ruler, compasses, protractor, felt tip pen (blue), paper (red), scissors, paints, paintbrush, water pot, glue stick.

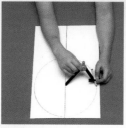

1 Draw a line down the centre of the piece of card. Place your compasses two-thirds of the way up the line. Draw a circle 23cm in diameter.

2 Add squared-off edges at the top of the circle, as shown. Now draw your handle (15cm long). The handle should be directly over the vertical line.

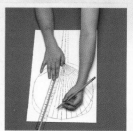

3 Place a protractor at the top of the handle and draw a semicircle around it. Now mark lines every 2.5 degrees. Draw pencil lines through these marks.

FEET OFF THE GROUND

To catch insects in a garden by lamplight these women are wearing *geta* (clogs). *Geta* were designed to protect the wearer's feet from mud and rain by raising them about 5–7cm above the ground. They were worn outdoors.

SILK *KIMONO*

This beautiful silk *kimono* was made in about 1600. Women wore a wide silk sash called an *obi* on top of their *kimono*. Men fastened their *kimono* with a narrow sash.

PAPER FAN

Folding fans, made of pleated paper, were a Japanese invention. They were carried by both men and women. This one is painted with gold leaf and chrysanthemum flowers.

It was the custom for Japanese noblewomen to hide their faces in court. They used decorated fans such as this one as a screen. Fans were also used to help people keep cool on hot, humid summer days.

BEAUTIFUL HAIR

Traditional palace fashions for men and women are shown in this scene from the imperial palace. The women have long, flowing hair that reaches to their waists – a sign of great beauty in early Japan.

4 Draw a blue line 1cm to the left of each line you have drawn. Then draw a blue line 2mm to the right of this line. Add a squiggle between sections.

5 Cut out your card fan. Now use this as a template. Draw around the fan top (not handle) on to your red paper. Cut out the red paper.

6 Now cut out the in-between sections on your card fan (those marked with a squiggle). Paint the card fan brown on both sides. Leave to dry.

7 Paint the red paper with white flowers and leave to dry. Paste glue on to one side of the card fan. Stick the undecorated side of the red paper to the fan.

Cold-climate Dress

IN THE FREEZING ARCTIC, clothes needed to be warm as well as beautiful. Strips or patches of different furs were used to form designs and geometric patterns on outer clothes. Fur trimmings, toggles and other decorative fastenings added the final touches to many clothes. Jewellery included pendants, bracelets, necklaces and brooches. These ornaments were traditionally made of natural materials, such as bone and walrus ivory.

In North America, Inuit women often decorated clothes with birds' beaks, tiny feathers or even porcupine quills. In Greenland, lace and glass beads were popular decorations. Saami clothes were the most colourful in the Arctic. Saami men, women and children wore blue outfits with a bright red and yellow trim. Mens' costumes included a tall hat and a short flared tunic. Womens' clothes included flared skirts with embroidered hems and colourful hats, shawls and scarves.

SAAMI COSTUME
A Saami man wears the traditional costume of his region, including a flared tunic trimmed with bright woven ribbon at the neck, shoulders, cuffs and hem. Outfits such as the one above were worn all year round. In winter, Saami people wore thick fur parkas, called *peskes,* over the bright tunics.

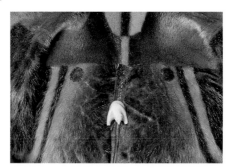

BEAR TOGGLE
An ivory toggle carved into the shape of a polar bear completes this traditional sealskin jacket. Arctic people took great pride in their appearance and loved to decorate their clothes in this way. In ancient times, the Inuit, for example, decorated their garments with hundreds of tiny feathers or the claws of mammals, such as foxes or hares. Women often decorated all the family's clothes.

MAKE A SAAMI HAT
You will need: red felt (58 x 30 cm), PVA glue, glue brush, black ribbon (58 x 2 cm), coloured ribbon, white felt, ruler, pencil, compass, red card, scissors, red, green and white ribbon (3 at 44 x 4 cm), red ribbon (58 x 4 cm).

1 Mark out the centre of the red felt along its length. Carefully glue the length of black ribbon along the centre line, as shown above.

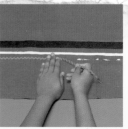

2 Continue to decorate the felt with different kinds of coloured ribbon and white felt, making a series of strips along the red felt, as shown above.

3 Cut out a circle of red card with a diameter of 18 cm. Draw a circle inside with a diameter of 15 cm. Cut into the larger circle to the 15 cm line.

CURVING BOOT

This picture shows a curved boot worn by the Saami people from Arctic Scandinavia. These boots are designed for use with skis and are decorated with traditional woollen pompoms. The curved boot tips stop the skier from slipping out of the skis when travelling uphill.

WEDDING FINERY

The bride, bridegroom and a guest at a Saami wedding in north Norway all wear the traditional outfits. Notice that the style of the man's wedding hat differs from the one shown in the picture on the opposite page. Both men and women wear brooches encrusted with metal disks. Saami women's wedding outfits include tall hats, tasselled shawls and ribbons.

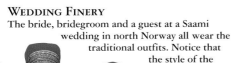

BEADS AND LACE

A woman from western Greenland wears the traditional beaded costume of her nation, which includes a top with a wide black collar and cuffs and high sealskin boots. After European settlers arrived in Greenland, glass beads and lace became traditional decorations on clothing. Hundreds of beads were sewn onto jackets to make intricate patterns.

The style of Saami hats varied from region to region. In southern Norway, men's hats were tall and rounded. Further north, their hats had four points.

4 Glue the ends of the decorated red felt together, as shown above. You will need to find the right size to fit around your head.

5 Fold down the tabs cut into the red card circle. Glue the tabs, then stick the card circle to the felt inside one end of the hat.

6 While the hat is drying, glue the coloured ribbon strips together. Glue these strips 15 cm from the end of the 58 cm long red ribbon band.

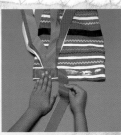

7 Glue the 58 cm band of red ribbon onto the base of the hat, making sure the shorter strips of red, green and white ribbons go over the top of the band.

Bold Designs in South America

FESTIVAL COSTUMES in the Andes today are in dazzling pinks, reds and blues. In the Inca period it was no different. People loved to wear brightly coloured braids, threads and ribbons. Sequins, beads, feathers and gold were sewn into fabric, while precious stones, red shells, silver and gold were made into beautiful earplugs, necklaces, pendants, nostril-rings and discs. However, it was only the nobles who were allowed to show off by wearing feathers, jewels and precious metals. Some of the most prized ornaments were gifts from the emperor for high-ranking service in the army.

Much of the finest craft work went into making small statues and objects for religious ceremonies, temples and shrines. During the Inca period, craft workers were employed by the State. They produced many beautiful treasures, but some of the best of these were the work of non-Inca peoples, particularly the Chimú. Treasures shipped to Spain after the Conquest astounded the Europeans by their fine craftsmanship.

PLUMES OF THE CHIEF
An impressive headdress like this would have belonged to a high-ranking Inca official or general in northern Chile over 500 years ago. The hat is made from coils of dyed llama wool. It is decorated with bold designs, and topped by a spray of feathers.

A SACRED PUMA
This gold pouch in the shape of a puma, a sacred animal, was made by the Moche people between 1,300 and 1,700 years ago. It may have been used to carry *coca* leaves. These were used as a drug during religious ceremonies. The pattern on the body is made up of two-headed snakes.

A GOLD AND SILVER NECKLACE
You will need: self-drying clay, cutting board, ruler, large blunt needle, gold and silver paint, paintbrush, water pot, card, pencil, scissors, strong thread.

1 Form pieces of clay into beads in the shape of monkey nuts. You will need 10 large beads (about 3.5cm x 2cm) and 10 smaller beads (about 2.5cm x 1.5cm).

2 Use the needle to mark patterns on the beads, so that they look like nut shells. Then carefully make a hole through the middle of each bead. Leave to dry.

3 Paint half the shells of each size gold and half of them silver. You should have 5 small and 5 large gold beads, and 5 small and 5 large silver beads.

PRECIOUS AND PRETTY

The most valued stone in the Andes was blue-green turquoise. It was cut and polished into beads and discs for necklaces, and inlaid in gold statues and masks. Blue lapis lazuli, black jet and other stones also found their way along trading routes. Colombia, on the northern edge of the Inca Empire, mined many precious stones and metals. Seashells were cut and polished into beautiful beads.

emerald *turquoise*

lapis lazuli

BIRDS OF A FEATHER

Birds and fish decorate this feather cape. It was made by the Chancay people of the central Peruvian coast between the 1300s and 1500s. It would have been worn for religious ceremonies. Feather work was a skilled craft in both Central and South America. In Inca times, the brilliantly coloured feathers of birds called macaws were sent to the emperor as tribute from the tribes of the Amazon forests.

Necklaces made of gold, silver and jewels would only have been worn by Inca royalty, such as the Quya *(Inca empress).*

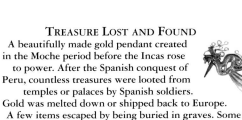

TREASURE LOST AND FOUND

A beautifully made gold pendant created in the Moche period before the Incas rose to power. After the Spanish conquest of Peru, countless treasures were looted from temples or palaces by Spanish soldiers. Gold was melted down or shipped back to Europe. A few items escaped by being buried in graves. Some have been discovered by archaeologists.

4 Paint some card gold on both sides. On it draw 11 rectangles (3cm x 1cm) with rounded ends. Cut them out and carefully prick a hole in each end.

5 Thread the needle and make a knot 10cm from the end of the thread. Then thread the card strips and large beads alternately, using the gold beads first.

6 Be sure to start and end with card strips. When you have finished, knot the thread tightly next to the last card strip. Cut the thread 10cm from the knot.

7 Repeat steps 5 and 6 using more thread and the small beads, so that the beads are joined as shown. Finally, knot the ends of the two threads together.

Interior Design in Assyria

WOMAN IN A WINDOW
A piece of carved ivory from Phoenicia. The Phoenicians probably supplied the Assyrians with most of their ivory. They were great traders from the eastern Mediterranean shores.

Assyrian kings in north Mesopotamia (present-day Iraq) loved the luxury of ivory furniture. They filled their palaces with ivory beds, arm chairs, foot stools and tables. No complete pieces of ivory furniture have survived to modern times, but archaeologists found part of an ivory throne during their excavations at the city of Nimrud in the 1840s. They also found some elephant tusks and many small, carved ivory plaques that were once attached to the wooden framework of pieces of furniture. Today, it is considered cruel to kill elephants for their ivory, and the animals have become an endangered species.

No textiles have survived but Assyrian palaces would probably have been made comfortable with cushions and woollen rugs. Stone entrances to the palace rooms carved in the form of floral-patterned carpets give us an idea of what the rugs may have looked like.

INSIDE THE PALACE
Palaces were built from mud brick, but the lower interior walls were decorated with carved and painted slabs of stone. Teams of sculptors and artists produced scenes showing the king's military campaigns and wild bull and lion hunts. The upper walls were plastered and painted with similar scenes to glorify the king and impress foreign visitors. Paints were ground from minerals. Red and brown paints were made from ochres, blues and greens from copper ores, azurite and malachite.

MAKE A BRONZE AND IVORY MIRROR

You will need: pencil, strong white and reflective card, ruler, scissors, thick dowel, masking tape, flour, water and newspaper to make papier mâché, paints, brushes, sandpaper, glue.

1 Draw around a saucer to mark a circle 12 cm across on to the strong white card. Add a handle about 6cm long and 2.5cm wide as shown. Cut out.

2 Take a length of dowel measuring about 20cm long. Fix the dowel to the handle using masking tape. Bend the card round the dowel as shown.

3 Scrunch up a piece of newspaper into a ball. Attach the newspaper ball to the top of the handle with masking tape as shown.

LUXURY IN THE GARDEN

King Ashurbanipal and his wife even had luxurious ivory furniture in the palace gardens at Nineveh. In this picture, the king is reclining on an elaborate ivory couch decorated with tiny carved and gilded lions. The queen is sitting on an ivory chair with a high back and resting her feet on a footstool. Cushions make the furniture more comfortable. Ivory workers used drills and chisels similar to those used by carpenters. The ivory plaques had signs on them to show how they should be slotted together.

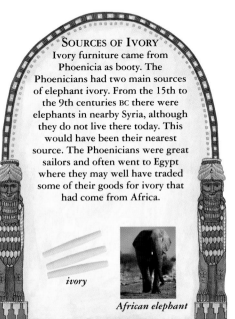

SOURCES OF IVORY

Ivory furniture came from Phoenicia as booty. The Phoenicians had two main sources of elephant ivory. From the 15th to the 9th centuries BC there were elephants in nearby Syria, although they do not live there today. This would have been their nearest source. The Phoenicians were great sailors and often went to Egypt where they may well have traded some of their goods for ivory that had come from Africa.

ivory

African elephant

Polished bronze was used for mirrors in ancient times. A mirror with a handle of carved ivory like this would have belonged to a wealthy woman.

BOY-EATER

This furniture plaque shows a boy being eaten by a lioness. Sometimes ivory was stained or inlaid with paste to imitate jewels. The boy's kilt is covered with gold leaf, and his curly hair is made of tiny gold pins. There are lotus flowers and papyrus plants in the background, inlaid with real lapis lazuli and carnelian.

4 Make a paste with flour and water. Tear the newspaper into strips and dip them into the paste. Cover the handle in the papier mâché strips.

5 Use newspaper to make the nose and ears. Add a strip of papier mâché at the top of the head for the crown. Leave to dry, then sandpaper until smooth.

6 Paint a base coat of grey paint on the face and bronze on the handle. Then add the details of the face and crown in black using a fine paintbrush.

7 Cut out a circle of reflective card to match the mirror shape. Glue the reflective card carefully on to the white card. This is your bronze mirror.

Egyptian Crafts

THE ANCIENT EGYPTIANS loved beautiful objects, and the craft items that have survived still amaze us today. There are shining gold rings and pendants, necklaces inlaid with glass and a dazzling blue glazed pottery called faience. Jars made of a smooth white stone called alabaster have been preserved in almost perfect condition, along with chairs and chests made of cedar wood imported from the Near East.

Egyptians made beautiful baskets and storage pots. Some pottery was made from river clay, but the finest pots were made from a chalky clay found at Quena. Pots were shaped by hand or, later, on a potter's wheel. Some were polished with a smooth pebble until their surface shone. We know so much about Egyptian craft work because many beautiful items were placed in tombs, so that the dead person could use them in the next world.

ALABASTER ART
Jars such as this would have held oils and perfumes. This elaborate jar was among the treasures in the tomb of King Tutankhamun (1334–1325BC).

GLASS FISH
This beautiful stripy fish looks as if it should be swimming in the reefs of the Red Sea. In fact, it is a glass jar used to store oils. Glass-making became popular in Egypt after 1500BC. The glass was made from sand and salty crystals. It would then have been coloured with metals and shaped while still hot.

MAKE A LOTUS TILE

You will need: card (2 sheets), pencil, ruler, scissors, self-drying clay, modelling tool, sandpaper acrylic paint (blue, gold, green, yellow ochre), water pot and brush. Optional: rolling pin & board.

1 Using the final picture as reference, draw both tile shapes onto card. Cut them out. Draw the whole pattern of tiles onto the sheet of card and cut around the border.

2 Roll out the clay on a board with a rolling pin or bottle. Place the overall outline over the clay and carefully trim off the edges. Discard the extra clay.

3 Mark the individual tile patterns into the clay, following the outlines carefully. Cut through the lines, but do not separate them out yet.

DESERT RICHES

The dwellers of the green Nile valley feared and disliked the desert. They called it the Red Land. However, the deserts did provide them with great mineral wealth, including blue-green turquoise, purple amethyst and blue agate.

blue agate   *turquoise*   *amethyst*

ROYAL TILES

Many beautiful Egyptian tiles have been discovered by archaeologists. It is thought that they were used to decorate furniture and floors in the palaces of the pharaohs.

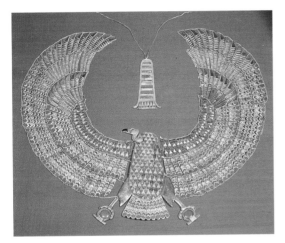

NEKHBET COLLAR

In this splendid collar, the spectacular wings of the vulture goddess Nekhbet include 250 feather sections made of coloured glass set in gold. The vulture's beak and eye are made from a black, volcanic glass called obsidian. It was one of 17 collars found in Tutankhamun's tomb. As one of many amazing objects found in the young king's tomb, it shows us the incredible skill of Egyptian craftsmen.

TUTANKHAMUN'S WAR CHEST

Tutankhamun is in battle against the Syrians and the Nubians on this painted chest. On the lid, the young king is seen hunting in the desert. The incredible detail of the painting shows that this was the work of a very skilled artist. When Tutankhamun's tomb was opened, the chest was found to contain children's clothes. The desert air was so dry that neither the wood, leather nor fabric had rotted.

4 Now use the tool to score patterns of leaves and flowers into the surface of the soft clay, as shown. Separate the pieces and allow them to dry.

5 When one side of each tile has dried, turn it over. Leave the other side to dry. Then sand down the edges of the tiles until they are smooth.

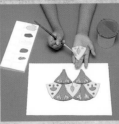

6 The tiles are now ready for painting. Carefully paint the patterns in green, yellow ochre, gold and blue. Leave them in a warm place to dry.

These tiles are similar to those found at a royal palace in Thebes. The design looks rather like a lotus, the sacred waterlily of ancient Egypt.

Chinese Pottery

Pottery making developed in the Far East long before it was mastered in north-west Europe. Over 5,000 years ago, Chinese potters had worked out how to shape clay, and bake it in kilns (ovens) at temperatures of about 900°C to make it hard. Gradually, they discovered how to bake better clays at much higher temperatures to make more hardwearing and water-resistant pottery, and to coat it with shiny, waterproof glazes. The toughest, most waterproof and most delicate ceramic of all was porcelain. This was invented by the Chinese about 800 years before it was produced in Europe. Porcelain was one of China's most important exports to Asia and Europe.

The Chinese were also the first to use lacquer, a smooth, hard varnish made from the sap of a tree. From about 1300BC, lacquer was used for coating wooden surfaces, such as house timbers, bowls or furniture. It could also be applied to leather and metal. Natural lacquer is grey, but in China pigment was added to make it black or bright red. It was applied in many layers until thick enough to be carved or inlaid with mother-of-pearl.

ENAMEL WARE
Ming dynasty craft workers created this ornate flask. They made a design with thin metal wire, then filled the wire compartments with drops of coloured, melted glass. The technique is called cloisonné.

CHINA'S HISTORY TOLD ON THE BIG SCREEN
A beautifully detailed, glossy lacquer screen shows a group of Portuguese merchants on a visit to China. It was made in the 1600s. Chinese crafts first became popular in Europe at this time, as European traders began doing business in southern China's ports.

FLORAL BOTTLE
This attractive Ming dynasty bottle is decorated with a coating of bright red lacquer. The lacquer is coloured with a mineral called cinnabar. It would have taken many long hours to apply and dry the many layers of lacquer. The bottle is carved with a design of peonies, which were a very popular flower in China.

FISH ON A PLATE

Pictures of fish decorate the border of this precious porcelain plate. It was made during the reign of the Qing emperor Yongzheng (1722–1736), a period famous for its elegant designs. It is coloured with enamel. Porcelain is made from a fine white clay called kaolin (china clay) and a mineral called feldspar. They are fired (baked) to a very high temperature.

A JUG OF WINE

An unknown Chinese potter made this beautiful wine jug about 1,000 years ago. It has been fired to such a high temperature that it has become strong and water-resistant. It was then coated with a grey-green glaze called celadon and fired again.

LIFE-LIKE FIGURES

A Ming dynasty entertainer smiles at his audience. All sorts of pottery figures have been found in Ming dynasty tombs. Potters made lively figures of merchants, musicians, court ladies and animals. Some are comic, while others are beautiful.

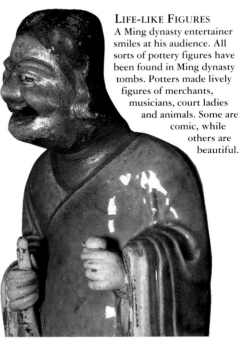

DEEP BLUE, PURE WHITE

Blue-and-white vases are typical of the late Ming dynasty (1368–1644). In the 1600s, large numbers were exported to Europe. Many were produced at the imperial potteries at Jingdezhen, in northern Jiangxi province. The workshops were set up in 1369, as the region had plentiful supplies of the very best clay. Some of the finest pottery ever made was produced there in the 1400s and 1500s.

Fine Crafts in Japan

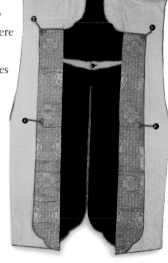

Tʜᴇʀᴇ ɪs ᴀ ʟᴏɴɢ ᴛʀᴀᴅɪᴛɪᴏɴ among Japanese craftworkers of making everyday things as beautiful as possible. Craftworkers created exquisite items for the wealthiest and most knowledgeable collectors. They used a wide variety of materials – pottery, metal, lacquer, cloth, paper and bamboo. Pottery ranged from plain, simple earthenware to delicate porcelain painted with brilliantly coloured glazes. Japanese metalworkers produced alloys (mixtures of metals) before they were known elsewhere in the world. Cloth was woven from fibres in elaborate designs. Bamboo and other plants from the grass family were woven into elegant *tatami* mats (floor mats) and containers of all different shapes and sizes. Japanese craftworkers also made beautifully decorated *inro* (little boxes, used like purses) which dangled from men's *kimono* sashes.

SHINY LACQUER

This samurai helmet was made for ceremonial use. It is covered in lacquer (varnish) and decorated with a diving dolphin. Producing shiny lacquerware was a slow process. An object was covered with many thin layers of lacquer. Each layer was allowed to dry, then polished, before more lacquer was applied. The lacquer could then be carved.

SAMURAI SURCOAT

Even the simplest garments were beautifully crafted. This surcoat (loose, sleeveless tunic) was made for a member of the noble Mori family, probably around 1800. Surcoats were worn by samurai on top of their armour.

MAKE A NETSUKE FOX

You will need: paper, pencil, ruler, self-drying clay, balsa wood, modelling tool, fine sandpaper, acrylic paint, paintbrush, water pot, darning needle, cord, small box (for an inro*), scissors, toggle, wide belt.*

1 Draw a square 5cm by 5cm on a piece of paper. Roll out a ball of clay to the size of the square. Shape the clay so that it comes to a point at one end.

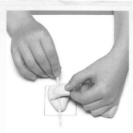

2 Turn your clay over. Lay a stick of balsa approximately 6cm long, along the back. Stick a thin sausage of clay over the stick. Press to secure.

3 Turn the clay over. Cut out two triangles of clay. Join them to the head using the tool. Make indentations to shape them into a fox's ears.

METALWORK

Craftworkers polish the sharp swords and knives they have made. It took many years of training to become a metalworker. Japanese craftsmen were famous for their fine skills at smelting and handling metals.

BOXES FOR BELTS

Inro were originally designed for storing medicines. The first *inro* were plain and simple, but after about 1700 they were often decorated with exquisite designs. These *inro* have been lacquered (coated with a shiny substance made from the sap of the lacquer tree). Inside, they contain several compartments stacked on top of each other.

MASTERWORK

This beautiful jar is decorated with a design of white flowers, painted over a shiny red and black glaze. It was painted by the master-craftsman Ogata Kenzan, who lived from 1663 to 1743.

Wear your inro *dangling from your belt. In early Japan,* inro *were usually worn by men. They were held in place with carved toggles called* netsuke.

4 Use the handle of your modelling tool to make your fox's mouth. Carve eyes, nostrils, teeth and a frown line. Use the top of a pencil to make eye holes.

5 Leave to dry. Gently sand the *netsuke* and remove the balsa wood stick. Paint it with several layers of acrylic paint. Leave in a warm place to dry.

6 Thread cord through the four corners of a small box with a darning needle. Then thread the cord through a toggle and the *netsuke,* as shown.

7 Put a wide belt round your waist. Thread the *netsuke* under the belt. It should rest on the top of it. The *inro* (box) should hang down, as shown.

Roman Decoration

DURING THE ROMAN ERA, houses and public places were decorated with paintings and statues. Mosaics were pictures made using *tesserae*, squares of stone, pottery or glass, which were pressed into soft cement. Mosaic pictures might show hunting scenes, the harvest or Roman gods. Geometric patterns were often used as borders.

Wall paintings, or murals, often showed garden scenes, birds and animals or heroes and goddesses. They were painted on to wooden panels or directly on to the wall. Roman artists loved to trick the eye by painting false columns, archways and shelves.

The Romans were skilled sculptors, using stone, marble and bronze. They imitated the ancient Greeks in putting up marble statues in public places and gardens. These might be of gods and goddesses or emperors and generals.

A COUNTRY SCENE
This man and wild boar are part of a mosaic made in Roman North Africa. Making a mosaic was quite tricky – rather like doing a jigsaw puzzle. Even so, skilled artists could create lifelike scenes from cubes of coloured glass, pottery and stone.

SCULPTURE
Statues of metal or stone were often placed in gardens. This bronze figure is in the remains of a house in Pompeii. It is of a faun, a god of the countryside.

FLOOR MOSAICS
Birds, animals, plants and country scenes were popular subjects for mosaics. These parrots are part of a much larger, and quite elaborate, floor mosaic from a Roman house.

MAKE A MOSAIC

You will need: rough paper, pencil, ruler, scissors, large sheet of card, self-drying clay, rolling pin, wooden board, modelling knife, acrylic paints, paintbrush, water pot, clear varnish and brush (optional), plaster paste, spreader, muslin rag.

1 Sketch out your mosaic design on rough paper. A simple design like this one is a good start. Cut the card so it measures 25cm x 10cm. Copy the design on to it.

2 Roll out the clay on the board. Measure out small squares on the clay. Cut them out with the modelling knife. Leave to dry. These will be your tesserae.

3 Paint the pieces in batches of different colours. When the paint is dry, coat them with clear varnish for extra strength and shine. Leave to dry.

MOSAIC MATERIALS

Mosaics were often made inside frames, in workshops, and then transported to where they were to be used. Sometimes, the tesserae were brought to the site and fitted on the spot by the workers. The floor of an average room in a Roman town house might need over 100,000 pieces.

tesserae

pot shards

MUSICIANS AND DANCERS

This dramatic painting is on the walls of an excavated villa in Pompeii. It is one in a series of paintings that show the secret rites, or mysteries, honouring the Greek god of wine, Dionysus, who was called Bacchus in Rome.

REAL OR FAKE?

Roman artists liked to make painted objects appear real enough to touch. This bowl of fruit on a shelf is typical of this style of painting. It was found on the wall of a villa that belonged to a wealthy Roman landowner.

4 Spread the plaster paste on to the card, a small part at a time. While it is still wet, press in your tesserae following your design, as shown above.

5 When the mosaic is dry, use the muslin rag to polish up the surface. Any other soft, dry cloth would also be suitable. Now your mosaic is ready for display.

The Romans liked to have mosaics in their homes. Wealthy people often had elaborate mosaics in their courtyards and dining rooms, as these were rooms that visitors would see.

Viking Picture Stories

THE VIKINGS WERE SKILLED ARTISTS and metalworkers as well as fierce warriors, although they rarely painted pictures. Instead, they embroidered tapestries, and carved pictures on wooden panels or stones.

Viking art often recorded events. Pieces of tapestry found in a Viking ship burial site in Oseberg, in Norway, show a procession of horses and wagons. The tradition of making tapestries to tell stories and events was continued by the Normans, descendants of the Vikings who settled in Normandy, in France, in the 8th century AD. Over 150 years later, the Bayeux Tapestry was made there. In 79 embroidered scenes, the Bayeux Tapestry told the story of the Norman conquest of England in 1066.

Many Viking artworks often describe the doom of the gods and destruction of the world in tales of great feuds and battles between gods, mythical monsters and giants. These often show bold, powerful figures, intricate, swirling patterns and graceful animals. They demonstrate the Viking artists' love of movement and line.

After the Viking Age, their style of art disappeared as Europeans brought different styles to the area.

TWILIGHT OF THE GODS
This stone carving from the Isle of Man shows the final battle of the gods. Odin, the father of the gods, is shown here armed with a spear and a raven on his shoulder. He is killed by Fenrir, the grey wolf.

ART FROM URNES
At Urnes, in Norway, there is a stave church that has old wood panels. They date from the final years of the Viking Age. This one shows a deer eating Yggdrasil, the tree that holds up the world. Urnes has given its name to the last and most graceful period of Viking art and design.

MAKE A SCARY FACE

You will need: pencil, paper, scissors, self-drying clay, rolling pin, board, modelling tool, sandpaper, thick brush, acrylic paints, fine brush, water pot.

1 Draw a scary monster face on paper. Copy this one or one from a book, or make up your own. Make your drawing big and bold. Then cut it out.

2 Roll out a large piece of modelling clay into a slab. Use a modelling tool to trim off the edges to look like the uneven shape of a rune stone.

3 Lay your design on top of the clay slab. Use a modelling tool to go over the lines of your drawing, pushing through the paper into the clay.

WOLF BITES GOD

In the picture below, Tyr, god of the assemblies and law-makers. His hand is being bitten off by Fenrir, the grey wolf. Fenrir is straining against a magic chain forged by the dwarfs. The chain is made from all sorts of impossible things, such as fish's breath and a mountain's roots. Tyr's name survives in the English word 'Tuesday'.

WHISTLE

This tiny whistle was made from a bird's leg bone. It may have been used to scare birds away from the crops.

WALL HANGING

The bold design on this tapestry shows the gods Odin, Thor and Frey. It comes from a church in Sweden and dates from the 1100s, just after the Viking Age. It is probably similar to the wall hangings woven for royal halls in the earlier Viking times.

4 Go over all the lines in the picture. Make sure the lines show up on the clay below. Remove the paper to see the monster's outline in clay.

5 Leave the clay to dry, turning it over to make sure it is well aired. When it is hard, smooth it down with fine sandpaper, then brush with a paintbrush.

6 Now paint the face as shown, using yellow ochre, black, red and blue. Let each colour dry completely before starting the next. Leave to dry.

Here's a face to scare off evil spirits on a dark night! Faces like this, with interlacing beard and moustache, appeared on stone memorials in the Viking Age.

Sport and Games in China

Fᴿᴼᴹ ᴇᴀʀʟʏ ɪɴ Cʜɪɴᴀ's history, kings and nobles loved to go hunting for pleasure. Horses and chariots were used to hunt deer and wild boar. Dogs and even cheetahs were trained to chase the prey. Spears, bows and arrows were then used to kill it. Falconry (using birds of prey to hunt animals) was commonplace by about 2000ʙᴄ.

In the Ming and Qing dynasties ancient spiritual disciplines used by Daoist monks were brought together with the battle training used by warriors. These martial arts (*wu shu*) were intended to train both mind and body. They came to include the body movements known as tai chi (*taijiquan*), sword play (*jianwu*) and the extreme combat known as kung fu (*gongfu*).

Archery was a popular sport in imperial China. The Chinese also loved gambling, and may have invented the first card games over 2,000 years ago.

CHINESE CHESS
The traditional Chinese game of xiang qi is similar to western chess. One army battles against another, with round discs used as playing pieces. To tell the discs apart, each is marked with a name.

pieces

xiang qi board

PEACE THROUGH MOVEMENT
A student of tai chi practises his art. The Chinese first developed the system of exercises known as tai chi more than 2,000 years ago. The techniques of tai chi were designed to help relax the human body and concentrate the mind.

MAKE A KITE

You will need: 30cm barbecue sticks (x12), ruler, scissors, glue and brush, plastic insulating tape, A1-size paper, pencil, paint (blue, red, yellow, black and pink), paintbrush, water pot, string, piece of wooden dowel, small metal ring.

1 Make a 40cm x 30cm rectangle by joining some of the sticks. Overlap the sticks for strength, then glue and tape together. Add a centre rod.

2 Make another rectangle 15cm x 40cm long. Overlay the second rectangle on top of the first one. Tape rectangles together, as shown above.

3 Place frame on to a sheet of white A1-size paper. Draw a 2.5cm border around outside of frame. Add curves around the end of the centre rod.

ALL-IN WRESTLING

This bronze figure of two wrestling muscle men was made in about 300BC. Wrestling was a very popular entertainment and sport in imperial China. It continues to be an attraction at country fairs and festivals.

BAMBOO BETTING

Gamblers place bets in a game of *liu po*. Bamboo sticks were thrown like dice to decide how far the counters on the board should move. Gambling was a widespread pastime during the Han dynasty. People would bet large sums of money on the outcome of card games, horse races and cock fights.

POLO PONIES

These women from the Tang dynasty are playing a fast and furious game of polo. They are probably noblewomen from the Emperor's royal court. The sport of polo was originally played in India and central Asia. It was invented as a training game to improve the riding skills of soldiers in cavalry units.

Chinese children today still play with home-made paper kites. Kites were invented in China in about 400BC.

4 Cut out the kite shape from the paper. Using a pencil, draw the details of your dragon design on the paper. Paint in your design and leave to dry.

5 Cut a triangular piece of paper to hang from the end of your kite as a tail. Fold tail over rod at bottom of kite, as shown. Tape tail into position.

6 Carefully tape and glue your design on to the frame. Fold over border that you allowed for when cutting out the paper. Tape to back of paper, as shown.

7 Wrap 10m of string around dowel. Tie other end to ring. Pass 2 pieces of string through kite from the back. Tie to centre rod. Tie other ends to ring.

Popular Music in Ancient Greece

MUSIC AND DANCE WERE important parts of Greek life. People sang, played and danced at religious ceremonies. Music was enjoyed for pleasure and entertainment at family celebrations, dramatic performances, feasts and drinking parties. Few written records remain of the notes played, but examples of the instruments do. The most popular instruments were the pipes. They were wind instruments similar to the oboe or clarinet. One pipe on its own was called the *aulos*, two played together were known as *auloi*. The stringed lyre and flute were other popular instruments. The stringed lyre produced solemn and dignified music. It was often played by men of noble birth to accompany a poetry recital. The flute was more usually played by slaves or dancing girls.

BREATH CONTROL
The leather strap tied around the auloi-player's cheeks helped to focus the power of his breath. One tube of the auloi supplied the melody, while the other produced an accompanying drone to give more depth to the sound. The aulos had as few as three or as many as 24 fingerholes for making the different notes.

Greek soldiers complained that lack of music was a hardship of war. Spartan soldiers resolved this problem by blowing tunes on pipes as they marched. Music was believed to have magical powers. Greek legend tells of Orpheus soothing savage beasts by playing his lyre. Another myth tells how Amphion (a son of Zeus) made stones move on their own and built a wall around the city of Thebes, by playing his lyre.

BANG! CRASH!
The bronze figurine above is playing the cymbals. They made a sound similar to castanets. The Greeks used the cymbals to accompany dancing. Other percussion instruments included wooden clappers and hand-held drums, like tambourines.

TIMPANON
You will need: scissors, corrugated card, tape measure, plate, white card, pair of compasses, pencil, PVA glue, tape, strips of newspaper, cream paper, red and purple felt-tip pens, ochre card, red and yellow ribbons.

1 Cut out a strip of corrugated card 5cm wide. Wrap it around a dinner plate. Add 6cm on to the length of this card and cut it off.

2 Put the plate upside down on the white card. Draw around it. Draw another circle 3cm inside the first. Cut this out to make a ring.

3 Glue the cardboard strip that you made in step 1 to the edge of the cardboard ring you made in step 2. Then tape them together for extra hold.

DIVINE MUSIC

Terpsichore was one of the Nine Muses, or spirits of the arts. She was the spirit of dance and music. Here Terpsichore plays a harp while her attendants hold the lyre and auloi. Other Muses included Polyhymnia, the spirit of hymns, and Euterpe, the spirit of flute-playing.

PERCUSSION

The timpanon was a tambourine made of animal skin, stretched over a frame. It was tapped to provide rhythmic accompaniment at dances or recitals. Stringed and wind instruments were thought superior because they made fitting music for solemn or exclusive occasions. Drums, cymbals and clappers were associated with buskers.

ENTERTAINING

In this plate painting a young man plays the auloi while his female companion dances. Professional musicians were often hired to entertain guests at dinner parties. Sometimes the musicians were household slaves.

To play the timpanon tap on it with your fingers, as the ancient Greeks would have done.

4 Make up some papier mâché solution with 1 part glue to 2 parts water. Soak strips of newspaper in it and cover the card ring with the wet strips.

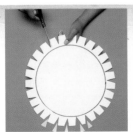

5 Draw around the plate on to cream paper. Draw another circle 5cm outside this. To make tabs, cut out about 28 small triangles around the edge.

6 Draw the design shown above on to the paper. Place the paper over the top of the card ring. Dab glue on each tab and stick on to the corrugated card.

7 Cut a strip of ochre card big enough to fit around the timpanon. Decorate it as above and glue on. Make 4 bows with the ribbons and glue around the edge.

Mythical Tales of Greece

GREEK MYTHOLOGY IS RICH in stories of victorious heroes and heroines, quarrelling gods and goddesses, and mysterious and unusual creatures. While keeping people entertained, the stories also tried to answer questions about how the world and humans came into existence. These powerful tales provided inspiration for ancient Greek art and material for their plays, which were performed to audiences of over 10,000. In addition, they were a valuable historical record and encouraged the Greeks to take pride in their cultural past.

Traditionally, mythical stories were passed down generations by word of mouth. Sometimes travelling bards were paid to recite poems, which they had learnt by heart. Eventually, these tales came to be written down. The earliest of these that survive are thought to be the work of the poet Homer (*c.*800BC). Two poems that we know about are *The Odyssey* and *The Iliad*. Both tell tales of heroes battling against supernatural forces.

MONSTER KILLER
According to Greek legend the Minotaur was half-bull and half-man. It lived in a maze called the labyrinth on the island of Crete. Many people had entered the maze but never come out. Each year the people of Athens were forced to send human sacrifices to feed the bull. The hero Theseus made it his mission to kill the Minotaur. A princess presented Theseus with a sword and a ball of string to help him. Theseus unwound the string as he walked through the maze. After killing the Minotaur he followed the string back to the entrance of the cave.

SNAKE STRANGLER
The super-strong Heracles was the only human being to become a Greek god. This Roman fresco shows him as a baby strangling serpents sent by the jealous goddess Hera to kill him.

HEAD OF MEDUSA
You will need: board, self-drying modelling clay, rolling pin, ruler, modelling tool, pencil, sandpaper, acrylic paints, one small and one large paintbrush, varnish (1 part water to 1 part PVA glue).

1 With a rolling pin, roll out a slab of clay 20cm by 20cm and 2cm thick. With the modelling tool, cut out a head in the shape shown in the picture.

2 Shape a small piece of clay into a nose. Mould it on to the head with your fingers. Use the modelling tool to smooth the edges into the face.

3 Carve a mouth with lots of teeth and two eyes and etch a gruesome design into the head. Press the end of a pencil into the eyes to make eyeballs.

STONY STARE

Medusa was a winged monster with hair of snakes. She was one of three such female gorgons. Medusa had a face so horrific that any human who looked directly at it was turned to stone. The only way to kill her was to cut off her head. Medusa, whose name means 'cunning', outwitted several would-be killers. The hero Perseus finally killed her with help from Athena and Hermes. They lent Perseus a magic cap to make him invisible, a sickle to cut off Medusa's head and a shield in which to see her reflection. Even dead, Medusa remained powerful. Perseus killed his enemy Polydectes by forcing him to look at her face.

FOOLING THE GIANT

King Odysseus was a mythical hero who had many adventures. One escapade found him captured in a cave by a one-eyed giant. To escape, Odysseus stabbed out the giant's eye and rode out of the cave clinging to the underside of a ram.

The word gorgon in Greek suggests the monster's glaring eyes.

FLYING HORSE

The winged horse Pegasus appeared on the coins of Corinth as the city's symbol. Pegasus helped Bellerophon, a Corinthian hero, in his battles. First against the Chimaera which was a monster with a lion's head, a goat's middle and a snake's tail and then against the Amazons, a race of female warriors.

4 Between the palms of your hands, roll out four thin strips of clay to represent the snakes on Medusa's head. Press them into place as shown above.

5 Press a finger down on the end of each roll to make a snake's head. Use the modelling tool and pencil to carve in scales on the snakes' bodies.

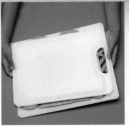

6 The head needs to dry completely before you can paint the face. To dry it, let it sit for a few hours on either side. Be careful when you turn it over.

7 When the head is completely dry, sand with fine sandpaper. Paint the face in black, red, white and gold as shown here. Leave to dry and varnish.

Roman Sport and Combat

MOST ROMANS preferred watching sport to taking part. There were some, however, who enjoyed athletics and keeping fit. They took their exercise at the public baths and at the sports ground or *palaestra*. Men competed at wrestling, the long jump and swimming. Women also exercised by working out with weights.

Boxing matches and chariot races were always well attended. The races took place on a long, oval racetrack, called a circus. The crowds watched with such excitement that violent riots often followed. Charioteers and their teams became big stars. Roman crowds also enjoyed watching displays of violence. Bloody battles between gladiators and fights among wild animals took place in a special oval arena, called an amphitheatre. Roman entertainments became more spectacular and bloodthirsty with time. The arenas of amphitheatres were sometimes flooded for mock sea battles.

A COLOSSEUM
This is the colosseum in the Roman city of El Djem, in Tunisia. A colosseum was a kind of amphitheatre. Arenas such as this were built all over the Empire. The largest and most famous is the Colosseum in Rome.

DEATH OR MERCY?
Gladiators usually fought to the death, but a wounded gladiator could appeal for mercy. The excited crowd would look for the emperor's signal. A thumbs-up meant his life was spared. A thumbs-down meant he must die.

COME ON YOU REDS!

Charioteers belonged to teams and wore their team's colours when they raced. Some also wore protective leather helmets, like the one in this mosaic. In Rome, there were four teams – the Reds, Blues, Whites and Greens. Each team had faithful fans and charioteers were every bit as popular as football stars today.

A DAY AT THE RACES

This terracotta carving records an exciting moment at the races. Chariot racing was a passion for most Romans. Chariots were usually pulled by four horses, though just two or as many as six could be used. Accidents and foul play were common as the chariots thundered round the track.

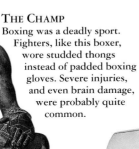

THE CHAMP

Boxing was a deadly sport. Fighters, like this boxer, wore studded thongs instead of padded boxing gloves. Severe injuries, and even brain damage, were probably quite common.

THE GREEK IDEAL

The Romans admired all things Greek, including their love of athletics. This painted Greek vase dates from about 333BC and shows long-distance runners. However, Roman crowds were not interested in athletic contests in the Greek style, such as the Olympic Games.

American Indian Storytelling

NORTH AMERICAN INDIANS LOVED storytelling. Many stories taught the children to respect nature and animals or described social behaviour. Stories were also a way of passing on tribal customs, rituals and religious beliefs. Some tribes considered it unlucky to tell tales of mythological events during the summer months. They looked forward to the long winter nights when they would gather in their tipis or lodges and huddle around the fire. Then, they listened to the storyteller who was often one of the elders. A story might recall past hunts and battles, or it could be complete fiction, although the listener could never be sure as the tales were always embellished. This was especially true if the storyteller was from the Yuma tribe. The Great Dreams of the Yuma people were fantastical tales, usually performed as plays and often based on tribal rituals and folklore.

SCROLL RECORDS

This is a fine example of a birchbark scroll. It is a Midewiwin (Grand Medicine Society) record of the Ojibwa. Most ceremonies were so long and complicated that a chart had to be made to remember all the songs and prayers in the right order. A document such as this was used to record the history and initiation rites of a tribe. Without it, knowledge of them might be lost forever.

STORY BEHIND THE PICTURES

A proud Mandan chief and his wife pose for a picture to be painted. It is not just the chief's headdress that reveals great prowess in battle. The painted skin displayed by the woman tells stories of the tribe's history. The war scenes show that the tribe has been involved in many victorious battles in the past. This group picture was painted between 1833 and 1835 by George Catlin. He was an artist whose paintings of North American Indians are themselves a form of storytelling. They are an important source of information about tribal lives, customs and dress, particularly as the Indians at that time did not write any books about themselves.

COLOURED SAND

Although many tribes made sandpaintings *(shown above)* it was the Navajo who developed the art. The painter trickled powders of yellow, white and red ochre and sandstone into patterns on the sand. Each picture described humans and spirits connected with creation stories and was usually used as part of a healing ceremony.

HEROIC TALES

The Sioux chief, seen at the bottom of this picture, must have been exceptionally brave as his headdress is very long. Painting warrior shields was an ancient art used to pass on tales of battle heroics. This shield may have been painted by one of the warriors involved. Shields were kept in the lodge and brought out when the warrior retold how brave he was. It would be given to his children to keep his memory alive.

WRITTEN IN STONE

These children are reading about the history of their ancestors in Colorado Springs. Stone Age North American Indians (the early Pueblo people) carved animals and designs on stone which told a little of their way of life.

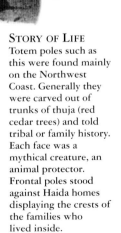

THE HISTORIAN

A young boy looks on as his father records tribal stories on dried animal hide. He is already learning the importance of recording the family history. Even in 1903, when this picture was painted, many tribes used picture writing, not the printed word of the white man.

STORY OF LIFE

Totem poles such as this were found mainly on the Northwest Coast. Generally they were carved out of trunks of thuja (red cedar trees) and told tribal or family history. Each face was a mythical creature, an animal protector. Frontal poles stood against Haida homes displaying the crests of the families who lived inside.

Celtic Bards and Musicians

THE CELTS ENJOYED MUSIC, poems and songs as entertainment, and for more serious purposes. Music accompanied Celtic warriors into battle and made them feel brave. Poems praised the achievements of a great chieftain or the adventures of bold raiders, and recorded the history of a tribe. Dead chieftains and heroes, and possibly even ordinary people, too, were mourned with sad laments. On special occasions, and in the homes of high-ranking Celts, poems and songs were performed by people called bards.

Roman writers described the many years of training to become a bard. Bards learned how to compose using all the different styles of poetry, and memorized hundreds of legends and songs. They also learned how to play an instrument, and to read and write, although most Celtic music and poetry was never written down. Becoming a bard was the first step towards being a druid (priest).

HOLY MUSIC

We do not know what part music played in Celtic religious ceremonies, but it was probably important. This stone statue shows a Celtic god playing a lyre. The Celts believed that religious knowledge, and music, was too holy to be written down. Sadly, this means that many Celtic poems and songs have been lost for ever.

GRACEFUL DANCER

Naked dancing girls may have entertained guests at important feasts. This little bronze statue, just 13cm high, dates from around 50BC. The Celts enjoyed dancing, and from the evidence of this statue it seems likely that their dances were quite wild in their movements.

MAKE A HARP

You will need: card 39 cm x 49 cm, pencil, ruler, scissors, cardboard 39 cm x 49 cm , felt-tip pen, paints, paintbrushes, bradawl, coloured string, paper fasteners.

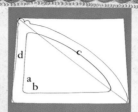

1 On the piece of card, draw a diagonal line from corner to corner. Draw a second, gently curving line, shaped at one end, as shown .

2 Draw two lines (a and b), 4.5 cm in from the edge of the paper. Join them with a curved line c. Finally add a curved line d parallel to *a*, as shown.

3 Cut out the harp shape. Place it on cardboard. Carefully draw round it with a felt-tip pen both inside and out. Cut the cardboard harp out.

HARPIST

This harpist is pictured on the Dupplin Cross, from Scotland. The harp itself is large and triangular in shape. It was placed on the ground and held between the harpist's knees. Such harps were popular at the end of the Celtic period.

MUSICAL GROUP

Musicians are shown playing at a religious ceremony on this stone carving from Scotland, dating from around AD900. The bottom panel shows a harpist plucking the strings of his harp, while a fellow musician plays a pipe. In the foreground is a drum, possibly made from a barrel with a skin stretched over it.

INSPIRED BY A DREAM

While a Celtic bard sleeps, he dreams of a beautiful woman from the world of the spirits. She will be the subject of his next song. Dreams and visions were a common theme in many ancient Celtic poems and legends. For example, Oisin, son of the great hero Finn MacCool, ran away with Niamh of the Golden Hair. Niamh was a spirit who appeared to Finn in a dream and invited him to come to a magic land across the waves.

Most Celtic poetry was not spoken, but sung or chanted to the music of a harp or a lyre. Bards used the music to create the right atmosphere to accompany their words, and to add extra dramatic effects, such as shivery sounds during a scary ghost tale.

4 Glue the one side of the card and and one side of the cardboard. Stick them together. Paint the harp brown and leave it in a warm place to dry.

5 Use a bradawl to make holes approximately 5 cm apart along the two straight sides of the harp. These will be the holes for the strings.

6 Cut a length of string 40 cm long. Cut 7 more pieces of string each 5 cm shorter than the last. Tie a paper fastener to both ends of each string.

7 Push the paper fasteners in to the harp frame so that the strings lie diagonally across the harp. Adjust the strings so that they are stretched tightly.

Games in Mesoamerica

MESOAMERICAN PEOPLE of Central America enjoyed sports and games after work and on festival days. Two favourite games were *tlachtli* or *ulama*, the famous Mesoamerican ball game, and *patolli*, a board game. The ball game was played in front of huge crowds, while *patolli* was a quieter game. Mesoamerican games were not just for fun. Both the ball game and *patolli* had religious meanings. In the first, the court symbolized the world, and the rubber ball stood for the Sun as it made its daily journey across the sky. Players were meant to keep the ball moving in order to give energy to the Sun. Losing teams were sometimes sacrificed as offerings to the Sun god. In *patolli*, the movement of counters on the board represented the passing years.

PATOLLI

A group of Aztecs are shown here playing the game of *patolli*. It was played by moving dried beans or clay counters along a cross-shaped board with 52 squares. It could be very exciting. Players often bet on the result.

THE ACROBAT

This Olmec statue shows a very supple acrobat. Mesoamericans admired youth, fitness and beauty. Sports were fun, but they could also be good training for the demands of war. Being fit was considered attractive.

FLYING MEN

Volador was a ceremony performed on religious festival days. Four men, dressed as birds and attached to ropes, jumped off a high pole. As they spun round, falling towards the ground, they circled the pole 13 times each. That made 52 circuits – the length of the Mesoamerican holy calendar cycle.

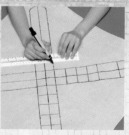

PLAY PATOLLI

You will need: thick card, pencil, ruler, black marker pen, paints, small paintbrush, water pot, coloured papers, scissors, PVA glue and glue brush, dried broad or butter beans, self-drying clay.

1 Measure a square of thick card about 50cm x 50cm. Using a marker pen and a ruler, draw three lines from corner to corner to make a cross-shape.

2 Draw seven pairs of spaces along each arm. The third space in from the end should be a double space. Paint triangles in it.

3 Draw eight jaguar heads and eight marigolds on differently coloured paper. Cut them out. Paint the face of the Sun god into the centre.

TARGET RING

This stone ring comes from Chichen-Itza. Ball-game players used only their hips and knees to hit a solid rubber ball through rings like this fixed high on the ball-court walls.

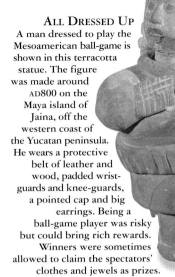

ALL DRESSED UP

A man dressed to play the Mesoamerican ball-game is shown in this terracotta statue. The figure was made around AD800 on the Maya island of Jaina, off the western coast of the Yucatan peninsula. He wears a protective belt of leather and wood, padded wrist-guards and knee-guards, a pointed cap and big earrings. Being a ball-game player was risky but could bring rich rewards. Winners were sometimes allowed to claim the spectators' clothes and jewels as prizes.

PLAY BALL

The ruins of a huge ball-court can still be seen in the Maya city of Uxmal. The biggest courts were up to 60m long and were built next to temples, in the centre of cities. People crowded inside the court to watch. Play was fast, furious and dangerous. Many players were injured as they clashed with opponents.

4 Stick the jaguars and marigolds randomly on the board. Paint a blue circle at the end of one arm, and a crown at the opposite end. Repeat in green on the other arms.

5 Paint five dried beans black with a white dot on one side. The beans will be thrown as dice. Make two counters from clay. Paint one green and one blue.

Most of the original rules for patolli have been lost. In this version, start each counter on the circle of the same colour. The aim is to move your counter to the crown of the same colour and back. Lose a turn if you land on a jaguar and get an extra turn if you land on a marigold.

At the Theatre in Japan

Going to the theatre and listening to music were popular in Japan among the wealthy. There were several kinds of Japanese drama. They developed from religious dances at temples and shrines, or from slow, stately dances performed at the emperor's court.

Noh is the oldest form of Japanese drama. It developed in the 1300s from rituals and dances that had been performed for centuries before. Noh plays were serious and dignified. The actors performed on a bare stage, with only a backdrop. They chanted or sang their words, accompanied by drums and a flute. Noh performances were traditionally held in the open air, often at a shrine.

Kabuki plays were first seen around 1600. In 1629, the shoguns banned women performers and so male actors took their places. Kabuki plays became very popular in the new, fast-growing towns.

GRACEFUL PLAYER
This woman entertainer is holding a *shamisen* – a three-stringed instrument, played by plucking the strings. The *shamisen* often formed part of a group, together with a *koto* (zither) and flute.

POPULAR PUPPETS
Bunraku (puppet plays) originated about 400 years ago, when *shamisen* music, dramatic chanting and hand-held puppets were combined. The puppets were so large and complex that it took three men to move them about on stage.

NOH THEATRE MASK
You will need: tape measure, balloon, newspaper, bowl, glue, petroleum jelly, pin, scissors, felt-tip pen, modelling clay, bradawl, paints (red, yellow, black, and white), paintbrush, water pot, cord.

1 Ask a friend to measure around your head above the ears. Blow up a balloon to fit this measurement. This will be the base for the papier-mâché.

2 Rip up strips of newspaper. Soak in a water and glue mixture (1 part glue to 2 parts water). Cover the balloon with a layer of petroleum jelly.

3 Cover the front and sides of your balloon with a layer of papier-mâché. Leave to dry. Repeat 2 or 3 times. When dry, pop the balloon.

TRAGIC THEATRE

An audience watches a scene from an outdoor performance of a Noh play. Noh drama was always about important and serious topics. Favourite subjects were death and the afterlife, and the plays were often very tragic.

LOUD AND FAST

Kabuki plays were a complete contrast to Noh. They were fast-moving, loud, flashy and very dramatic. Audiences admired the skills of the actors as much as the cleverness or thoughtfulness of the plots.

BEHIND THE MASK

This Noh mask represents a warrior's face. Noh drama did not try to be lifelike. The actors all wore masks and moved very slowly using stiff, stylized gestures to express their feelings. Noh plays were all performed by men. Actors playing women's parts wore female clothes and masks.

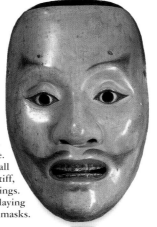

Put on your mask and feel like an actor in an ancient Noh play. Imagine that you are wearing his long, swirling robes, too.

4 Trim the papier-mâché so that it forms a mask shape. Ask a friend to mark where your eyes, nose and mouth are when you hold it to your face.

5 Cut out the face holes with scissors. Put clay beneath the side of the mask at eye level. Use a bradawl to make two holes on each side.

6 Paint the face of a calm young lady from Noh theatre on your mask. Use this picture as your guide. The mask would have been worn by a man.

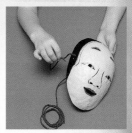

7 Fit the cord through the holes at each side. Tie one end. Once you have adjusted the mask so that it fits, tie the other end.

Entertaining Royal India

MUSIC AND DANCE have long entertained noble people in the royal courts. In Mughal India (1526–1857), courtiers listened to poetry and music every day. They loved riddles and word games, and in contests, poets were given half a verse and asked to complete it. Different art forms were connected to one another. For example, the *Natyashastra*, an ancient text on dance and drama, includes a long section on music. Dancers were also storytellers, using hand gestures to show meaning. North and south India developed their own musical traditions – Hindustani in the north and Karnatak in the south. Islam introduced new instruments, such as the sitar (a stringed instrument) and the tabla (a drum). Outside the courts, religion played a part in the development of singing. Muslim mystics sang and played musical pieces called *qawwali*, while Hindus sang songs to the god, Krishna.

JOYFUL OCCASION

Drummers and trumpeters at the Mughal court joyfully proclaim the birth of Akbar's son, Prince Salim. Music was often used to announce celebrations. Though they enjoyed royal patronage and were often renowned for their talent, musicians, dancers and actors were generally considered to be of low social standing.

INSTRUMENTAL BIRD

An instrument called a *sarongi* has been finely carved in the shape of a peacock. The *sarongi* was played with a bow and usually accompanied the dance performances of courtesans during late Mughal times.

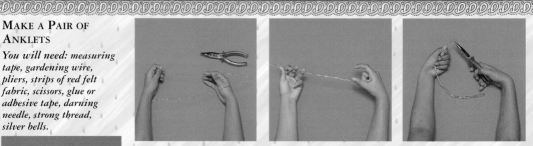

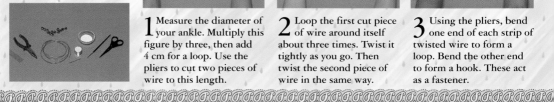

MAKE A PAIR OF ANKLETS

You will need: measuring tape, gardening wire, pliers, strips of red felt fabric, scissors, glue or adhesive tape, darning needle, strong thread, silver bells.

1 Measure the diameter of your ankle. Multiply this figure by three, then add 4 cm for a loop. Use the pliers to cut two pieces of wire to this length.

2 Loop the first cut piece of wire around itself about three times. Twist it tightly as you go. Then twist the second piece of wire in the same way.

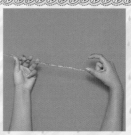

3 Using the pliers, bend one end of each strip of twisted wire to form a loop. Bend the other end to form a hook. These act as a fastener.

FOLK DANCING

This tapestry shows a folk dance in the Punjab. Folk dances were common in the villages, among ordinary people. Each dance usually involved lots of performers. People danced to celebrate births, weddings and many other special occasions.

ENTERTAINING AT COURT

Dancers perform the style of dance known as a Kathak for the great Mughal emperor Akbar. Dance was a popular form of entertainment at court. Many of the complicated dance styles known in India today originated at the courts of kings in ancient times. The dances performed at court often told a story.

ON A STRING

A woman from Rajasthan plays with a yo-yo. Games with balls and strings were not expensive, so they could be enjoyed by both rich and poor people. Many other kinds of games were afforded only by the wealthy.

Anklets were worn by dancers who performed at ceremonies in the royal courts of the Mughals.

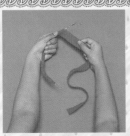

4 Cut out two strips of felt fabric that are slightly longer than your strips of wire. Glue or tape a felt strip on to the end of the twisted wire.

5 Wrap the felt around the wire, overlapping the edges of the felt. Glue the end of the felt to the place where you began. Wrap the second wire strip.

6 Thread a darning needle with sewing thread. Sew lots of tiny silver bells to the felt fabric covering your wire loops.

7 Repeat your stitches several times to make sure that the bells stay firmly in place. Add more bells, so that you cover both anklets completely.

Picture-writing in Mesopotamia

WRITING, AS A MEANS of recording information, first developed in the ancient worlds of Mesopotamia (present-day Iraq), Egypt and China. The earliest examples are about 5,000 years old and come from the Sumerian city-state of Uruk. At first, writing was in the form of pictures and numbers. It was used to make lists of produce such as barley, wine and cheese, or numbers of cattle and donkeys. Gradually, this picture-writing was replaced by groups of wedge-shaped strokes formed by a reed pen as it was pressed into the clay. This type of writing is called cuneiform, which means 'wedge-shaped'. To begin with, cuneiform was only used to write Sumerian, but later it was adapted to write several other languages, including Assyrian and Babylonian.

CLAY TABLET
Writing was done on clay tablets with a stylus (pen) made from a reed. The writer pressed the stylus into a slab of damp clay. This was left to dry and harden. The clay tablet in the picture, from around 3000BC, has symbols on it. One symbol looks like a hand and others resemble trees or plants. It is not clear which language they represent, although it is likely to be Sumerian.

TWO SCRIBES
The scribe on the right is writing on a clay tablet with a stylus. He is making a list of all the booty and prisoners that his king has captured in battle. He is writing in Akkadian, one of the languages used by the Assyrians. The other scribe is writing on a leather roll, possibly in Aramaic, another language the Assyrians used. Aramaic was an easier language to write because it used an alphabet unlike Akkadian, which used about 600 different signs.

SHAPES AND SIZES
Differently shaped clay tablets, including prisms and cylinders, were used for writing. Many tablets were flat but some were three-dimensional and hollow like vases. One like this, that narrows at each end, is called a prism. It is about 30cm long and records the military campaigns of King Sargon of Assyria.

A CLAY TABLET
You will need: pen, stiff card, ruler, scissors, modelling clay, cutting board, rolling pin, blunt knife, paper, paint and paintbrush, cloth.

1 Draw a pointed stylus 20cm by 1.5cm on to the stiff card with the pen. Use the shape in the picture as a guide. Cut the shape out with the scissors.

2 Roll out the clay on the cutting board with the rolling pin until it measures about 30cm by 15cm. Use the knife to cut out the clay as shown.

3 Take your card stylus and start writing cuneiform script on your clay tablet. Use the wedge shape of your stylus to make the strokes.

COMMUNICATING IDEAS

Cuneiform signs gradually came to be used for ideas as well as objects. At first, a drawing of a head meant simply 'head', but later came to mean 'front' and 'first'. The symbols also came to represent spoken sounds and could be used to make new words. For example, in English, you could make the word 'belief' by drawing the symbols for a bee and a leaf. The chart shows how cuneiform writing developed. On the top row are simple drawings. In the middle row the pictures have been replaced by groups of wedges, and in the bottom row are the even more simplified versions of the signs.

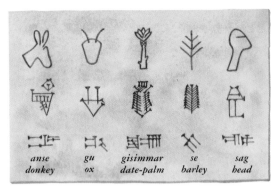

anse donkey	gu ox	gisimmar date-palm	se barley	sag head

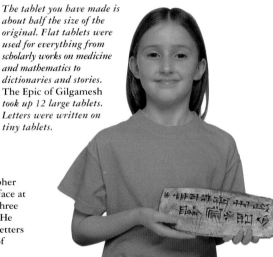

The tablet you have made is about half the size of the original. Flat tablets were used for everything from scholarly works on medicine and mathematics to dictionaries and stories. The Epic of Gilgamesh took up 12 large tablets. Letters were written on tiny tablets.

WRITING ON THE ROCK FACE

Henry Rawlinson, a British army officer who helped decipher cuneiform in the mid-1800s, risks his life climbing a cliff face at Behistun to copy the writing there. The inscription was in three languages, Old Persian, Elamite and Babylonian (Akkadian). He guessed that the cuneiform signs in Old Persian represented letters of the alphabet and found the name of Darius, the King of Persia. This helped scholars work out all three languages.

4 Copy the wedge-shapes of the cuneiform script shown here. See how each group of strokes combines to make a particular letter or word.

5 Move your tablet on to a piece of clean paper. Take the paintbrush and paint and cover the clay, working the paint well into the cuneiform script.

6 When the painting is finished, wipe across the clay with the cloth. Most of the paint should come off, leaving the lettering a darker colour.

7 Leave the clay and the paint to dry. The lettering on your finished tablet reads: Nebuchadnezzar King of Babylon.

Decoding Egyptian Script

MOST OF WHAT WE KNOW about the people of the past comes from the written language they left behind. Inscriptions providing information about the ancient Egyptians can be found on everything from obelisks to tombs. From 3100BC the Egyptians used pictures called hieroglyphs. Each picture stood for an object, an idea or a sound. There were around 1,000 hieroglyphic symbols. The term hiero means sacred. This is because it was initially used by the Egyptians for religious texts.

By 1780BC, hieroglyphs had evolved into hieratic, a more flowing text. In the latter days of ancient Egypt, an even simpler script called demotic (popular) was used. However, by AD600, long after the last of the pharaohs, no one understood hieroglyphs. The secrets of ancient Egypt were lost for 1,200 years, until the discovery of the Rosetta Stone.

THE ROSETTA STONE

The discovery of the Rosetta Stone was a lucky accident. In 1799, a French soldier discovered a piece of stone at an Egyptian village called el-Rashid or Rosetta. On the stone, the same words were written in three scripts representing two languages. Hieroglyphic text is at the top, demotic text is in the centre, and Greek is at the bottom.

EGYPTIAN CODE CRACKED

French scholar Jean-François Champollion cracked the Rosetta Stone code in 1822. The stone contains a royal decree written in 196BC when the Greek king Ptolemy V was in power in Egypt. The Greek on the stone enabled Champollion to translate the hieroglyphs. This one discovery is central to our understanding of the way the ancient Egyptians used to live.

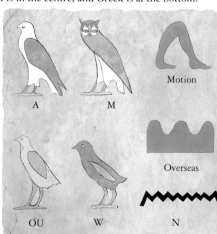

A   M   Motion

OU   W   Overseas   N

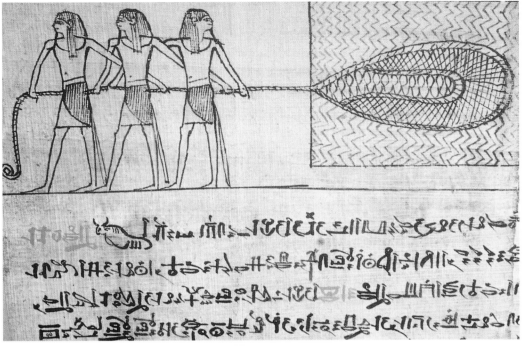

HIERATIC SCRIPT

The picture symbols of hieroglyphs, developed into hieratic script (above), which had signs that were more like letters. This script was more flowing and could be written quickly. It was used for stories, letters and business contracts. It was always read from right to left.

DEMOTIC SCRIPT

A new script, demotic (*left*), was introduced towards the end of the New Kingdom (1550–1070BC). This could be written even more quickly than hieratic script. Initially it was used for business, but soon it was also being used for religious and scientific writings. It disappeared when Egypt came under Roman rule in 30BC.

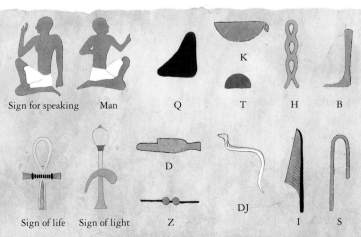

Sign for speaking   Man   Q   T   H   B

K

Sign of life   Sign of light   Z   D   DJ   I   S

HIEROGLYPHS

Made up of small pictures, hieroglyphs were based on simplified sketches of birds and snakes, plants, parts of the body, boats and houses. Some hieroglyphs represented complete ideas such as light, travel or life. Others stood for letters or sounds that could be combined to make words.

Chinese Word Symbols

THE CHINESE LANGUAGE is written with symbols (characters) that stand for sounds and words. The first-known Chinese writing dates to more than 1000 years after the invention of writing in Egypt and Mesopotamia. With few outside influences, these early symbols changed little over the ages, making modern Chinese the oldest writing in use today. A dictionary from 1716 lists over 40,000 characters. Each character was written with a brush, using 11 basic strokes. The painting of these beautiful characters is called calligraphy, and was always seen as a form of art.

Before the Chinese began using woodblocks for printing in 1600BC, books were often handwritten on bamboo strips. Movable type was invented in the AD1040s. The Chinese also invented paper, nearly 2,000 years ago. Cloth or bark was shredded, pulped and dried on frames. Ancient writings included poetry, practical handbooks and encyclopedias. During the 1500s, popular folk tales such as *The Water Margin* were published, and about 200 years later, the writer Cao Xuequin produced the novel, *A Dream of Red Mansions*.

MAGICAL MESSAGES
The earliest surviving Chinese script appears on animal bones. They were used for telling fortunes in about 1200BC. The script was made up of small pictures representing objects or ideas. Modern Chinese script is made up of patterns of lines.

ART OF CALLIGRAPHY
This text was handwritten during the Tang dynasty (AD618–906). Traditional Chinese writing reads down from right to left, starting in the top right-hand corner.

MAKE PRINTING BLOCKS

You will need: plain white paper, pencil, paint, soft Chinese brush or thin paintbrush, water pot, tracing paper, board, self-drying clay (15cm x 20cm, 2.5cm thick), modelling tool, wood glue, block printing ink, damp rag.

1 Copy or trace the characters from the reversed image block (see opposite). Start off with a pencil outline, then fill in with paint. Leave to dry.

2 Copy design on to tracing paper. Turn the paper over. Place it on the clay. Scribble on the clean side of the paper to leave a mirror image in the clay.

3 Use a modelling tool to carve out characters. Cut away clay all around characters to make a relief (raised pattern). Smooth clay base with your fingertips.

THE BEST WAY TO WRITE
A calligrapher of the 1840s begins to write, surrounded by his assistants. The brush must be held upright for the writing of Chinese characters. The wrist is never rested on the table. Many years of practice and study are necessary to become a good calligrapher.

INKS AND COLOURS
The watercolours and inks used for Chinese calligraphy were based on plant and mineral pigments in reds, blues, greens and yellows. Black ink was made from carbon, obtained from soot. This was mixed with glue to form a solid block. The ink block was wetted during use. Brushes were made from animal hair fitted into bamboo handles.

Chinese brushes

THE PRINTED PAGE
The Buddhist scripture called the *Diamond Sutra (shown right)* is probably the oldest surviving printed book in the world. It includes both text and pictures. The book was printed from a wood block on 11 May AD868 and was intended to be distributed to the public free of charge.

reversed image *actual image*

Moon Ruler

Mouth Sun

Block rubbings of characters were an early form of printing.

4 When the relief has dried, paint the clay block with wood glue. Leave it to dry thoroughly. When dry, the glue seals and protects the pattern.

5 Now paint the design. Apply a thick layer of printing ink to the raised parts of the clay with a Chinese brush or a soft paintbrush.

6 Lay a thin piece of plain white paper over the inked block. Use a dry brush to press the paper into the ink, so that the paper takes up the design.

7 Lift up the paper to reveal your design. Look after your printing block by cleaning it with a damp rag. You can then use it again and again.

Celtic Messages in Stone

I N EUROPE, the Celts had several different languages, but no single Celtic alphabet. To write something down, the Celts had to borrow other peoples' scripts. Sometimes they used Greek letters, sometimes Latin (the Romans' language). In the British Isles, a script known as Ogham was based on the Latin alphabet, but used straight lines instead of letters. Celtic craftworkers used all these different ways of writing to carve messages in stone. Their inscriptions might commemorate an important event, or a person who had died, or be a proud symbol of a leader's power. Craftworkers also decorated stones with beautiful patterns, sometimes copied from jewellery and metalworking designs. In some parts of Celtic Europe, standing stones and lumps of rock were carved with special symbols. Historians believe that these picture-carvings were designed to increase respect for powerful leaders, and for the gods.

STANDING STONE
Tall, carved standing stones were a special feature of Celtic lands in north-west France and Ireland. Archaeologists are not sure why they were put up or decorated, but they probably marked boundaries or holy sites. This stone comes from Turoe, in Ireland.

PRACTICE MAKES PERFECT
Before using precious metals such as gold, or starting to chip away at hard, valuable materials such as stone, craftworkers made sketches and worked out patterns on little pieces of bone. These bone fragments, marked with compass designs, were found in Ireland. They belonged to craftworkers from around AD50.

MAKE AN OGHAM STONE

You will need: modelling clay, board, rolling pin, ruler, modelling tool, sandpaper, white paint, paintbrush, green card, scissors, PVA glue.

1 Roll out the modelling clay to make a strip roughly 33 cm long, 5 cm wide and 3 cm thick. Carefully shape the top as shown.

2 Take the modelling tool and make a hole in the top end of the strip. This tall "holed" Ogham stone is based on one in southern Ireland from AD400.

3 These are some of the Ogham letters.

ON LIVING ROCK

This rough slab of stone is decorated with a carving of a wild boar. It was found in Dunadd, Scotland. Archaeologists have many theories as to why it was carved. It may have been a memorial to a dead leader or a notice announcing an alliance between friendly clans. An alternative view is that it was a tribal symbol, put up as a proud boast of the local peoples' power or a sign of a local chieftain's land.

THE CELTS LIVE ON

The Picts were a mysterious people who lived in Scotland from about AD300 to 900. They were descended from Celtic people and they continued many of the Celts' customs and traditions. In particular, they carved picture-symbols and Ogham letters on stone slabs, in caves and on lumps of rock. This stone monument, from Orkney, Scotland, shows three warriors and various other common Pictish symbols.

ALL CHANGE

Many tall, carved stones had religious power for the Celts. When Christian missionaries arrived in Celtic lands, they sometimes decided to make old carved stones into Christian monuments. They hoped this might help people understand that the Christian God was more important than the old Celtic ones. This stone is at Oronsay in the Orkney Islands off the north-east coast of Scotland.

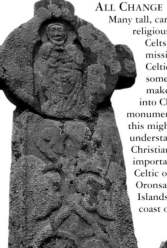

Ogham is sometimes referred to as the "tree alphabet" because each letter takes the name of a tree. In many cases the Ogham inscription on a stone is read from the bottom up and contains the name of the person being commemorated and that of the carver.

4 Ogham writing is done as a series of lines or notches scored across a long stem. Use the alphabet in step 3 to help you write something on your stone.

5 Ogham inscriptions are often found on memorials featuring a person's name. You could try writing your name on your model Ogham stone.

6 Sand the modelling clay gently to remove any rough edges. Then paint one side of your stone. Leave to dry, turn over and paint the other side.

7 Cut a circular base out of green card, roughly 14 cm wide. Glue the bottom of your stone on to the base, as shown. Now leave the stone to dry.

Mesoamerican Writing

THE MAYA OF CENTRAL AMERICA were the first – and only –
Mesoamerican people to invent a complete writing system. By AD250,
Maya picture-symbols and sound-symbols were written in books, carved on
buildings, painted on pottery and inscribed on precious stones. Maya scribes
also developed an advanced number system, including a sign for zero,
which Europeans at the time did not have.

Maya writing used glyphs (pictures standing for words) and also
picture-signs that stood for sounds. The sound-signs could be joined
together, like the letters of the Roman alphabet, to make words and
complete sentences. The Aztecs used picture-writing too, but theirs
was much simpler and less flexible. Maya and Aztec picture-symbols
were difficult to learn. Only specially trained scribes could write them,
and only priests or rich people
could read them. They could
spare time for study and
afford to pay a good teacher.

MAYA READER
A Maya statue showing a wealthy
woman seated cross-legged with a
codex (folding book) on her lap. A
Maya or Aztec codex was made of
long strips of fig-bark paper,
folded like a concertina. The
writing was read from top to
bottom and left to right.

CITY EMBLEM
Four separate images make up
this emblem-glyph for the Maya city-
state of Copan. Together they give a
message meaning 'the home of the
rulers of the royal blood of Copan'. At
the bottom, you can see a bat, the
special picture-sign for the city.

MAKE A CODEX
*You will need: thin card,
ruler, pencil, scissors, white
acrylic paint, eraser, large
and small paintbrushes,
water pot, paints in red,
yellow, blue and black,
palette, tracing paper.*

1 Draw a rectangle about
100cm x 25cm on to
thin card. Cut the
rectangle out. Cover it
evenly with white acrylic
paint. Leave it to dry.

2 Using a pencil and ruler,
lightly draw in four
fold-lines 20cm apart.
This will divide the
painted card into five
equal sections.

3 Carefully fold along the
pencil lines to make a
zig-zag book, as shown.
Unfold the card and rub
out the pencil lines with
an eraser.

MAYA CODEX
Maya scribes wrote thousands of codices (folding, hand-painted books), but only four survive. All the rest were destroyed by Spanish missionaries. These pages from a Maya codex show the activities of several different gods. The figure at the top, painted black with a long nose, is Ek Chuah, the god of merchants.

zero	one	four	five	eleven	eighteen

AZTEC ENCYCLOPEDIA
These pictures of Aztec gods come from a book known as the Florentine Codex. This encyclopedia was compiled between 1547 and 1569 by Father Bernardino de Sahagun, a Spanish friar. He was fascinated by Aztec civilization and wanted to record it before it disappeared. This codex is the most complete written record of Aztec life we have.

MAYA NUMBERS
The Maya number system used only three signs – a dot for one, a bar for five, and the shell-symbol for zero. Other numbers were made by using a combination of those signs. When writing down large numbers, Maya scribes put the different symbols on top of one another, rather than side by side as we do today.

4 Trace or copy Aztec or Maya codex drawings from this book. Alternatively, make up your own, based on Mesoamerican examples.

5 Paint your tracings or drawings, using light, bright colours. Using the Maya numbers on this page as a guide, add some numbers to your codex.

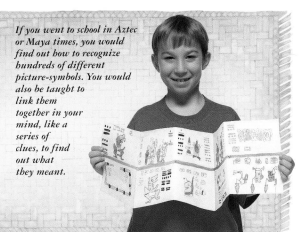

If you went to school in Aztec or Maya times, you would find out how to recognize hundreds of different picture-symbols. You would also be taught to link them together in your mind, like a series of clues, to find out what they meant.

Gods, Beliefs & Ceremonies

Discover the background to the world's
ancient religions and how they are
celebrated

Religion, Ritual and Myth

Throughout the world, in different centuries, people have expressed their religious beliefs through prayers, ceremonies, offerings, festivals, drama, music and dancing. We do not know precisely what the ancestors of modern humans thought or felt. However, archaeologists have found evidence of burial rituals dating from more than half a million years ago. Sites discovered in France and the Zagros Mountains in Iran show carefully buried bodies with animal horns and bones around them. If people took the trouble to honour the remains of the dead, they may have believed that a person's spirit lived on, in this world or another one, after their body had decayed. People who hunted for food painted pictures of animals they wanted to find. The paintings may have been for decoration.

Prehistoric goddess figurines may have been worshipped as symbols of fertility by early Stone Age people.

Some experts believe that they may have been a way in which people tried to contact powerful spirits from the natural world.

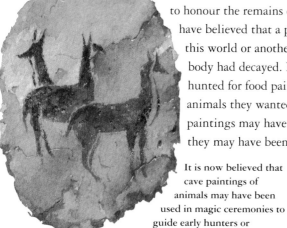
It is now believed that cave paintings of animals may have been used in magic ceremonies to guide early hunters or promote fertility.

Rituals and human activities such as art, magic, myth and ceremonies provide clues to past beliefs. They show us that people gradually developed more complex ways of

Timeline 500,000–2000BC

*c.*500,000BC Early humans living in China perform rituals using the skulls of dead people. This suggests that they either honour the dead person's spirit or fear it.

*c.*75,000BC People in the Middle East start burying some of their dead. They may have believed that a person's spirit lived on, in this world or another one, after their body had decayed.

*c.*30,000BC Cave-paintings in Europe show men and women living as hunter-gatherers trying to make contact with powerful spirits from the natural world, to guide and protect them.

*c.*10,000BC People migrate to live in all parts of North and South America. Over the centuries, Native Americans develop many

Animal cave painting

religious beliefs. Some are shared among them all, such as reverence for the natural world, and belief in shamans – magic healers who can communicate with the spirit world. Others relate to each peoples' own lifestyle and homeland.

Shamanic mask worn for special rituals

500,000BC   30,000BC   10,000BC   9000BC

explaining the world around them. Many rituals were linked to key stages in peoples' lives, such as birth, death, becoming an adult or important community events. When people began to farm and live in settled villages, from around 8000BC, religion reflected a close relationship with the plants and the seasons. The Aztecs of Mexico, the Celts of Europe and the Incas of Peru made objects of goddesses who symbolized fertility. Offerings were made to "mother earth" in the hope that in return, divine help would be given to ensure successful crops. Chinese customs encouraged hard work, order and respect on earth as this created a harmony between heaven, earth and human beings.

The Inca earth goddess, shown on this gold plate, played an important role in the beliefs of farming peoples, living in the windswept Andes mountains.

Religions bind societies together. Many settlements grew into market towns, dependent on trade and craftwork and often became centres of religion, too. In Egypt, Greece and Aztec Mexico, cities were homes to priests and scribes, who guarded religious knowledge and contained splendid temples for worshipping gods. Festivals in India, China and South America, were opportunities for people to celebrate the gods and natural events, such as the coming of spring or the harvest. As societies grew, people began to ask questions about what religion meant to them personally. What is the meaning of life? Why does

During Egyptian ceremonies, priests had to pour sacred water over offerings made to the gods to purify them.

c.8000BC People begin to live in settled farming villages. New religious beliefs develop, based on the close relationship between farmers, the land, growing plants and the seasons.

c.5000BC People begin to live in towns. They build splendid temples for their gods, and to pay for

Stonehenge, a prehistoric stone circle, may have been used for worship

priests to say prayers and make sacrifices (offerings) on the community's behalf.

c.3100–30BC The ancient Egyptians worship many gods and goddesses, build magnificent temples, and preserve dead bodies by mummification, so that their spirit will live on after death.

c.2300–500BC The civilizations of Akkad, Sumer, Babylon and Assyria flourish in Mesopotamia (Iraq). Their people worship gods of the sun and moon, and special gods and goddesses who protected their cities and kings.

Sun worshipper

8000BC   5000BC   3000BC   2000BC

suffering exist? What happens after death? Does God exist?

Many religions had human versions of their gods on earth. The pharaohs of Egypt and the emperors of China were worshipped as gods. In tribal North America, shamans (healers) had the most important role in the community because they communicated with the spiritual world, thought to control people's daily lives.

In the ancient world, many – rather than one – gods were worshipped. Around 600BC, religious leaders appeared in several regions of the world including the Buddha in India and Zoroaster in Persia (Iran). Leaders taught that fulfilment lay beyond this world, in heaven, or in seeking unity with a single God.

People at Holi, the Hindu spring festival, throw coloured powders over each other.

Philosophers (thinkers), such as Plato in ancient Greece and Confucius in China, began to discuss with their followers the best way to live. Collections of holy scriptures, such as the Hindu Upanishads from India and the Jewish Bible (Torah), were written down to guide believers. This tradition was continued in the 1st century AD by the followers of Jesus of Nazareth (Christians) and, in the 7th century AD by the prophet Mohammed from Arabia. Mohammed taught Muslims to follow the Quran, a holy text that was believed to be the actual word of God.

Confucius lived at a time of great change in China. He taught people to respect their elders and to work hard.

TIMELINE 1600BC–AD1500

c.1600–1122BC The Shang dynasty rules China. People honour the spirits of dead ancestors, and make offerings. They foretell the future by consulting oracle bones.

c.1200–600BC The earliest Hindu holy texts, called

Chinese fireworks

Vedas, are written in Sanskrit, the language of the Aryan people who migrate to India at this time.

c.800BC–AD100 The Celts are powerful in Europe. They honour nature gods, and make human sacrifices to them. They believe in magic, and are guided by learned priests, called druids.

c.604BC Birth of Laozi, religious teacher who founded the Daoist religion in China.

c.600–200BC Peak of ancient Greek civilization. The Greeks honour a family of 12 gods, who live on Mount Olympus, and resemble human beings, but possess great powers.

c.563–483BC Life of Indian religious leader Siddartha Gautama, known as "Buddha" (the enlightened one). After his death, his teachings spread to many parts of Asia.

c.551–479BC Life of Confucius, moral and ethical teacher in China.

1600BC   800BC   600BC   500BC

This section explores the main religious beliefs from around the world. It starts with the earliest evidence of ceremonies and rituals, and moves through time to see how religions developed in different ways from land to land. The religions of ancient Egypt, Greece and Rome, the Inca, Maya and Aztec peoples of Central and South America, with their many gods, have disappeared with the civilizations that created them. But some ancient tribal beliefs and ceremonies survive to this day in parts of Africa, the Americas, Australia and Asia.

The Celts worshipped their various gods in the form of sculpted images. This clenched-fisted bearded god appears on a large metal bowl.

You will be able to see how religious beliefs have played an important role in everyday life through the ages. You will be able to compare the ways in which people expressed their faith and depicted their gods – in paintings, music and festivals, legends, and traditions that can still be seen today. Most of all, you will have a sense of the rich and varied ways in which people have tried to explain the existence of good and evil, and the reasons for life and death.

The Egyptian pyramids remain a legacy to some of the great beliefs of the past. The Egyptians believed their pharaohs were gods who lived after their bodies had died. They built the pyramids to safeguard their bodies and buried them with their treasures to be used in the afterlife.

Shiva, the Hindu god of creation and destruction

*c.*500BC–300AD Roman power spreads in Europe. The Romans worship most Greek gods, but give them Roman names, and also family gods of their own.

AD200 Hinduism is widespread in India. Hindus honour one of two gods, Vishnu or Shiva, as lord of creation.

AD570–632 Life of the Prophet Mohammed, who founded the faith of Islam. This spread from Arabia and is one of the leading world religions.

*c.*AD700–1100 The Vikings are powerful in Europe. They worship many gods and heroes, and their rich collection of myths and legends explains how the world was created and how it will end.

*c.*AD960 Christianity starts to spread through the Viking lands.

1469–1539 Life of Guru Nanak, founder of the Sikh religion in India.

1487 Aztecs sacrifice 20,000 captives to consecrate (make holy) the great new temple in their capital city, Tenochtitlan.

Aztec blood sacrifices

AD200   AD500   1400   1500

Stone Age Beliefs

W E CAN ONLY GUESS at the beliefs of Stone Age people, the earliest ancestors to modern humans. These were the Neanderthal people who lived from 120,000 to 33,000 years ago in Europe and Asia. There is evidence that they were burying their dead, which suggests that they believed in a spirit world. They probably worshipped the spirits of the animals they hunted and other natural things. They made paintings and engravings on rocks and in caves, which may have a magical or religious purpose.

ANCIENT BURIAL
The skull of the skeleton from this burial found in France has been scattered with red ochre earth. Red may have represented blood or life for Stone Age people. Bodies were often buried on their sides, with their knees pulled up to their chins. Tools, ornaments, food and weapons were put in the graves. Later Stone Age people built elaborate tombs for their dead.

Stone Age people probably thought illnesses and accidents were caused by evil spirits. It may have been the job of a shaman (witch doctor), to speak to the spirits and interpret what should be done.

As farming spread and settlements grew into towns, more organized religions began. Shrines decorated with religious pictures have been found at Çatal Hüyük in Turkey, the site of a well-preserved town dating from around 7000BC.

RITUAL ANTLERS
These antlers are from a red stag and were found at Star Carr in England. Some experts think that antlers were worn by a kind of priest called a shaman, perhaps in a coming-of-age ceremony or to bring good luck in that season's hunt.

CLAY GODDESS
This female figure is made from clay and was found at Pazardzik in Bulgaria. Many prehistoric societies worshipped images of the Earth Goddess, or Great Mother. As the mother of the world, she gave life to plants, animals and humans, and so ensured the future of the human race.

TREPANNING

Cutting a hole in a person's head is called trepanning. It was practised in prehistoric times from about 5000BC. A sharp flint tool was used to cut a hole in the skull in order to let illness escape from the body. Several skulls have been found that show the hole starting to close – evidence that some patients even survived the blood-curdling procedure!

SPELLS AND POTIONS

In many hunter-gatherer societies today, a shaman (witch doctor) can speak with the spirits from the world of the dead. In cultures such as that of the Amazonian Indians, shamen also administer potions from plants to cure illness. They use plants such as quinine, coca and curare.

Stone Age people probably behaved in a similar way. There is evidence that neolithic farmers in north-western Europe grew poppies and hemp, possibly for use in magic potions and rituals.

poppy

ANCESTOR WORSHIP

Before the people of Jericho in the Near East buried their dead, they removed the skulls. This skull found in Jericho dates from about 6500BC. These were covered with plaster and painted to look like the features of the dead person. Cowrie shells were used for eyes. Some experts believe that this was done as a form of ancestor worship.

RITUAL DANCE

A modern painting shows a traditional Australian Aboriginal dance. Traditional ceremonies are an important part of Aboriginal life. Evidence of them has been found on prehistoric sites in Australia. Aboriginal beliefs are designed to maintain the delicate balance between people and their environment.

City Gods of Mesopotamia

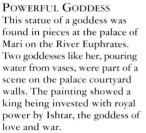

AS SETTLEMENTS GREW INTO TOWNS AND CITIES, religious rituals became more complex. Some of the first cities in the world developed in Mesopotamia, most of which is now modern-day Iraq. Each city had it's own guardian god and temples were built especially for that god.

There were often temples dedicated to members of the god's family, too. The Sumerians, Assyrians, Babylonians and Akkadian-speaking peoples who lived in Mesopotamia worshipped the same gods and goddesses, but had different names for them. The Sumerians called the Moon-god Nanna, but in Akkadian his name was Sin. The chief Sumerian god was called Enlil, who was often also referred to as King, Supreme Lord, Father, or Creator. According to one Sumerian poem, no one was allowed to look at Enlil, not even the other gods. The Sumerian kings believed that they had been chosen by Enlil.

The god's chief sanctuary was at the city of Nippur. Legends tell that when the Nippur temple was raided by the army of the King of Agade, Enlil was so angry that he caused the Agade dynasty to end.

POWERFUL GODDESS
This statue of a goddess was found in pieces at the palace of Mari on the River Euphrates. Two goddesses like her, pouring water from vases, were part of a scene on the palace courtyard walls. The painting showed a king being invested with royal power by Ishtar, the goddess of love and war.

BEFORE THE GOD
A scene on a 4000-year-old seal shows an official called Lamabazi being led into the presence of a great god by a lesser god. The great god is sitting on the throne, and before him is a brazier for burning incense. Lamabazi is holding his hand in front of his face as a sign of respect for the god.

IN THE BEGINNING
Marduk was the god of Babylon. He is shown here standing on his mushushshu (snake dragon). In the *Epic of Creation*, a Babylonian story about how Marduk created the world, he fought against a female monster, Tiamat, and her son, Kingu. After Marduk had killed them, the other gods made him their king. Marduk then brought the rest of creation into existence. He made models of human beings by mixing some clay with the blood of Kingu and then brought them to life.

CLUES TO IDENTITY

Most of our ideas about what the Mesopotamian gods and goddesses looked like come from their pictures on cylinder seals. This one shows Ishtar, the goddess of love and war, carrying her weapons. She is accompanied by a lion, which was her sacred animal. Shamash, the sun god, is recognizable by the flames coming from him, as he rises between two mountains. Ea the water god, has streams of water gushing from his shoulders.

FERTILE MIND

Nisaba was originally a goddess of fertility and agriculture, although she later became the goddess of writing. Good harvests were very important to the people of Mesopotamia, and almost everyone ate barley bread and dates. This carving of Nisaba shows her covered with plants. She is wearing an elaborate headdress composed of a horned crown and ears of barley. Flowers sprout from her shoulders, and she is holding a bunch of dates.

GOD OF ASSYRIA

Ashur was the chief god of the Assyrians. It was thought that he was the god who chose the Assyrian kings and went before them into battle. He is often symbolized by the same horned cap as Enlil, the chief Sumerian god. Sometimes he is shown standing on a winged bull or on a mushushshu (snake dragon) like Marduk, the god of Babylon. Both gods were honoured in New Year festivals when their priests slapped the reigning king's face, pulled his ears and made him bow low. The king then said he had served his people properly and was re-crowned for another year.

Bible Links to Mesopotamia

FLOODS

A tale like the Old Testament story of Noah's Ark was found in the library at Nineveh. King Utnapishtim was warned that the god Enlil was going to send a flood and was told to make a boat and take his family, all the animals and craftsworkers on board. It rained for seven days and seven nights. When it stopped, the king sent out birds to see if the water had gone down. The goddess Ishtar put her necklace in the sky as a sign that this would never happen again.

WHILE THE MESOPOTAMIANS HAD MANY GODS, a faith based on one god developed among the Jews in the area. Many of the people, places and events in the Jewish holy scriptures (the Old Testament of the Bible) are also told in Mesopotamian history. Several laws and customs relating to marriage and adoption mentioned in the Old Testament are like those of Mesopotamia. Abraham, the father of the Israelite and Arab nations, lived in the Sumerian city of Ur before setting off for the Promised Land. The prophet Jonah was instructed by God to go to the Assyrian city of Nineveh, and the Jewish people were exiled from their Promised Land to Babylon. Assyrian records often include kings and events mentioned in the Old Testament.

One Assyrian king, Shalmaneser III, records his victory at the Battle of Qarqar in Syria. He says he fought against 12 kings, one of whom was Ahab of Israel. This is the first time a king of Israel appears in the history of another country.

DESERT JOURNEY

Abraham, the father of the Jewish and Arab nations, travels from the Sumerian city of Ur to the country God has promised his people. In this painting of the 1800s, Abraham is leading a wandering existence in a desert landscape with his flock of sheep moving from one area to another in search of grazing ground for his animals. However, there would have been no camels at the time he is thought to have lived, about 2000BC. They were not used for transport in Mesopotamia until about 1000BC.

BLACK OBELISK

The man bowing in front of the Assyrian king, Shalmaneser III, could be Jehu, King of Israel. Israel had been an enemy of Assyria, but Jehu has decided to change sides and become an ally of Assyria. The picture appears on the Black Obelisk, which tells of Shalmaneser III's conquests at war. The writing says that the gifts of the Israelite king are being presented to show his loyalty and win Shalmaneser's approval.

WAR CORRESPONDENTS

The Bible reports that the Assyrian king Sennacherib laid siege to Jerusalem when Hezekiah was king of Judah. It says he withdrew from the siege when an angel attacked his army. In Sennacherib's version of events on this clay prism (a hollow tablet), he does not say he was defeated or that he captured Jerusalem. All he says is that he shut Hezekiah up like a bird in a cage.

EXILE IN BABYLON

The great Babylonian king of the 500s BC was Nebuchadnezzar II who took over many parts of the ancient world that had formerly been part of the Assyrian Empire. In 597BC he attacked Jerusalem, the chief city of the kingdom of Judah, a scene imagined here by a medieval painter. At the end of a successful siege, he took the king, his courtiers, the army and all the craftworkers to Babylon. There they spent many years far from home, a time known among Jewish people as the Exile. Nebuchadnezzar took treasures from the temple in Jerusalem as booty. He appointed another king, Zedekiah, to rule in Jerusalem. Nebuchadnezzar returned some years later when Zedekiah rebelled and punished him severely.

Pharaoh Gods

HORUS
Horus the falcon god was the son of Isis. He was god of the sky and protector of the reigning pharaoh. The name Horus meant 'He who is far above'. Here he holds an *ankh*, the symbol of life. The holder of an *ankh* had the power to give life or take it away. Only pharaohs and gods were allowed to carry them.

THE ANCIENT EGYPTIANS believed that the ordered world in which they lived had been created out of chaos. They carried out rituals to prevent chaos and darkness from returning. The pharaohs were honoured as god-kings because it was believed the spirit of the gods lived in them. They looked after the everyday world for the gods. Over 2,000 gods were worshipped in ancient Egypt. Many gods were linked to a particular region. The mighty Amun was the god of Thebes. Some gods appeared as animals – Sebek the water god was a crocodile. Gods were also connected with jobs and interests. The hippopotamus goddess, Tawaret, looked after babies and childbirth.

Many ordinary Egyptians understood little about the religion of the court and nobles. They believed in magic, local spirits and superstitions.

LOTUS FLOWER
The lotus was a very important flower to the Egyptians. This sacred symbol was used to represent Upper Egypt.

THE GODDESS NUT
Nut, covered in stars, was goddess of the heavens. She is often shown with her body stretched across the sky. The Egyptians believed that Nut swallowed the Sun each evening and gave birth to it the next morning. She was married to the Earth god, Geb, and gave birth to the gods Isis and Osiris.

AMUN OF THEBES

Amun was originally the god of the city of Thebes. He later became popular throughout Egypt as the god of creation. By the time of the New Kingdom, Amun was combined with other powerful gods such as Ra, god of the Sun, and became known as Amun-Ra. He was believed to be the most powerful god of all. Amun is sometimes shown as a ram.

HOLY BEETLES

Scarabs are beetles that were sacred to the ancient Egyptians. Pottery or stone scarabs were used as lucky charms, seals, or as ring decorations. The base of these scarabs was often inscribed with stories telling of some great event.

OSIRIS, KING OF THE UNDERWORLD

The great god Osiris stands dressed as a king. He was one of the most important gods in ancient Egypt, the master of life and the spirit world. He was also the god of farming. Egyptian tales told how Osiris was murdered and cut into pieces by his brother Seth, the god of chaos. Anubis, the jackal-headed god of embalming, gathered the pieces together and his sister, Isis, brought Osiris back to life.

CAT MUMMIES

The Egyptians worshipped gods in the forms of animals from the Old Kingdom onwards. The cat goddess Bastet was said to be the daughter of the great Sun god, Ra. Cats were so holy to the Egyptians that at one time many of them were embalmed, wrapped in linen bandages and preserved as mummies. It is thought that bronze cat figures and these mummified cats were left as offerings to Bastet at her temple.

MIW THE CAT

Cats were holy animals in ancient Egypt. They even had their own god! The Egyptians' love of cats dated back to the early farmers who tamed cats to protect stores of grain from mice. Cats soon became popular pets. The Egyptian word for cat was *miw*, which was rather like a mew or miaow!

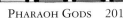

Preparing for the Afterlife

THE EGYPTIANS believed that the dead would need to use their bodies in the next life. They discovered that bodies buried in the desert were often preserved in the dry sand. The bodies dried out and became mummified. Over the ages, the Egyptians became experts at preserving bodies by embalming them.

The methods of mummification varied. The process usually took about 70 days. The brains were hooked out through the nose and the other organs were removed and placed in special jars. Only the heart was left so that it could be weighed in the next life. The body was embalmed by being dried out with salty crystals of natron. Afterwards it was stuffed and covered with oils and ointments and then wrapped in bandages. The mummy was then placed inside a series of coffins in the shape of the body.

MUMMY CASE
This beautiful gold case contains the mummy of a priestess. Once the embalmed body had been wrapped in bandages it was placed in a richly decorated coffin. Both the inside and outside would be covered in spells to help the dead person in the underworld. Sometimes more than one coffin was used. The inner coffins would be of brightly painted or gilded wood (*as left*) and the outer coffin would be a stone sarcophagus.

CANOPIC JARS
Special jars were used to store the body's organs. The human-headed jar held the liver. The baboon jar contained the lungs. The stomach was put in the jackal-headed jar and finally the guts were placed in the falcon-headed jar.

CANOPIC JARS

You will need: self-drying clay, rolling pin and board, ruler, modelling tool, sandpaper, masking tape, acrylic paint (white, blue, green, yellow, black), water pot and brush.

1 Roll out ³/₄ of the clay and cut out a circle about 7cm in diameter. This is the base of the jar. Now roll out thin strips of clay. Coil these from the base to make the sides.

2 Carefully press out the bumps between the coils until the sides of the jar are smooth and round. Finally trim the top of the jar with a modelling tool.

3 Now make a lid for the jar. Measure the size needed and cut out a circle of the remaining clay. Mould it into a dome. Model the head of a baboon on to the lid.

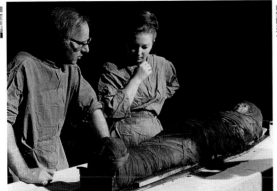

BENEATH THE BANDAGES

Unwrapping a mummy is a delicate operation. Today, archaeologists can use scanning or X-ray equipment to examine the mummies' bodies. It is possible to tell what food they once ate, the work they did and the illnesses they suffered from. X-rays also show the stuffing used to replace the internal organs.

RAMESSES II

This is the unwrapped head of the mummy of Ramesses II. Wadding was placed in his eye sockets to stop the natron (preserving salts) from destroying his features.

It was believed that any part of a person's body could be used against them. For this reason the organs were removed and stored in canopic jars. Spells written on the jars protected them.

THE OPENING OF THE MOUTH CEREMONY

The last ritual before burial was led by a priest wearing the mask of the god Anubis. The human-shaped coffin was held upright and its face was touched with magical instruments. This ceremony enabled the mummy to speak, see and hear in the next world.

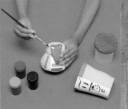

4 Hapy the baboon guarded the mummy's lungs. Use the modelling tool to make the baboon's eyes and long nose. Leave the lid in a warm place to dry.

5 When both the jar and the lid are completely dry, rub them down with sandpaper until they are smooth. The lid should fit snugly on to the jar.

6 It is now time to paint your jar. Use the masking tape to protect the baboon's face and to help you get the stripes straight. Follow the colours in the picture above.

7 Paint hieroglyphs down the front of the jar as shown. Use the design shown above to help you. The canopic jar is now ready for the funeral.

Grand Temples of Egypt

MASSIVE TEMPLES were built in honour of the Egyptian gods. Many can still be seen today. They have great pillars and massive gates, courtyards and avenues of statues. Once, these would have led to a shrine that was believed to be the home of a god.

Ordinary people did not gather to worship in an Egyptian temple as they might today in a church. Only priests were allowed in the temples. They carried out rituals on behalf of the pharaoh, making offerings of food, burning incense, playing music and singing. They had complicated rules about washing and shaving their heads, and some had to wear special clothes such as leopard skins. Noblewomen served as priestesses during some ceremonies. Many priests had little knowledge of religion and just served in the temple for three months before returning to their normal work. Other priests studied the stars and spells.

There were many religious festivals during which the god's shrine would be carried to other temples in a great procession. This was when ordinary Egyptians joined in worship. Offerings of food made to the gods were given back to the people for public feasting.

SACRED RITUALS
A priest engaged in a religious ritual wears a leopard skin garment. He is carrying a vase containing sacred water from the temple's holy lake. During ceremonies, this water would have been poured over offering tables to ensure the purity of the gifts made to the gods. Incense would also have been burned to purify the atmosphere of the temple.

KARNAK
This painting by David Roberts shows the massive temple of Karnak as it appeared in 1850. It still stands just outside the modern town of Luxor. The temple's most important god was Amun-Ra. The site also includes courts and buildings sacred to other gods and goddesses, including Mut (a vulture goddess, wife of Amun) and Khons (the Moon god, son of Amun). The Great Temple was enlarged and rebuilt over about 2,000 years.

TEMPLE OF HORUS

A statue of Horus, the falcon god, guards the temple at Edfu. There was a temple on this site during the New Kingdom. However, the building that still stands today dates back to the period of Greek rule. This temple was dedicated to Horus and his wife, the cow goddess Hathor. Inside the temple there are stone carvings showing Horus fighting the enemies of Osiris, his father.

ANUBIS THE EMBALMER

A priest wears the mask of Anubis to embalm a body. This jackal-headed god was said to have prepared the body of the god Osiris for burial. He and his priests had strong links with mummies and the practice of embalming.

KALABSHA TEMPLE

The Kalabsha temple was one of the largest temples in Lower Nubia. In the 1960s, the Aswan Dam was built and Lower Nubia was flooded. Many monuments such as the temples at Abu Simbel and Philae had to be moved. The temple at Kalabsha was dismantled, and its 13,000 blocks of stone were moved to New Kalabsha, where it was rebuilt.

GATEWAY TO ISIS

The temple of Philae (*above*) was built in honour of Isis, the mother goddess. Isis was worshipped all over Egypt and in many other lands, too. Massive gateways called pylons guard the temple of Philae. Pylons guard the way to many Egyptian temples and were used for special ceremonies.

Religions of India

MANY RELIGIONS DEVELOPED IN INDIA. The Aryan people, who settled in northern India from around 1500BC, had customs which influenced India's later beliefs. In 500BC, a spiritual leader called the Buddha founded Buddhism. This religion was dominant for the next 700 years. In time, the Aryan religion evolved into Hinduism. Many beliefs were the same, but Hinduism discouraged the practice of making animal sacrifices, and introduced new gods to replace the Aryan deities. Gradually, Hinduism took over from Buddhism, and has been India's dominant religion ever since.

In the two main types of Hinduism – Vaishnavism and Shaivism – Hindus believe that one god (Vishnu or Shiva) rules the universe. From AD1000, some worshipped the goddess Devi instead. As a result, Hindu mythology seems to have many different gods, but to most Hindus, they are versions of Vishnu, Shiva or Devi.

TERRIFYING GOD
Shiva appears in the form of a terrifying being wielding a trident. At times, Shiva is associated with the destructive forces of the universe and commands demonic beings, called ganas.

HAPPY GOD
The conch shell and the discus are the symbols of the god Vishnu, who is often shown with blue skin. Vishnu mostly brings happiness, preservation and kingship. He stands on a lotus flower.

MAKE A GARLAND OF FLOWERS
You will need: Tissue paper in orange, yellow, red, pink and white, pencil, scissors, PVA glue, paintbrush, length of string, darning needle.

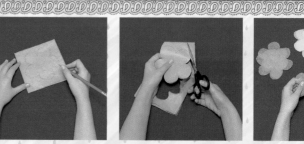

1 Draw simple flower shapes on to sheets of coloured tissue paper. If you like, you can lay the sheets of paper in layers, one on top of the other.

2 Using scissors, cut out your flower shapes. Take care not to tear the tissue paper. Cut the same number of flowers in each colour.

3 Scrunch up the tissue flower shapes with your hands. Then uncrumple them, but don't smooth them out too much.

GANESHA
The elephant god, Ganesha, is the son of Shiva. He is god of wisdom and prosperity and is known for his love of sweets. Ganesha is always shown travelling with a rat.

KRISHNA AND RADHA
The god Krishna was an incarnation of Vishnu on earth. Krishna was born as a cowherder. In his youth, he is said to have been adored by many women, but his favourite was Radha. The love of Radha and Krishna is the theme of many Hindu religious songs.

GODDESS OF DEATH AND WAR
Shiva's wife had many forms. The fiercest was Kali, goddess of death. Here, she holds an array of weapons in her many arms. Kings often worshipped Kali before going into battle.

Hindus make garlands of fresh flowers to wear at festivals to honour their gods.

4 Glue the flower shapes together loosely in layers to make larger, single flowers. Use eight layers of tissue paper for each finished flower.

5 Now gently fluff up the layers of tissue paper with your fingers. This will make your flowers look much more impressive.

6 Measure a length of string that is long enough to go around your neck. Start to thread the flowers on to the string to make a garland.

7 Thread all the tissue flowers on to the length of string. When you have secured all the flowers, tie a double knot in the string to finish.

RELIGIONS OF INDIA   207

Islam Reaches India

THE MUSLIM RELIGION, called Islam – which means submission to God – was founded in Arabia (present-day Saudi Arabia) by a man named Mohammed in AD622. It spread quickly into the countries around Arabia, and nearly 400 years later, reached India.

In AD1007 Sultan Mahmud, the Muslim leader of the city of Ghazni in Afghanistan, started a series of attacks on northern India to loot the rich temples there. More Islamic leaders followed his example, and by AD1206, Muslim Turks from Central Asia had founded a new kingdom, or Sultanate, based in the city of Delhi. The Delhi Sultanate ruled the region for 300 years.

Islam gradually spread among ordinary Indian people. Islamic sufis (mystics) played an important role in spreading the message of God's love for all people. They worshipped in a very emotional style at their countryside shrines, in a way that the Hindu peasants could understand. By the 1700s, nearly a quarter of India's population was Muslim. They showed great tolerance to other religions and cultures, especially the Hindu faith.

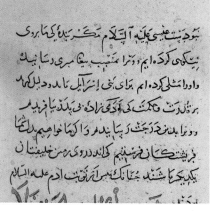

BEAUTIFUL WRITING
This page is from a Persian commentary on the holy book of Muslims, the *Quran*. Muslims were not allowed to represent images, such as humans, animals or flowers, in art. Instead they developed calligraphy (the art of beautiful writing).

SEAFARING SETTLERS
The Indian Ocean was controlled by Muslim traders from about AD700. They arrived along the south-western coast of India on their way to Indonesia and China, and were among the earliest Muslims to settle in India. These traders followed Muslim law. Different Muslim laws spread in India through further Muslim invasions from Turkey and Afghanistan in the 1100s and 1200s.

FROM TEMPLE TO MOSQUE

The Quwat al-Islam, a large mosque in Delhi, was built out of parts of destroyed temples of older faiths. It has two architectural features that were introduced to India by Islam. One feature is the arch, the other is the use of mortar for sticking bricks together. The mosque was built by the Delhi Sultanate in 1193.

HOLY MEN

Sufis (mystics) gather together to pray. Sufism was a type of Islam that preached that people's souls can communicate to God through ecstatic music, singing and dancing. Sufism came into prominence in Persia in the AD900s. By about 1100 it had also gained a foothold in the north-west of India.

FAMILY TOMB

A man cycles towards a tomb of one of the later Sultans of Delhi. The tomb is in the gardens of the Lodi family, the last rulers of the Delhi Sultanate. The last Lodi Sultan was defeated in battle by the Mughal prince Babur, in 1526.

SUFI SHRINE

This tomb-shrine, or dargah, in Rajgir, honours a famous sufi saint. Sufi teachers were called pirs, or shaikhs. They often had a large number of followers.

Sikhs of India

As ISLAM SPREAD through northern India, Hinduism and Islam existed side by side. In the Punjab region of northern India, a new religion emerged that had elements of both. It was called Sikhism, and was founded by a man called Guru (teacher) Nanak (1469–1539). Sikhism rejected the strict Hindu caste system and adopted the Islamic idea that all people are equal before God, but kept many aspects of Hindu ritual. Sikhs worshipped in temples called gurdwaras (abode of the gurus). After Nanak, there were nine more gurus. The fifth, Arjan, founded the Golden Temple at Amritsar, which later became the holiest of all gurdwaras. He also wrote the Sikh holy book, or *Adi Granth*.

In the 1600s, the Muslim Mughal rulers in Delhi became concerned about the growth of this new religion. They began to persecute the Sikhs and killed Arjan and another guru. The tenth guru, Gobind Singh, decided that Sikhs should protect themselves and founded a military order called the khalsa. Members carried a comb and dagger, wore a steel bangle, breeches, and did not cut their hair. Sikh men took the title Singh (lion). After the death of Gobind Singh in 1708, there were no more gurus, but Sikhs continued to live by the teachings of the *Adi Granth.*

LETHAL TURBAN
A Sikh war turban is decorated with weapons that could be removed and used against the enemy during battle. Metal throwing rings could slice heads off, while 'claws' were for disembowelling people.

THE GOLDEN TEMPLE
The greatest Sikh temple is the Golden Temple in the Sikh holy city of Amritsar. The temple was built by Guru Arjan Singh (1581–1606). Its white marble walls and domes are decorated with gold. The city of Amritsar is named after the lake that surrounds the temple. Sikhs worship in their temples in large congregations (groups). Free kitchens are attached to Sikh temples, where all can eat.

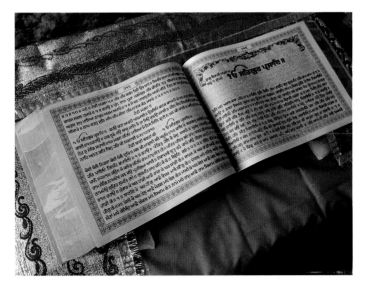

SYMBOLIC COMB
This close-up picture of a Sikh turban shows the kangha, a comb that is pinned to the centre. The kangha is one of the five signs of the Sikh religion. Sikh men do not cut their hair – another sign of Sikhism.

THE SACRED BOOK
The *Adi Granth* is the sacred book of the Sikhs. Its text was compiled by Guru Arjan Singh in the late 1500s. After the death of the last teacher, Guru Gobind Singh, Sikhs came to accept these scriptures as the symbol of God. They took over the role of the teacher from the Gurus.

A MILITARY MAHARAJA
The Maharaja Ranjit Singh (1799–1838) holds court. The water tank of the Golden Temple can be seen in the background. Ranjit Singh led the Sikh army to victory against Afghan warlords and the collapsing Mughal Empire. He established a separate Sikh kingdom in the Punjab region of India.

AN ABLE WARRIOR
A Sikh soldier sits on a cushion in this portrait from the 1800s. When the British ruled India, they recruited many Sikhs into their army. Sikhs were regarded as one of India's most warlike peoples.

Festivals and Ceremonies in India

Ritual ceremonies in India go back to Aryan times (1500BC), when there were fire sacrifices throughout the year. After the growth of Buddhism, priests developed a set of rites for important events such as marriages, caste initiations and funerals, which Hindus then used for centuries. Many temple festivals developed too. Some, such as Navaratri and Dasara, honoured fierce goddesses. Diwali was a festival of lights in honour of the goddess Lakshmi. In spring, people played games at the fertility festival of Holi.

Generally, Muslims had fewer and less elaborate rituals. Islamic festivals included Eid al-Fitr after Ramadan, the month of fasting, and Eid al-Adha to commemorate Abraham's attempted sacrifice of his son, Isaac. Muslims also adopted some of the customs and practices of the Hindus.

HANDY HENNA
Using henna to mark the hands and feet was a common practice in India, and is still part of marriage ceremonies. Henna is a plant extract that is mixed into a paste with water and used to make patterns on the skin. The paste dyes the skin red.

A FESTIVAL OF FUN
The Vasantotsava (or modern Holi) was a festival of play and courtship which took place in the spring. Men and women threw coloured powders and squirted coloured waters over one another with syringes as they ran about the streets and gardens of the city.

TABLA DRUM

You will need: A2 sheet of thick card, measuring tape, scissors, pair of compasses, pencil, sticky tape, strips of newspaper, flour and water or wallpaper paste, bowl, fine sandpaper, calico fabric, bradawl, red-brown and blue paint, paintbrushes, darning needle, twine, PVA glue.

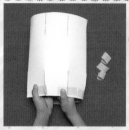

1 Cut out a card rectangle 55 x 21 cm. Cut slits along both long edges. Use the compasses to measure a card circle with a diameter of 16 cm. Cut out the circle.

2 Roll the rectangle to form a cylinder with a diameter of 16 cm and tape. Tape the slits so that the drum tapers at each end. Tape the circle to one end.

3 Cover the cylinder with 3 layers of newspaper strips soaked in paste or flour and water. Leave it to dry between layers. Smooth the edges with sandpaper.

CEREMONY AROUND THE FIRE

A bride, with her face covered, is led into the marriage pandal (ceremonial awning), which is covered with mango and lime leaves to bring good luck. The bride will follow her husband around the fire. Hindu marriages still take place in the home around a sacrificial fire, and are administered by a Brahmin priest.

END OF FASTING

Muslim men take part in Eid festivities, in Bombay. Muslim men pray in public congregations at a mosque and give zakat (gifts) to the poor. Then they celebrate with friends and families.

PILGRIMAGE TO MECCA

Muslim pilgrims travel by camel to the city of Mecca, in Arabia (modern Saudi Arabia). Muslims must travel to Mecca once in their lifetime, if possible. The journey is called the haj.

DEATH OF AN IMAM

A passion play with music and drumming is enacted in the streets to celebrate Muharram, the first month of the Muslim calender. For Shia Muslims, the tenth day of Muharram is one of dramatic public mourning to commemorate the death of an imam (spiritual leader) named Husain.

The tabla drum was played at ceremonies and festivals.

4 Cut a circle of calico with a diameter of 25 cm. Prick holes around the edge with a bradawl. Paint the tabla with two coats of red-brown paint.

5 Thread the needle with a long piece of twine and knot. Place the calico over the tabla's open end. Push the needle and thread through a hole in the calico.

6 Pass the twine across the base and through a hole on the other side of the fabric. Pull the twine tight, to stretch the fabric. Repeat all the way around the tabla.

7 Paint a pattern on to the calico. Then apply a coat of watered down PVA glue. This will help to shrink the calico and pull it tight over the tabla.

Chinese Religions

"**T**HREE TEACHINGS FLOW INTO ONE" is an old saying in China. The three teachings are Daoism, Confucianism and Buddhism. In China they gradually merged together over the ages.

The first Chinese peoples believed in various gods and goddesses of nature, in spirits and demons. The spirit of nature and the flow of life inspired the writings that are said to be the work of Laozi (born *c.*604BC). His ideas formed the basis of the Daoist religion.

The teachings of Kong Fuzi (Confucius) come from the same period of history but they stress the importance of social order and respect for ancestors as a source of happiness. At this time another great religious teacher, the Buddha, was preaching in India. Within 500 years, Buddhist teachings had reached China and by the Tang dynasty (AD618–906), Buddhism was the most popular religion. Islam arrived at this time and won followers in the north-west. Christianity also came into China from Persia, but few Chinese were converted to this religion until the 1900s.

THE MERCIFUL GODDESS
Guanyin was the goddess of mercy and the bringer of children. She was a holy figure for all Chinese Buddhists.

DAOISM – A RELIGION OF HARMONY
A young boy is taught the Daoist belief in the harmony of nature. Daoists believe that the natural world is in a state of balance between two forces – yin and yang. Yin is dark, cool and feminine, while yang is light, hot and masculine. The two forces are combined in the black and white symbol on the scroll.

PEACE THROUGH SOCIAL ORDER
Kong Fuzi (Confucius) looks out on to an ordered world. He taught that the well-being of society depends on duty and respect. Children should obey their parents and wives should obey their husbands. The people should obey their rulers, and rulers should respect the gods. All of the emperors followed the teachings of Confucianism.

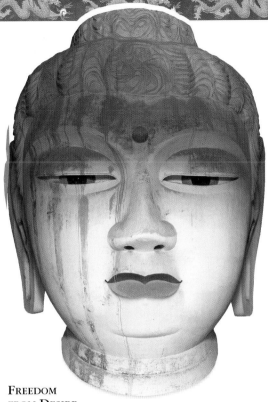

FREEDOM FROM DESIRE

Chinese monks carved huge statues of the Buddha from rock. Some can be seen at the Mogao caves near Dunhuang, where temples were built as early as AD366. The Buddha taught that suffering is caused by our love of material things. Buddhists believe that we are born over and over again until we learn to conquer this desire.

ISLAM IN CHINA

This is part of the Great Mosque in Xian (ancient Chang'an), built in the Chinese style. The mosque was founded in AD742, but most of the buildings in use today date from the Ming dynasty (1368–1644). Islam first took root in China in about AD700. Moslem traders from Central Asia brought with them the Koran, the holy book of Islam. It teaches that there is only one god, Allah, and that Mohammed is his prophet.

TEMPLE GUARDIANS

Gilded statues of Buddhist saints ward off evil spirits at Puningsi, the Temple of Universal Peace, near Chengde. The temple was built in 1755 in the Tibetan style. It is famed for its Mahayana Hall, a tower roofed in gilded bronze.

Celebrations in China

THE CHINESE FESTIVAL best known around the world today is the New Year or Spring Festival. Its date varies according to the traditional Chinese calendar, which is based on the phases of the moon. The festival is marked by dancers carrying a long dragon through the streets, accompanied by loud, crackling firecrackers to scare away evil spirits. The festival has been celebrated for over 2,000 years and has always been a time for family feasts and village carnivals. The doorways of buildings are traditionally decorated with handwritten poetry on strips of red paper to bring luck and good fortune for the coming year.

Soon after New Year, sweet dumplings made of rice flour are prepared for the Lantern Festival. Paper lanterns are hung out to mirror the first full moon of the year. This festival began during the Tang dynasty (AD618–906). In the eighth month of the year, the autumn full moon is marked by the eating of special moon cakes.

Chinese festivals are linked to agricultural seasons. They include celebrations of sowing and harvest, dances, horse races and the eating of specially prepared foods.

DANCING ANIMALS
Chinese New Year parades are often headed by a lion *(shown above)* or dragon. These are carried by dancers accompanied by crashing cymbals. The first month of the Chinese calendar begins on the first full moon between 21 January and 19 February.

HORSE RACING
The Mongols, who invaded China in the 1200s, brought with them their love of horses and superb riding skills. Today, children as young as three years old take part in horse-racing festivals in northern China and Mongolia. Archery and wrestling competitions are also regularly held.

MAKE A LANTERN

You will need: thick card, pencil, ruler, scissors, compasses, glue and brush, red tissue paper, blue paint, paintbrush, water pot, thin blue and yellow card, wire, tape, bamboo stick, torch, fringing fabric.

Frame (x4) — 25cm — 18cm

Side (x4) — 1cm — 2.5cm — 16cm

End (x2) — 18cm — 18cm

Using the measurements above, draw the 10 pieces on to thick card (pieces not drawn to scale). Cut out pieces with scissors.

1 Using compasses, draw an 8cm diameter circle in the middle of one of the end pieces. Cut out the circle with scissors. Glue on the 4 sides, as shown.

2 Glue together the frame pieces. Then glue the end pieces on to the frame. When dry, cover frame with red tissue paper. Glue one side at a time.

DRAGON BOATS

In the fifth month of the Chinese year, races are held in the Dragon Boat festival. This is in memory of a famous statesman called Qu Yuan, who drowned himself in 278BC when his advice to his ruler was ignored. Rice dumplings are eaten at the Dragon Boat festival every year in his memory.

CHINESE LANTERNS

Elaborate paper lanterns brighten up a wedding in the 1800s during the Qing dynasty. Lanterns were also strung up or paraded on poles at other private celebrations and during Chinese festivals.

3 Paint top of lantern blue. Cut borders out of blue card. Glue to top and bottom of frame. Stick a thin strip of yellow card to bottom border.

4 Make 2 small holes opposite each other at top of lantern. Pass the ends of a loop of wire through each hole. Bend and tape ends to secure wire.

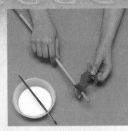

5 Make a hook from thick card. Split end opposite hook. Glue and wrap around bamboo stick. Hang lantern by wire loop from hook.

Light up your lantern by placing a small torch inside it. Decorate with a fringe. Now you can join in Chinese celebrations!

Ancient Japanese Faith

Almost all Japanese people in history followed a very ancient religious faith called Shinto. Shinto means the way of the gods. It developed from a central idea that all natural things had a spiritual side. These natural spirits – called *kami* in Japanese – were often kindly, but could be powerful or even dangerous. They needed to be respected and worshipped. Shinto also encouraged the worship of ancestors, spirits who could guide, help and warn. Special priests, called shamans, made contact with the spirits by chanting, fasting, or by falling into a trance.

Shinto spirits were honoured at shrines that were often built close to sites of beauty or power, such as waterfalls or volcanoes. Priests guarded the purity of each shrine, and held rituals to make offerings to the spirits. Each Shinto shrine was entered through a *torii* (large gateway) which marked the start of the sacred space. *Torii* always had the same design – they were based on the ancient perches of birds waiting to be sacrificed.

At the Shrine
A priest worships by striking a drum at the Grand Shrine at Izu, one of the oldest Shinto shrines in Japan. A festival is held there every August, with processions, offerings and prayers. An *omikoshi* (portable shrine) is carried through the streets, so that the spirits can bring blessings to everyone.

Offerings to the Spirits
Worshippers at Shinto shrines leave offerings for the *kami* (spirits) that live there. These offerings are neatly wrapped barrels of *sake* (rice wine). Today, worshippers also leave little wooden plaques with prayers on them.

Votive Dolls
You will need: self-drying clay, 2 balsa wood sticks (12cm long), ruler, paints, paintbrush, water pot, modelling clay, silver foil, red paper, gold paper, scissors, pencil, glue stick, optional basket and dowelling stick.

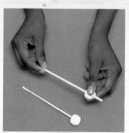

1 Place a ball of clay on the end of each of the balsa sticks. On one of the sticks, push the clay down so that it is 5mm from the end. This will be the man.

2 Paint hair and features on the man. Stand it up in modelling clay to dry. Repeat with the woman. Cover the 5mm excess stick on the man's head in foil.

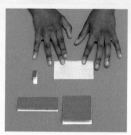

3 Take two pieces of red paper, 6.5cm x 14cm and 6cm x 10cm. Fold them in half. Take two pieces of gold paper, 10.5cm x 10cm and 1cm x 7cm. Fold in half.

HOLY VOLCANO

Fuji-San (Mount Fuji) has been honoured as a holy place since the first people arrived in Japan. Until 1867, women were not allowed to set foot on Fuji's holy ground.

LUCKY GOD

Daikoku is one of seven lucky gods from India, China and Japan that are associated with good fortune. In Japan, he is the special god of farmers, wealth, and of the kitchen. Daikoku is recognized by both Shinto and Buddhist religions.

FLOATING GATE

This *torii* at Miyajima (Island of Shrines), in southern Japan, is built on the seashore. It appears to float on the water as the tide flows in. Miyajima was sacred to the three daughters of the Sun.

In some regions of Japan, dolls like these are put on display in baskets every year at Hinamatsuri (Girls' Day), on 3 March.

4 Take the folded red paper (6.5cm x 14cm). This is the man's *kimono*. Cut a triangular shape out of the bottom. Cut a neck hole out at the folded end.

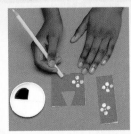

5 Dip the blunt end of the pencil in white paint. Stipple a pattern on to the red paper. Add the central dots using the pencil tip dipped in paint.

6 Slip the man's head and body into the red paper *kimono*. Then take the larger piece of gold paper and fold around the stick, as shown. Glue in place.

7 Now stick the gold paper (1cm x 7cm) on to the woman's *kimono*, in the middle. Slip the woman's head and body into the *kimono*. Glue in place.

Gods of Ancient Greece

THE GODS OF THE ANCIENT GREEKS had many human characteristics. They looked like ordinary people and felt emotions that led them to quarrel and fall in love. However, the gods also had magical powers and were immortal (they could live forever). With these powers, the gods could become invisible, or disguise themselves, or turn people into animals. The gods were thought to influence all parts of human life. They were kept busy with requests for help, from curing illness to ensuring a victory in war. In order to keep on the right side of the gods, the Greek people made sacrifices, left offerings and said prayers. Communities financed the building of temples, such as the Parthenon in Athens. They paid for priests to look after the buildings and to organize festivals in honour of the gods.

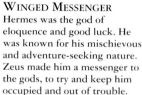

WINGED MESSENGER
Hermes was the god of eloquence and good luck. He was known for his mischievous and adventure-seeking nature. Zeus made him a messenger to the gods, to try and keep him occupied and out of trouble.

KING OF THE GODS
Zeus ruled over earth and heaven from Mount Olympus, (a real place on the border of Macedonia). He was thought to be a fair god who upheld order and justice. Wrongdoers could be punished with thunderbolts thrown by him.

WILD GODDESS
Artemis was the goddess of wild places and animals, hunting and the moon. She was a skilful archer, whose arrows caused death and plagues. The power to heal was another of her attributes.

PARTHENON
You will need: two pieces of white card 62cm by 38.5cm, ruler, black felt-tip pen, shoebox, scissors, blue, red and cream paint, paintbrush, PVA glue, piece of red corrugated card (approximately 39cm x 28.5cm), masking tape, craft knife, 160cm of balsa wood.

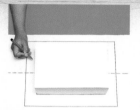

1 Draw a horizontal line across the centre of the card. Place the shoebox in the middle. Draw around it. Draw a second box 7cm away from this.

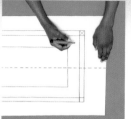

2 Draw a third box 2cm away from the second. Extend the lines of the second box to meet the third, to form four tabs, one in each corner.

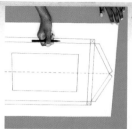

3 To make the ends of the roof, draw half a diamond shape along the edge of the second box. Add on two rectangular tabs 1cm deep.

SYMBOLS

Each god and goddess was thought to be responsible for particular aspects of daily life. Each was represented by a symbol. Wheat symbolized Demeter, goddess of living things. Dionysus, god of the vine and wine, was appropriately represented by grapes.

wheat   grapes

LOVE AND PROTECTION

Aphrodite was the goddess of love and beauty. Her vanity was instrumental in causing one of the biggest campaigns in Greek folklore, the Trojan War. Aphrodite promised to win Paris (son of the king of Troy) the love of the most beautiful mortal woman in the world – Helen. In return, Paris was to name Aphrodite as the most beautiful of all the goddesses. However, Helen was already married to the king of Sparta. When she left him to join Paris, the Greeks declared war on Troy. A bloodthirsty war followed in which heroes and gods clashed.

A POWERFUL FAMILY

Hera was the wife of Zeus and goddess of marriage. She was revered by women as the protector of their married lives. Her own marriage was marked by conflicts between herself and her husband. Her jealousy of rivals for her unfaithful husband's affections led her to persecute them. She was also jealous of Heracles, who was Zeus' son by another woman. Hera sent snakes to kill Heracles when he was a baby. Fortunately for Heracles, he had inherited his father's strength and killed the snakes before they harmed him.

GRAPES OF JOY

The god Dionysus was admired for his sense of fun. As god of fertility, the vine and wine, he was popular with both male and female worshippers. However, his followers were too enthusiastic for some city-states which banned celebrations in his name.

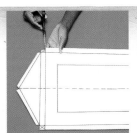

4 Repeat step 3 for the other end of the roof. Cut out both ends of the roof and cut into the four corner tabs. Get your painting equipment ready.

5 Turn the roof piece over. Draw and then paint the above design on to each end piece. Paint a blue, 1cm margin along each side. Leave to dry.

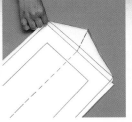

6 Turn the card over. Fold up all the sides of the second box. Fold in each corner tab and glue to its adjoining side. Fold down the rectangular tabs.

7 Cut the piece of red corrugated card in half. Stick them together with tape, along the unridged side. Turn them over and fold along the middle.

Temples and Festivals in Greece

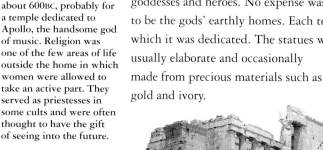

Festivals to honour the gods were important public occasions in ancient Greece. At the heart of each festival was a temple. At festival time, people flocked to the cities from the countryside. The greatest festivals were occasions of splendour and celebration. They involved processions, music, sports, prayers, animal sacrifices and offerings of food, all of which took place at the temple.

The earliest Greek temples were built of wood, and none have survived. Later, temples built from stone echoed the simplicity of tree trunks in their columns and beams. The finest temples were made from marble. They were often decorated with brightly painted friezes, showing mythical stories of gods, goddesses and heroes. No expense was spared because temples were thought to be the gods' earthly homes. Each temple housed a statue of the god to which it was dedicated. The statues were usually elaborate and occasionally made from precious materials such as gold and ivory.

A WOMAN'S ROLE
This vase in the shape of a woman's head was made about 600BC, probably for a temple dedicated to Apollo, the handsome god of music. Religion was one of the few areas of life outside the home in which women were allowed to take an active part. They served as priestesses in some cults and were often thought to have the gift of seeing into the future.

GRAND ENTRANCE
The monumental gateway to the temple complex at the Acropolis in Athens was called the Propylaea. The temple beside it honoured the city's guardian goddess, Athena.

8 Glue the ends of the corrugated card to the folded up edges of the painted card. Leave to dry. This piece forms the roof to your temple.

9 Draw around the shoebox, on to the second piece of card. Draw another box 7cm away. Cut it out, leaving a 1cm border. This is the temple base.

10 Ask an adult to help you with this step. Cut out 32 columns from balsa wood. Each must be 5cm in height. Paint them cream and leave to dry.

11 Mark eight points along each edge of the second box by drawing around a column piece. Draw them an equal distance from each other.

A BIRTHDAY PARADE

A parade of horsemen, chariots and people leading sacrificial animals all formed part of the procession of the Panathenaic festival. This was held once a year, in Athens, to celebrate the goddess Athena's birthday. Every fourth year, the occasion involved an even more elaborate ceremony which lasted for six days. During the festivities, the statue of Athena was presented with a new robe.

A TEMPLE FOR THREE GODS

The Erectheum was built on the Acropolis, looking down on Athens 100 m below. Unusually for a Greek temple, it housed the worship of more than one god: the legendary king Erectheus; Athena, guardian goddess of the city of Athens, and Poseidon, god of the sea. The columns in the shape of women are called caryatids.

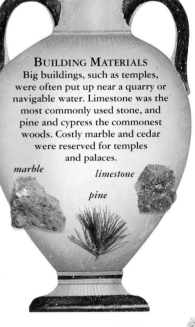

BUILDING MATERIALS

Big buildings, such as temples, were often put up near a quarry or navigable water. Limestone was the most commonly used stone, and pine and cypress the commonest woods. Costly marble and cedar were reserved for temples and palaces.

marble

limestone

pine

THE LION'S MOUTH

This gaping lion is actually a waterspout from an Athenian temple built in about 570BC. Although rainfall in Greece is low, waterspouts were necessary to allow storm water to drain off buildings with flat roofs. The lion was chosen as a symbol of strength and power.

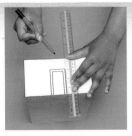

12 Draw a door on to a short end of the shoebox. Glue the roof on to the top of the shoebox. Paint the 1cm border on the temple base, blue.

13 Glue the columns into place, between the roof and the base. Dab glue on to their ends. Position them on the circles marked out in step 11.

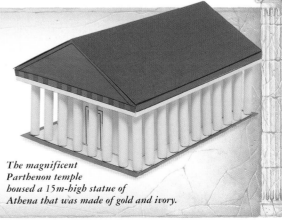

The magnificent Parthenon temple housed a 15m-high statue of Athena that was made of gold and ivory.

The Ancient Greek Underworld

P EOPLE IN ANCIENT GREECE lived only about half as long as people in the West do today. It was common for sickly children to die in infancy. Large numbers of men were killed in battle, women often died in childbirth and epidemics could wipe out whole communities.

Most Greeks believed that after death, their souls roamed the Underworld, a cold and gloomy region where the wicked were sent to be punished. Achilles, the hero in the Greek epic poem, *The Odyssey,* says, "I'd rather be a common labourer on earth working for a poor man than lord of all the legions of the dead". Few people were thought good enough to be sent to the Isles of the Blessed. If they were, they could spend eternity amusing themselves with sports and music. People who had led exceptional lives (such as the hero Heracles) were destined to become gods and live on Mount Olympus, the home of the gods.

FRAGRANT FAREWELL
Graves were sometimes marked with lekythoi, white clay flasks holding a perfumed oil that had been used to anoint the body. The lekythoi were usually painted with farewell scenes, funerals or images of the dead.

When someone died, their body was either buried or cremated. The Greeks believed that only when the body or ashes had been covered with earth, could its spirit leave for the Underworld. Graves contained possessions for use in the afterlife, and women left offerings of food and drink at the graveside to help the spirits.

FOOD FOR THOUGHT
The tradition of leaving food at gravesides began in Mycenaean times. Then people could be buried with their armour, cooking pots and even pets and slaves to accompany them. By 300BC the Greeks were leaving food such as wine and eggs at gravesides as nourishment for the dead.

wine

eggs

A DIVE INTO THE UNKNOWN
The figure on the painting above is shown leaping from life into the ocean of death. The pillars were put up by Heracles to mark the end of the known, living world. This diver was found painted on the walls of a tomb.

TUG OF LOVE

This painting from a vase shows Persephone with her husband, Hades, ruler of the underworld. Hades dragged Persephone from earth down to the Underworld. Her distraught mother, the goddess Demeter, neglected the crops to search for her. Zeus intervened and decided that Persephone would spend six months of every year with her mother and the other six with Hades. Whenever her daughter returned in spring, Demeter would look after the crops. However, Demeter grew sad each time her daughter went back to the Underworld and wintertime would set in.

LAST JOURNEY

The body of a dead person was taken from the home to the grave by mourners bearing tributes. To express their grief, they might cut off their hair, tear at their cheeks with their nails until blood flowed, and wear black robes. If there was a funeral feast at the graveside, the dishes were smashed afterwards and left there.

ROYAL TOMB

Women were less likely to be honoured by tombstone portraits than men. Philis, seen above, was an exception to this rule, possibly because she was the daughter of a powerful Spartan king. Athens enforced a law against extravagant tombs. No more than ten men could be employed for any more than three days to build one.

Roman Gods

WHEN THE ROMANS conquered Greece in 146BC, they adopted many of the ancient Greek gods. Some gods were renamed in Latin, the language of the Roman Empire. Jupiter (Zeus in Greek), the sky god, was the most powerful god. Venus (Aphrodite) was the goddess of love, Mars (Ares) was the god of war, Ceres (Demeter) goddess of the harvest and Mercury god of merchants. Household gods protected the home. Splendid temples were built in honour of the gods, and special festivals were held during the year, with processions, music, offerings and animal sacrifices. The festivals were often public holidays. The mid-winter festival of Saturnalia, in honour of Saturn, lasted up to seven days. As the Roman Empire grew, many Romans adopted the religions of other peoples, such as the Egyptians and the Persians.

CHIEF GOD
Jupiter was the chief god of the Romans. He was the all-powerful god of the sky. The Romans believed he showed his anger by hurling a thunderbolt to the ground.

DIANA THE HUNTRESS
Diana was the goddess of hunting and the Moon. In this detail from a floor mosaic, she is shown poised with a bow and arrow, ready for the hunt. Roman gods were often the same as the Greek ones, but were given different names. Diana's Greek name was Artemis.

ONE TO ALL
The Pantheon in Rome was a temple to all the gods. It was built between AD118 and 128. Its mosaic floor, interior columns and high dome still remain exactly as they were built.

A TEMPLE TO THE GODS

You will need: thick stiff card, thin card, old newspaper, scissors, balloon, PVA glue, ruler, pencils, masking tape, drinking straws, acrylic paints, paintbrush, water pot, Plasticine.

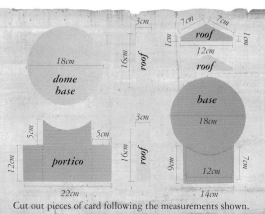

18cm
dome base

3cm
16cm *floor*
1cm
roof
7cm 7cm
1cm
12cm
roof

base
18cm

5cm
12cm
5cm
portico
3cm
16cm *floor*
9cm
12cm
7cm

22cm
14cm

Cut out pieces of card following the measurements shown.

1 Blow up the balloon. Cover it in strips of newspaper pasted on with glue. Keep pasting until you have a thick layer. Leave to dry. Then burst the balloon and cut out a dome.

Priests of Isis

The Egyptian mother-goddess Isis had many followers throughout the Roman Empire. This painting shows priests and worshippers of Isis taking part in a water purification ceremony. The ceremony would have been performed every afternoon.

Bless This House

This is a bronze statue of a *lar* or household god. Originally gods of the countryside, the *lares* were believed to look after the family and the home. Every Roman home had a shrine to the *lares*. The family, including the children, would make daily offerings to the gods.

Mithras the Bull-Slayer

Mithras was the Persian god of light. He is shown here, in a marble relief from a temple, slaying a bull. This bull's blood was believed to have brought life to the Earth. The cult of Mithras spread through the whole Empire, and was particularly popular with Roman soldiers. However, only men were allowed to worship Mithras.

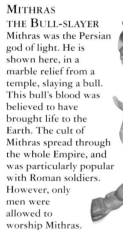

The Pantheon was built of brick and then clad in stone and marble. Its huge dome, with a diameter of over 43m, was the largest ever constructed until the 1900s.

2 Put the dome on its card base and draw its outline. Cut out the centre of the base to make a halo shape. Make a hole in the top of the dome. Bind the pieces together, as shown.

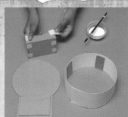

3 Glue together the base pieces. Cut a piece of thin card long enough to go round the base circle. This will be the circular wall. Use masking tape to hold the portico in shape.

4 Cut some straws into eight pieces, each 6cm long. These will be the columns for the entrance colonnade. Glue together the roof for the entrance. Secure with tape.

5 Glue together the larger pieces, as shown. Position each straw column with a small piece of Plasticine at its base. Glue on the entrance roof. Paint your model.

Protectors of Celtic Tribes

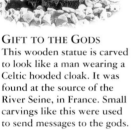

THERE ARE MANY surviving traces of Celtic religion, in descriptions by Roman writers, in carvings and statues, in place names, in collections of religious offerings and in myths and legends. Yet there are many things we do not know or fully understand about Celtic beliefs. This is because the Celts believed that holy knowledge was too important to be written down. It seems almost certain, however, that they worshipped gods who protected the tribe and gave strength in war, and goddesses who protected homes and brought fertility. Some gods were associated with the sky, and some goddesses with the earth. Gods and spirits controlled the elements and natural forces, such as water and thunder. They were given different names in different parts of the Celtic world, which covered large areas of central and north-western Europe. Gods and goddesses were worshipped close to water and in groves of trees. The Celts believed that dreadful things would happen if they did not make sacrifices of their most valuable possessions, including living things, to the gods.

GIFT TO THE GODS
This wooden statue is carved to look like a man wearing a Celtic hooded cloak. It was found at the source of the River Seine, in France. Small carvings like this were used to send messages to the gods.

HANDS HELD HIGH
From the Gundestrup bowl, this bearded god holds his hands up. Such a gesture may have been used by druids (Celtic priests) when praying. The clenched fists are a sign of power.

MAKE THE GUNDESTRUP BOWL

You will need: plastic bowl, silver foil, scissors, cardboard strip 12 cm x 84 cm, felt-tip pen, plasticine, PVA glue, double-sided tape, bradawl, paper fasteners.

1 Find a plastic bowl that measures about 26 cm in diameter across the top. Cover the bowl on the inside and outside with silver foil.

2 Use the pair of scissors to trim any excess foil, as shown. Ensure that you leave enough foil to turn over the top edge neatly.

3 Divide the card into six sections. Leave 3 cm at the end of the card. Draw a god figure in each section. Make a plasticine version of the figure. Glue it on top.

BURIED IN A BOG

The remains of this Celtic man were found in a peat bog in northern England. He died some time between AD1 and AD200. He was sacrificed by being killed in three different ways, having been strangled, had his throat cut, and struck on the head. Like the three-mothers carving, this shows the Celts' use of the number three for religious purposes.

HORSES AND WAR

According to Roman writers, Epona was the Celtic goddess of war. Epona was worshipped by many Roman soldiers who spent time on duty in Celtic lands. This Roman-style carving shows Epona with a horse. It was found in northern France.

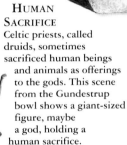

HUMAN SACRIFICE

Celtic priests, called druids, sometimes sacrificed human beings and animals as offerings to the gods. This scene from the Gundestrup bowl shows a giant-sized figure, maybe a god, holding a human sacrifice.

THREE MOTHERS

To the Celts, the number three was a sign of power, so they often portrayed their gods and goddesses in triple form. This stone carving shows three mother-goddesses. It was made in Britain, probably between AD50 and AD400. The figures stand for the three female qualities of strength, power and fertility.

The famous Gundestrup bowl, which inspired your model, was made in eastern Europe some time between 200BC and 1BC. It was found many years later in a Danish bog.

4 Cover both sides of the card strip and the plasticine figures with glue. Then cover with silver foil. Make sure that the foil is well glued to the figures.

5 Stick double-sided tape to the back of the foil-covered strip along the bottom and side edges. This will be used to join the sides of the bowl.

6 Make holes with a bradawl every few centimetres through the bottom of the strip. Make matching holes along the top of the bowl, as shown.

7 Attach the strip to the bowl with the double-sided tape. Stick the ends together, as shown. Secure by putting paper fasteners through both sets of holes.

Annual Celtic Festivals

As FARMERS, the Celts needed to be able to measure time, so that they would know when to plough their fields and sow their crops. The Celtic year (354 days) was divided into 12 months, each 29 or 30 days long. Every two-and-a-half years, an extra month was added, so that the calendar kept pace with the natural seasons. The Celts marked the passing of time by holding religious festivals. Samain (1 November) was the most important. It was the beginning of the Celtic year, and was a time for sacrifices and community gatherings. It was a dangerous time, when spirits walked the earth. Samain has survived today in Christian form as All Souls' Day, and Hallowe'en. Imbolc (1 February) marked the beginning of springtime and fertility. Beltane (1 May) was observed by lighting bonfires. Their smoke had purifying powers, and was used to kill pests on cattle. The final festival of the year was Lugnasad (1 August).

GODDESS AND SAINT
This statue is of the Celtic goddess Brigit (later known as St Brigit in Ireland) who was honoured at the Imbolc festival. The Celts believed that she brought fertility and fresh growth. She was also the goddess of learning, and had healing powers.

HOLY DAYS
Celtic calendars were kept by druids (priests). They believed that some days were fortunate, while others brought bad luck. This picture, painted about 150 years ago, shows how one artist thought a druid might look. However, it is mostly imaginary.

MAKE A PIG
You will need: modelling clay, board, modelling tool, ruler, 4 x balsa-wood sticks, metallic paint, paintbrush.

1 Make the body of the pig by rolling a piece of modelling clay into a sausage shape roughly 13 cm x 3.5 cm. Make a head shape at one end.

2 With your thumb and index finger, carefully flatten out a ridge along the back of the pig. The ridge should be about 1 cm high.

3 Now use the modelling tool to make a pattern along the ridge section. The pattern should have straight vertical lines on both sides of the ridge.

CLEVER GOD

Archaeologists think that this stone head, found in North Wales, may represent Lug, the Celtic god of all the arts. According to legend, Lug was clever at everything. He was honoured at Lugnasad, the fourth and final festival of the Celtic year when offerings were made to all the earth spirits and goddesses, to ask them for a plentiful harvest.

MISTLETOE AND OAK

Both mistletoe and oak were sacred to the Celts. Druids made sacrifices at wooden temples or in sacred oak groves. Even the druids' name meant "knowledge of the oak". Mistletoe was magic and mysterious. It could only be cut with a golden sickle. Mistletoe growing on oak trees was the most holy and powerful of all.

mistletoe

oak tree leaves

DRUID CEREMONY

This picture from the 1800s shows an imaginary view of druids at a Celtic religious ceremony. We have very little detailed information about how these ceremonies were performed. According to Roman writers, there were three different kinds of druids, each with different duties. Some were soothsayers, who told the future and issued warnings. Some held sacrifices. Some wrote and performed songs in honour of the gods.

To the Celts, wild boars were magic symbols of strength, fertility and power. The Celts also enjoyed roast boar at feasts held to celebrate the great festivals of the Celtic year, such as Samain, Imbolc, Beltane and Lugnasad.

4 Roll out four legs roughly 4.5 cm long. Push a balsa-wood stick into each leg. Leave about 1 cm of balsa wood exposed, as shown.

5 Now roll out a small amount of modelling clay. Cut out two triangular shapes using your modelling tool. These will be the pig's ears.

6 Carefully attach the ears on either side of the pig's head. Mould them on using a little water and your modelling tool, as shown.

7 Attach the legs to the pig, pushing the balsa wood sticks into the body. Leave the modelling clay to dry. When it is dry, paint the whole pig.

Gods of the Vikings

THE VIKINGS believed that the universe was held up by a great ash tree called Yggdrasil. The universe was made up of several separate worlds. Niflheim was the underworld, a misty realm of snow and ice. The upper world was Asgard, home of the gods. Its great hall was called Valholl (Valhalla), and it was here that warriors who died bravely in battle came to feast. The world of humans was called Midgard. It was surrounded by a sea of monsters and linked to Asgard by a rainbow bridge. Beyond the sea lay Utgard, the forest home of the Giants, deadly enemies of the gods.

The Vikings believed in many gods. They thought that Odin, father of the gods, rode through the night sky. Odin's wife was Frigg (a day of the week – Friday – is named after her) and his son was Baldr, god of the summer Sun. Powerful, red-bearded Thor was the god of thunder. Like many of the Vikings themselves, he enjoyed laughing, but was quick to anger. The twins Frey and Freya were god and goddess of fertility and love. Trouble was stirred up by Loki, a mischief-making god.

WORSHIPPING FREYA
This silver charm shows Freya. She was the goddess of love and marriage and was particularly popular in Sweden. Freya was the sister of Frey, the god of farming. It was also believed that when women died, Freya would welcome them into the next world. In *Egil's Saga*, a dying woman says "I have not eaten and shall not till I am with Freya".

THOR'S HAMMER
This lucky charm from Iceland shows Thor. He used his magic hammer to fight the giants. Thor was strong and brave.

BALDR IS SLAIN
Stories tell how the wicked Loki told the blind god Hod to aim a mistletoe spear at Baldr, god of the Sun and light.

MAKE A LUCKY CHARM

You will need: thick paper or card, pencil, scissors, self-drying clay, board, felt-tip pen, modelling tool, rolling pin, fine sandpaper, silver acrylic paint, brush, water pot, a length of cord.

1 Draw the outline of Thor's hammer onto thick paper or card and cut it out. Use this as the pattern for making your lucky charm, or amulet.

2 Place a lump of the clay on the board and roll it flat. Press your card pattern into the clay so that it leaves an outline of the hammer.

3 Remove the card. Use a modelling tool to cut into the clay. Follow around the edge of the imprint as shown, and peel away the hammer shape.

SLEIPNIR

Odin rode across the sky on Sleipnir, a grey, eight-legged horse. A pair of wolves travelled with Odin. In this carved stone from Sweden, Odin and Sleipnir are arriving at Valholl. They would have been welcomed by a *valkyrie*, or servant of the gods, bearing wine for Odin to drink.

Vikings wore lucky charms or amulets to protect themselves from evil. Many of the charms, such as this hammer, honoured the god Thor.

ODIN

One-eyed Odin was the wisest gods. He had two ravens called Hugin, meaning thought, and Mugin, meaning memory. Each day the ravens flew across the world. Every evening they flew back to Odin to perch on his shoulders and report to him the deeds that they had seen.

4 Model a flattened end to the hammer, as shown. Use a modelling tool to make a hole at the end, to thread the cord through when it is dry.

5 Use the end of a felt-tip pen, a pencil or modelling tool to press a series of patterns into the clay, as shown. Leave the clay to dry and harden.

6 When the amulet is dry, smooth any rough edges with sandpaper. Paint one side silver. Leave it to dry before painting the other side.

7 When the paint has dried, take enough cord to fit your neck and thread it through the hole in the hammer. Cut it with the scissors and tie a knot.

Vikings Convert to Christianity

B Y THE BEGINNING of the Viking Age, most of western Europe had become Christian. The early Vikings despised the Christian monks for being meek and mild. The warriors looted church treasures on their raids and murdered many priests or sold them into slavery. However, over the years, some Vikings found it convenient to become Christian. This made it easier for them to trade with merchants in western Europe and to hire themselves out as soldiers with Christian armies.

Christian missionaries went to Scandinavia from Germany and the British Isles. Monks from Constantinople preached to the Vikings living in the Ukraine and Russia. They soon gained followers. In about 960, King Harald Bluetooth of Denmark became a Christian. In 995, Olaf Tryggvason, a Christian king, came to the throne of Norway. He pulled down many of the shrines to the old gods. In 1000 the Viking colonists on Iceland also voted to become Christian. The new faith spread from there to Greenland. Sweden was the last Viking country to become Christian. People gave up worshipping pagan gods in the old temples of the settlement at Uppsala

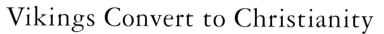

NEW FAITH
This silver crucifix was found in the Gotland region of Sweden. It is nearly 1,000 years old. It shows Christ wearing breeches, like those worn by Viking men.

STAVE CHURCH
This Christian church is made of staves, or split tree trunks. It was built in Gol, in Norway, in about 1200. The very first Christian churches in Scandinavia were built in this way. When the wooden foundations rotted away, the churches were rebuilt.

SIGN OF THE CROSS
This stone was raised at Jelling in Denmark by King Harald Bluetooth, in honour of his parents. It dates from about 985. The stone marks a turning-point in Viking history – the conversion of the Danes to Christianity. One side of the stone shows a dragon-like beast fighting with a snake. The other side is a Christian scene (*above*), showing Jesus on the cross.

crucifix

Thor's hammer charms

CHOICE OF GODS

The mould below was made from a soft mineral called soapstone. It was used to shape metal pendants 1,000 years ago. The mould could produce both hammer-of-Thor designs and crosses (*above*). The two religions – the old and the new – existed side-by-side for many years in the Viking world. It was a long time before Christianity really took hold. Many of the early converts to Christianity still turned to Thor for help in the heat of battle.

mould

AGAINST EVIL

Is this a silver cross, or a hammer-of-Thor charm with a dragon's head? Perhaps it was both. It was certainly intended to protect the wearer from evil and bad luck. Even after they became Christians, the Vikings remained very superstitious people. Helgi the Lean is described in a Viking saga as believing in Christ 'yet he still asked Thor for help on sea voyages and when facing danger'.

BAPTISM IN A BARREL

The Danish king, Harald Bluetooth, was converted to Christianity in about 960. This gold altar piece shows Harald being baptized in a barrel of holy water by Bishop Poppo. Harald went on to build a Christian church on the ancient site of the royal burial mound at Jelling.

STONE CROSS

This cross is from Kirkinner Church, in Scotland. It is about 1,000 years old. Its carving shows a mixture of Anglian and Norwegian Viking styles. The Christians in Britain, France and Germany were horrified by the Vikings' pagan religion, and they tried to persuade them to give it up. Eventually, Viking kings saw that becoming Christian could make them more powerful.

Spirits in North America

To North American Indian tribes, everything in the world had a soul or spirit that was very powerful and could help or harm humans. They believed that the changing seasons and events surrounding them were caused by different spirits. Spirits had to be treated with respect, so prayers, songs, chants and dances would be offered to please them. The most important spirit to Sioux tribes was Wakan Tanka, the Great Spirit or Great Mysterious, who was in charge of all other spirits. The Navajo tribes believed in the Holy People. These were Sky, Earth, Moon, Sun, Hero Twins, Thunders, Winds and Changing Woman. Some tribes believed in ghosts. Western Shoshonis, Salish (Flathead) people and Ojibwas considered ghosts to be spirit helpers who acted as bodyguards in battle. The leader of ceremonies was the shaman (medicine man) who conducted the dances and rites. He also acted as a doctor. The shamans of California would treat a sick person by sucking out the pain, spitting it out and sending it away.

CHARMED LIFE
A whale's tusk was used to carve this Inuit shaman's charm. Spirits called tuneraks were thought to help the angakok, as the Inuit shaman was called, in his duties. The role of shaman was passed from father to son. In Padlimuit, Copper and Iglulik tribes, women could also be shamans.

BEAR NECESSITIES OF LIFE
This shaman is nicknamed Bear's Belly and belonged to the Arikara Plains tribe. Shamans were powerful, providing the link between humans and spirits. After years of training, they could cure ill health, tell the future or speak to the dead.

MAKE A RATTLE

You will need: thick card, pencil, ruler, scissors, masking tape, compasses, PVA glue, brush, two balsa wood strips 2–3cm wide and about 18cm long, raffia or string, air-drying clay, barbecue stick, cream, black, orange/red and brown paint, paintbrushes, water pot, black thread, needle.

1 Cut two pieces of card 1.5cm wide, one 46cm long and one 58cm long. Cover both in masking tape. Make holes about 3cm apart along the strips.

2 Bend each strip into a ring. Glue and tape the ends together to make two rings. Fix the two strips of balsa wood into a cross to fit across the large ring.

3 Glue the two sticks together then strap them with raffia or string. Wrap the string round one side then cross it over the centre. Repeat on all sides.

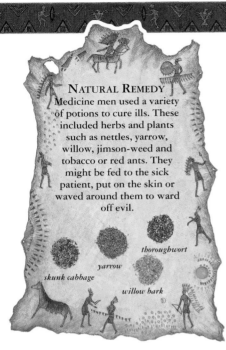

NATURAL REMEDY

Medicine men used a variety of potions to cure ills. These included herbs and plants such as nettles, yarrow, willow, jimson-weed and tobacco or red ants. They might be fed to the sick patient, put on the skin or waved around them to ward off evil.

thoroughwort

yarrow

skunk cabbage

willow bark

THE HAPPY COUPLE

Menominee people of the Woodlands made these dolls to celebrate the marriage of a couple. The miniature man and woman were tied face to face to keep husband and wife faithful. Dolls feature in the customs of many tribes, not least the Hopi and Zuni of the Southwest. Their katchina dolls are spirits shown in the form of animals, humans or plants.

MEDICINE BAGS

Crystals, animal parts, feathers and powders made of ground up plants and vegetables might be inside these bundles. They were used to make cures and spells by a shaman (medicine man) of the Winnebago tribe from the Woodlands.

SACRED BIRD

Rattles such as this Thunderbird rattle from the Northwest Coast were considered sacred objects and carved with the images of spirits. They were made of animal hoofs, rawhide or turtle shells, and filled with seeds or pebbles. Some were hand held, others were put on necklaces.

Rattles were an important part of any ceremony. In some tribes only shamans could hold one.

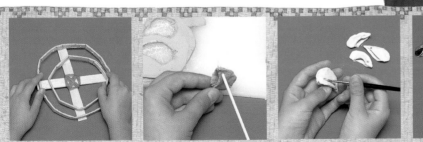

4 Glue the two card rings on to the cross, as here. The larger ring sits on the outer ends of the cross. The smaller one is roughly 1–2cm inside of that.

5 Roll out the modelling clay to a 1cm thickness. Cut out 20 to 30 semicircle shapes to resemble penguin beaks. Use a stick to make a hole at one end.

6 When the beaks are dry, paint them cream. Leave to dry. Paint the tips black then paint red or orange stripes. Next, paint the two rings brown.

7 Thread the black cotton through the hole in a painted beak, then tie it through one of the holes in the rings. Repeat with each beak, filling both rings.

American Indian Purifying Rites

SWEATING PURIFIED THE BODY AND MIND according to North American Indians. The Sioux called it "fire without end". The sweat was one of the most important and ancient of all North American religious rituals. They were among the first people to use heat to cleanse the body. But for tribe members, it was not simply a question of hygiene. The sweat lodge rite was performed before and after other ceremonies to symbolize moving into and out of a sacred world. Warriors prepared their spirits before the Sun Dance ceremony by taking a sweat bath. This was a dance to give thanks for food and gifts received during the year, and often featured self-mutilation. Sweats were also taken as a medical treatment to cure illness, and as a rite of passage through a stage in life such as from childhood to adulthood. A young boy who was about to make his transition into warrior-life was invited to spend time with the tribe's males. They would offer him the sacred pipe, which was usually smoked to send prayers. This was called Hunka's ceremony and showed the tribe's acceptance that the boy was ready. Some warrior initiation rites were brutal – such as the Mandan's custom of suspending young men by wooden hooks pierced through their chest, or scarring them, known as Okipa. Both girls and boys prepared for passing into adolescence by spending time alone and fasting (not eating).

STEAM AND SMOKE
A holy man, such as this Pima shaman, would be in charge of sweats. Prayers and chants were offered and the sacred pipe was passed around each time the door was opened.

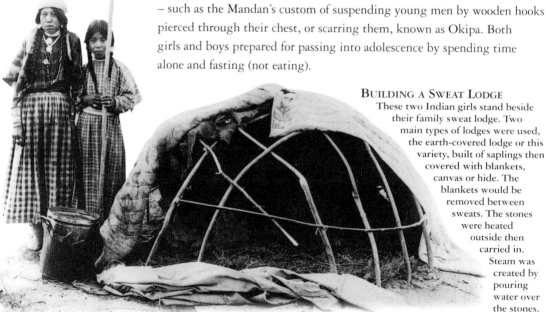

BUILDING A SWEAT LODGE
These two Indian girls stand beside their family sweat lodge. Two main types of lodges were used, the earth-covered lodge or this variety, built of saplings then covered with blankets, canvas or hide. The blankets would be removed between sweats. The stones were heated outside then carried in. Steam was created by pouring water over the stones.

BATHS IN EARTH

An Indian crawls out from an earth-covered sweat lodge for air. Six to eight people could sit around the hot stones inside, depending on the size of the sweat lodge. Males and females would both take part in sweats but it was customary to do so separately. In some tribes, families built their own family lodges and some larger sweat lodges were also used as homes or temples. Sticks and wood formed the frame. This was covered in mud or clay. The fire would be built in the lodge causing a dry heat. It was dark, stuffy and hot, similar to the saunas used in Europe. However, a sweat lodge was used to cleanse the spirit as well as the skin.

CLEANSED AND REFRESHED

Herbs, such as sweetgrass and cedar, were often put on the hot stones inside a sweat lodge. When the water was poured over the stones, the smell and essence of the herbs were released into the lodge with the steam. Herbs helped to clear the nasal passages. They could also be selected to treat particular ills. As the heat from the steam opened up the skin's pores, the herbs could enter the body and work at the illness or help purify the spirit. Sweating removed toxins (poisons in the body) and, the Indians believed, forced out disease.

GROWING UP

A young Apache girl is dressed up for a modern tribal ceremony. The lives of North American Indians were filled with rituals to mark each milestone in a person's life or important tribal events. There were ceremonies for birth, for becoming an adult or to mark changing seasons.

INSTRUMENTS TELL A STORY

This Tsimshian rattle has been involved in many ceremonies. Tribes had a vast amount of ceremonial objects, from rattles to headdresses, clothing and wands. Their decorations were usually of spiritual significance. In some tribes, the frog was respected since it would croak when danger was near. Others believed that their long tongues could suck out evil. A frog also features in the creation myths of the Nez Perce.

Shamans in the Arctic World

LONG BEFORE CHRISTIAN MISSIONARIES arrived in the Arctic, local people had developed their own beliefs. Arctic people thought that all living creatures possessed a spirit or *inua*. When an animal died, its spirit lived on and was reborn in another creature. Powerful spirits were thought to control the natural world, and these invisible forces influenced people's everyday lives. Some spirits were believed to be friendly towards humans. Others were malevolent or harmful. People showed their respect for the spirits by obeying taboos – rules that surrounded every aspect of life. If a taboo was broken the spirits would be angered. People called shamans could communicate with the spirit world. Shamans had many different roles in the community. They performed rituals to bring good luck in hunting, predicted the weather and the movements of the reindeer herds and helped to heal the sick. They worked as doctors, priests and prophets, all rolled into one.

SHAMAN AND DRUM
An engraving from the early 1800s shows a female shaman from Siberia. Most, but not all, shamans were male. Shamans often sang and beat on special drums, such as the one shown above, to enter a trance. Some drums had symbols drawn on them and helped the shamans to predict the future.

TUPILAK CARVING
This little ivory carving from Greenland shows a monster called a *tupilak*. *Tupilaks* were evil spirits. If someone wished an enemy harm, he might secretly make a little carving similar to this, which would bring a real *tupilak* to life. It would destroy the enemy unless the person possessed even more powerful magic to ward it off.

SHAMAN'S DRUM

You will need: ruler, scissors, thick card, PVA glue, glue brush, masking tape, compass, pencil, shammy leather, brown paint, paint brush, water pot, brown thread or string

1 Cut out two strips of thick card, each strip measuring 77 cm long and 3 cm wide. Glue the two strips together to give the card extra thickness.

2 Once the glue has dried, use masking tape to cover the edges of the double-thickness card. Try to make the edges as neat as possible.

3 Using a compass, draw a circle with a 24 cm diameter on a piece of shammy leather. Cut it out, leaving a 2 cm strip around the edge of the circle.

HERBAL MEDICINES

An Innu woman collects pitcher plants that she will use to make herbal medicines. In ancient times, shamans acted as community doctors. They made medicines from plants and gave them to sick people to heal them. They also entered trances to soothe angry spirits, which helped the sick to recover from their illness.

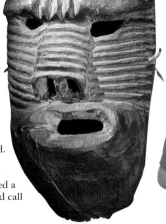

SEA SPIRIT

This beautiful Inuit sculpture shows a powerful spirit called Sedna. The Inuit believed that Sedna controlled storms and all sea creatures. If anyone offended Sedna, she withheld her blessing and hunting was poor. Here Sedna is portrayed with a mermaid's tail and accompanied by a narwhal and two seals. This very delicate carving has been made from a piece of reindeer antler.

MAGIC MASK

This mask is from Arctic North America. It was worn by Inuit shamans during a special ritual to communicate with the spirit world. Shamans wore wooden masks similar to this one. They also wore headdresses. Each mask represented a powerful spirit. The shaman would call on the spirit by chanting, dancing and beating on a special drum.

Shamans' drums were made of deerskin stretched over a round wooden frame. The shaman sometimes drew pictures of people, animals and stars on the side of the drum.

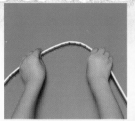

4 Using your fingers, curve the strip of card, as shown above. Make sure you curve the card slowly so that it does not crease.

5 Glue the card onto the circle. Ask someone to help keep the shammy leather stretched as you go. Tape the ends of the card together.

6 Make cuts 3 cm apart along the edge of the excess shammy leather towards the card, as shown above. Glue the edges to the cardboard ring.

7 Paint the card with dark brown paint and leave it to dry. Decorate the drum with thick brown thread or string by tying it around the edges.

Aztec Myths and Omens

THE AZTECS OF CENTRAL AMERICA lived in constant fear that their world might come to an end. Ancient legends told that this had happened four times before. Each time, the world had been born again. Yet Aztec priests and astrologers did not believe that this would happen next time. If the world ended again, it would be forever. The souls of all Aztec people would be banished to a dark, gloomy underworld. The Wind of Knives would cut the flesh from their bones, and living skeletons would feast and dance with the Lord of the Dead. Then the Aztecs would vanish forever when they reached Mictlan (hell). The Maya people told similar stories about the underworld – which they called Xibalba (the Place of Fright) in a great epic poem, the *Popol Vuh*. This poem featured two brothers, called the Hero Twins.

Aztec legends also told that the end of the world would be heralded by strange signs. In AD1519, these gloomy prophecies seemed to be coming true. Ruler Moctezuma II had weird, worrying dreams. Astronomers also observed eclipses of the Sun and a moving comet with a fiery tail.

FEATHERED SERPENT
Quetzalcoatl was an ancient god-king. His name meant feathered-serpent. He was worshipped by many Mesoamerican people, but especially by the Toltecs. They believed that he had sacrificed himself to help his people. A Toltec legend said that one day he would return, heralding the end of the world.

HEROES AND LEGENDS
This ball court is in Copan, Guatemala. The ball-game featured in many Maya legends about the Hero Twins. They were skilled ball-game players and also expert hunters with deadly blow guns.

CREATURES OF LEGEND

This Maya bowl is decorated with a picture of a spider-monkey. Many different kinds of monkeys lived in the rainforests of Mesoamerica. Monkey-gods played an important part in Maya myths and legends. Because monkeys were quick and clever, the Maya believed that monkey-gods protected clever people, such as scribes.

THE NEW FIRE CEREMONY

Every 52 years, the Aztecs believed that the world might come to an end. To stop this happening, they held a special ceremony. People put out their fires and stayed indoors. At sunset, priests climbed to the top of a hill and waited for the planet Venus to appear in the sky. At the moment it appeared, a captive was sacrificed to the gods. His heart was ripped out and a fire lit in his chest. The priests then sent messengers all over the Aztec lands, carrying torches to relight the fires. People then believed the world was safe for another 52 years.

HEAVENLY MESSENGER

Ruler Moctezuma is shown here observing the brilliant comet that appeared in the Mexican sky in 1519. Priests and Aztec people carefully studied the stars for messages from the gods. They remembered the old Toltec legend that said one day, the god Quetzalcoatl would return and bring the world to an end.

AZTEC HERITAGE

Many Aztec and Maya traditions still survive today. Millions of people speak Nahuatl (the Aztecs' language) or Maya languages. Aztec and Maya beliefs have mingled with Christian traditions to create new religious festivals. The most famous of these festivals is the Day of the Dead. Families bring presents of flowers and sweets shaped like skulls to their ancestors' graves.

Blood Sacrifices of Mesoamerica

Mesoamerican people, such as the Aztecs and Maya, believed that unless they made offerings of blood and human lives to the gods, the Sun would die and the world would come to an end. Maya rulers pricked themselves with cactus thorns and sting-ray spines, or drew spiked cords through their tongues to draw blood. They pulled out captives' fingernails so the blood flowed. Aztecs pricked their ear-lobes each morning and collected two drops of blood to give to the gods. They also went to war to capture prisoners. On special occasions, vast numbers of captives were needed for sacrifice. It was reported that 20,000 victims were sacrificed to celebrate the completion of the Great Temple at Tenochtitlan in 1487. It took four days to kill them all. Mesoamerican temples were tombs as well as places of sacrifice. Rulers and their wives were buried inside. Each ruler aimed to build a great temple as a memorial to his reign.

TEMPLE TOMB
Pyramid Temple 1 at Tikal was built in the AD700s as a memorial to a Maya king. Nine stone platforms were built above the burial chamber, to create a tall pyramid shape reaching up to the sky.

HOLY KNIFE
This sacrificial knife has a blade of a semi-precious stone called chalcedony. It was made by Mixtecs from south Mexico. Mesoamerican priests used finely decorated knives of flint, obsidian and other hard stones to kill captives for sacrifice. These were trimmed to be as sharp as glass.

A PYRAMID TEMPLE

You will need: pencil, ruler, thick card, scissors, PVA glue, glue brush, masking tape, thin strips of balsa wood, thin card, corrugated card, water bowl, paintbrushes, paints.

Bottom level A x2 — 45 cm / 45 cm

Top level C — 21 cm / 21 cm

A x4 — 45 cm / 5 cm / 3cm

Middle level B x2 — 33 cm / 33 cm

B 33cm x4 / 2cm

C x4 — 21 cm

6cm / 9cm / 9cm x6 / 7cm Shrine walls

6cm / Shrine roof x 2 — 6cm / 7cm 6cm

Cut out pieces for the pyramid and temple-top shrines from thick card, as shown above.

1 Use PVA glue and masking tape to join the thick card pieces to make three flat boxes (A, B and C). Leave the boxes until the glue is completely dry.

2 From the remaining pieces of card, make the two temple-top shrines, as shown. You could add extra details with strips of balsa wood or thin card.

Skull Shrine

Rows of human skulls, carved in stone, decorate this shrine outside the Aztecs' Great Temple in the centre of Tenochtitlan. Most Aztec temples also had skull-racks, where rows of real human heads were displayed. They were cut from the bodies of sacrificed captives.

Perfection

The ideal victim for human sacrifice was a fit and healthy young man.

Religious Gifts

Mesoamerican people also made offerings of food and flowers as gifts to the gods. Maize was a valuable gift because it was the Mesoamerican people's most important food. Bright orange marigolds were a sign of the Sun, on which every person's life depended.

maize

marigolds

Human Sacrifice

This Aztec codex painting shows captives being sacrificed. At the top, you can see a priest cutting open a captive's chest and removing the heart as an offering to the gods.

This model is based on the Great Temple that stood in the centre of Tenochtitlan.

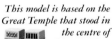

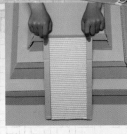

3 Glue the boxes, one on top of the next. Cut out pieces of card the same size as each side of your boxes. They should be about 1–2cm wide. Stick down, as shown.

4 Cut out two strips of card 2cm x 26cm. Glue them to a third piece of card 14cm x 26cm. Glue corrugated card 9.5cm x 26cm in position, as shown.

5 Stick the staircase to the front of the temple, as shown. Use a ruler to check that the staircase is an equal distance from either side of the temple.

6 Paint the whole temple a cream colour to look like natural stone. Add details, such as carvings or wall paintings, using brightly coloured paint.

Inca Feasts and Celebrations

IN COMMON WITH OTHER CENTRAL AMERICAN PEOPLE, the Incas loved to celebrate the natural world and its changing seasons. They marked them with special festivals and religious rituals. Some celebrations were held in villages and fields, others took place at religious sites or in the cities. It is said that the Incas had as many as 150 festivals each year. The biggest festival of all was *Inti Raymi*, the Feast of the Sun. It was held in June, to mark midwinter in the southern part of the world. *Qapaq Raymi*, the Splendid Festival, was held in December to mark the southern midsummer. This was when boys were recognized as adult warriors or young nobles. Crop festivals included the Great Ripening each February, the Earth Ripening each March and the Great Cultivation each May. The sowing of new maize was celebrated in August. The Feast of the Moon, held in September, was a special festival for women, while the Day of the Dead, in November, was a time to honour one's ancestors.

FEAST OF THE SUN
The Quechua people of Peru have revived the ancient festival of *Inti Raymi*. They gather each year at Sacsahuaman fortress, Cuzco, to celebrate the light and warmth of the Sun during the southern midwinter. In Inca times, a golden bowl was raised to the rising Sun. The Sun's rays would be used to make fire.

BRINGER OF RAIN
Drought was feared throughout the Empire, especially in the dry lands of the coast. If rain failed to fall, the life-giving irrigation channels dried up. In desperation, people visited the temples of Apu Illapu, bringer of rain. The priests made offerings and sacrifices, and the pilgrims prayed. The purpose of most Inca ceremonies and festivals was to prevent disaster and to ensure that life carried on.

THE AUGUST FESTIVAL
Quya Raymi (August) was a rainy month. A special festival called *Situa* was held to ward off the sicknesses that were common at that time of year. The people dressed for battle and went out into the streets. They hoped to drive away the evil spirits that made them ill. They carried torches of burning straw and plastered their faces with cornmeal or llama blood.

DANCERS AND MASKS

Drums, music and dance were always an important part of *Inti Raymi*, the Sun Festival. The Incas played rattles and whistles, drums and hand-drums, flutes and panpipes to help them celebrate the festival. Musicians played all day long without taking a break, and some of their ancient tunes are still known. Today, masks representing the Spanish invaders are added to the festivities. The modern festival proves that the old way of life has not been forgotten. Modern Peruvians are proud of their Inca past.

THE EMPEROR'S DAY

The modern festival of *Inti Raymi* attracts thousands to Cuzco. In the days of the Incas, too, nobles poured into the Inca capital from every corner of the Empire. Their aim was to honour the emperor as much as the Sun god. They came carrying tributes from the regions and personal gifts, hoping for the Emperor's favour in return.

FIESTA TIME

A drawing from the 1700s shows Peruvian dancers dressed as devils. Many of them are playing musical instruments or carrying long whips. After the conquest, festivals were known by the Spanish term, *fiestas*, and officially celebrated Christian beliefs. However, many of the festivities were still rooted in an Inca past. The dances and costumes often had their origins in Inca traditions.

Glossary

A

adobe Plaster, made from clay and straw, used by Pueblo Indians of central America, Egyptians and Mesopotamians in buildings.

agriculture Farming – the activity of growing crops and breeding animals.

alabaster A gleaming white stone, a type of gypsum.

alloy A mixture of metals melted together to create a new substance.

amaut Black pouch used by Inuit tribes of the north American Arctic to carry babies and young children.

amethyst A purple crystal, a type of quartz.

ancestor A family member who died long ago.

archaeologist Someone who studies ancient ruins and objects to learn about the past.

archaeology The scientific study of the past looking at the things people left behind, such as tools.

Arctic The region in the far north of our planet, surrounding the North Pole.

atrium The hallway or courtyard of a Roman house. The centre of the atrium was open to the sky.

auloi A pair of musical pipes used in ancient Greece. One pipe produced the melody while the other produced a background drone.

Aztecs Mesoamerican people who lived in northern and central Mexico. They were at their most powerful between AD1350 and AD1520.

B

banquet A rich, elaborate feast served with great ceremony.

bard A poet, or someone who recites poetry. Becoming a bard was the first stage in the training of a druid (a Celtic priest).

barter The exchange of goods, one for another.

booty Valuable things taken away by a victorious army.

brahmins The priests, members of the first caste (social class) in India.

bronze A metal made by mixing tin with copper.

Buddha An Indian prince who left his family to seek enlightenment. Founder of the Buddhist way of life.

burial ship Finely decorated ships in which Vikings were sometimes buried or cremated.

C

calpulli An Aztec family or neighbourhood group. The calpulli enforced law and order. It also arranged education, training and welfare benefits for its members.

caste One of four social classes into which Hindus in India were divided.

chalcedony A reddish, semi-precious stone.

chinampa An Aztec garden built on the fertile, reclaimed land on the lake shore.

chullpa A burial chamber in the form of a tower.

city-state A city, and its surrounding villages, with its own god and ruler.

civil servant Official who carries out government administration.

civilization A society that has made advances in arts, science and technology, law and government.

codex An early form of book; the Aztec codex was a folding book.

collyrium A black paste used as an eyeliner.

colony A settlement of people outside their own country.

Confucianism The western name for the teachings of the Chinese philosopher Kong Fuzi (Confucius), which call for social respect for one's family and ancestors.

courtier A person attending at royal court.

cowrie A seashell used as currency.

cremation The burning of dead bodies.

currency Form of exchange for goods, such as money.

D

daikon A white radish vegetable grown in Japan.

Daoism Chinese philosophy based on contemplation of the natural world. It later became a religion with a belief in magic.

deity A god or goddess.

delta A coastal region where the river slips into coastal waterways before flowing into the sea.

dhoti Traditional Indian dress worn by Hindu men.

die A tool for punching a design into metal.

dowry Money that is given to a newly married couple, usually by the bride's father.

drought A long period of time without rainfall.

druid Celtic priest. According to Roman writers, there were three different grades of druids. Some studied the natural world and claimed to foretell the future. Some were bards who knew about history. Some led Celtic worship, made sacrifices to the gods and administered holy laws.

dynasty A period of rule by the same royal family.

E

embalm To preserve a dead body.

emperor The ruler of an empire.

empire An area including many cities and countries and ruled by one person.

excavate To dig in the ground to discover ancient ruins and remains.

F

faience A type of opaque glaze that is often blue or green. It is made from quartz or sand, lime, ash and natron.

festival A special day set aside to honour a god or goddess.

feud A long-standing quarrel, especially between two families.

flax A plant that yields fibres, which are woven into a fabric called linen.

flint A hard stone that flakes easily, creating sharp edges. It is used to make tools and weapons.

G

geometry A branch of mathematics concerning the measurements of lines, angles and surfaces. It was pioneered by Euclid, a Greek scientist. In Greek it means measuring the land.

gladiator A professional fighter in Roman times who, as a slave or a criminal, fought to the death for public entertainment.

gorgon A Greek female monster of such horrific appearance that anyone who looked at her died.

gypsum A type of limestone used for sculpture.

H

hemp A fibrous plant used to make coarse clothes or textiles in China.

henna A reddish dye for the hair or skin, made from the leaves of a shrub.

Hinduism Religion that includes the worship of several gods and belief in reincarnation.

human sacrifice Killing humans as an offering to a god.

hunter-gatherer A person whose way of life involves hunting wild animals and gathering plant foods.

I

igloo An Inuit word meaning house, often used to refer to Inuit shelters built of ice or snow blocks.

immortal An idea or person that can live forever.

imperial Relating to the rule of an emperor or empress.

inro A small, decorated box, worn hanging from the belt in Japan.

inua An Inuit word for spirit.

Inuit The native people of the Arctic regions of North America, Canada and Greenland as distinguished from those of Asia and the Aleutian Islands.

irrigation Bringing water to dry lands so that crops can grow.

Islam The religion of the Muslim people.

ivory The hard, smooth, cream-coloured part of the tusks of elephants or walruses.

K

kabuki Popular plays, performed in Japan from about AD1600. They were fast moving and noisy.

kami Japanese holy spirits.

kaolin A fine white clay used in porcelain and paper making.

kero An Inca drinking vessel.

L

lacquer A thick, coloured varnish, used to coat wood, metal or leather.

lapis lazuli A dark blue, semi-precious stone used for jewellery.

llama A camel-like creature of south America. It is shorn for its wool and was sacrificed in ceremonies by the Inca people of south America.

longhouse The chief building of a Viking and Native American homestead.

loom A wooden frame used for weaving cloth.

lyre One of the various harp-like instruments played in Mesopotamia, Greece and Rome.

M

maki sushi Japanese rolls of vinegared rice made with fish and vegetable fillings.

mammals A type of warm-blooded animal such as human beings, whales, bats and cats.

marl Natural lime, dug from under the ground.

martial arts Physical exercises that are often based on combat, such as sword play and kung fu. Chinese martial arts bring together spiritual and physical disciplines.

Maya People who lived in south-western Mexico, Guatemala and Belize. The Maya lands were conquered by the Spanish between 1524 and 1546.

merchant A person who buys and sells goods for a profit.

Mesoamerica Central America.

metronomi Greek officials whose job it was to stop merchants and traders from cheating one another. They oversaw the weighing out of dry goods.

midden A rubbish tip or dunghill.

millet A grass type of grain plant that produces edible seeds.

minotaur A mythical beast, half man, half bull, that lived in a maze under a palace in Crete. It was slain by the Greek hero, Theseus.

mosaic A picture or decorated object made up of many small

squares or cubes of glass, stone or pottery, set in soft concrete.

mother-of-pearl A hard, shiny substance found in shells, also known as nacre. It was often used in inlays by skilled Chinese craftworkers.

mummification The process of preserving a human or animal body, by drying.

mummy A dead body preserved by being dried out in the sun, by extreme cold, or by a mixture of chemicals.

myth An ancient story about gods and heroes.

N

Neanderthals A group of *Homo sapiens* who were the first people to bury their dead.

Near East The area known today as the Middle East, comprising the countries of the eastern Mediterranean.

Nenet A reindeer herding people of southern Siberia.

Neolithic (New Stone Age) A period that began about 2 million years ago when the first stone tools were made.

netsuke Small toggles, carved from ivory and used to attach items to belts in Japan.

New Kingdom The period of Egyptian history between 1550–1070BC.

nobles People who are high in social rank.

Noh A serious, dignified drama that originated in Japan in around 1300.

Normans Descendants of the Vikings in Europe, who settled in northern France.

O

obi A wide sash, worn only by women in Japan.

ochre A yellow- or red-coloured earth used as pigment in paint.

Odin The most powerful and mysterious Viking god. He was the god of war, magic and poetry.

olive The fruit of the olive tree. An important crop in ancient Greece, olives were eaten as an appetizer or pressed to make olive oil.

Olmec A Mesoamerican people who lived in southern central Mexico. Their civilization existed between 1200BC and 400BC.

Olympic Games A sporting competition held every year at Olympia in ancient Greece in honour of the god Zeus. The first games were held in 776BC.

oppida The Roman name for fortified Celtic towns.

P

Panathenaic festival A yearly procession with sacrifices in honour of of the goddess Athena, which took place at the Parthenon in Athens.

papyrus A tall reed that grows in the river Nile, used to make a kind of paper by the ancient Egyptians.

paratha A fried wheat bread eaten in northern India.

Parthenon A temple in Greece on the Acropolis in Athens dedicated to the city's goddess, Athena.

peasant A farm worker.

peske Thick fur parka worn by Saami people in the Arctic over their tunics.

pharaoh Ruler of ancient Egypt.

pigment Any material used to provide colour for paint or ink.

pilgrim A person who makes a journey to a holy place.

plateau High, flat land, usually among mountains.

plumbline A weighted cord, held up to see if a wall or other construction is vertical.

porcelain The finest quality of pottery. It was made from kaolin and baked at a high temperature.

potcheca Aztec merchants.

priest Someone who offered prayers and sacrifices on behalf of worshippers at a temple.

prehistoric Belonging to the time before written records were made.

propylaea The momumental gateways to the temple complex on top of the Acropolis in Athens in Greece.

Pueblo People from the southwestern Mexico who lived in villages built of mud and stone.

pyramid A large pointed monument with a square base and triangular sides.

pyxis A box used for storing face powder or other cosmetics in Greece.

Q

quern A simple machine, made from two stones, that is used to grind corn.

R

relief A carved stone slab.

rites Solemn procedures carried out for a religious purpose or ceremony.

rituals An often repeated set of actions carried out during a religious ceremony.

S

sacrifice The killing of a living thing in honour of the gods.

sanctuary The most holy place in a temple.

sari Traditional dress for women in India.

scribe A professional writer, a clerk or civil servant.

serfs People who are not free to move from the land they farm without the permission of their landlord.

shaduf A bucket on a weighted pole,

used by the Egyptians to move water from the river Nile into the fields on the banks.

shamans Medicine men and women in tribal cultures. These people were healers, doctors, spiritual, and ceremonial leaders.

shamisen A traditional Japanese three-stringed musical instrument.

Shinto An ancient Japanese religion, known as "the way of the gods", based on honoring holy spirits.

shogun A Japanese army commander. From 1185–1868, shoguns ruled Japan.

shrine A container of holy relics or a place for worship.

sickle A tool with a curved blade used to harvest crops.

Silk Road The overland trading route that stretched from northern China through Asia to Europe.

silt Fine grains of soil found at the bottom of rivers and lakes.

slaves People who were owned by their masters as opposed to being free.

smelt To extract a metal from its ore by heating it in a furnace.

sphinx A creature with a human's head and a lion's body.

sultan A Muslim ruler.

surcoat A long, loose tunic worn over armor.

survey To measure land or buildings. Land is surveyed before the construction of a building, road, and any other sructure.

symbol A mark that has a special meaning.

T

tabla A drum played in north Indian classical music.

tablet A flat piece of clay of varying shape and size used for writing.

taboo A rule or custom linked with a religious belief that shows respect to the spirit.

tanbo Flooded fields where rice was grown in Asia.

tapestry A cloth with a picture or design woven by hand on its threads.

tax Goods, money, and services paid to the government.

temple A special building where a god or goddess is worshipped.

terracotta Baked, unglazed, orange-red clay.

textile Any cloth that has been woven, such as silk and cotton.

Thor The fierce Viking god of thunder.

threshing To beat or thrash out grain from corn.

timpanon A tambourine made with animal skin.

tipi Conical tent with a frame of poles, covered with animal skins, used by Plains Indians.

Torii The traditional gateway to a Shinto shrine.

totem pole A tall post carved with good luck charms.

tribe A group of families who owe loyalty to a chief and who share a common language and way of life.

tribute Goods given by a country to its conquerors, as a mark of submission.

turban Headdress worn by Muslim, Sikh, and some Hindu men.

U

uictli A Mesoamerican digging stick used like a spade.

Underworld This was the place to which the spirits of the dead were supposed to travel in ancient Greece.

V

Vaishnavism Hindu belief in Vishnu as lord of the Universe.

vallus The Roman name for a Celtic farm machine, used for reaping (cutting) grain crops.

Veda Ancient Aryan texts.

Venus figurine A statue of a woman, usually shown with large hips, breasts and buttocks, and a full stomach. The figurines may have been worshipped as symbols of fertility or plenty, and carried as good luck charms.

vicuña A llama-like animal whose wool was used to make cloth.

Viking One of the Scandinavian peoples who lived by sea-raiding in the Middle Ages.

Vishnu A chief Hindu god.

vizier The treasurer or highest ranking official in the Egyptian court.

W

walrus A sea mammal with long tusks.

wampum Shells strung together and used as currency or to record a historical event, by Native Americans.

warrior A man who fights in wars.

wigwam A Native American house made of bark, rushes, or skins spread over arched poles lashed together.

winnowing Separating grains of wheat and rice from their papery outer layer, called chaff.

X

xiang qi A traditional Chinese board game, similar to chess.

Y

yoke A long piece of wood or bamboo, used to help carry heavy loads. The yoke was placed across the shoulders and a load was hung from each end to balance it.

Z

zakat Alms that must be given to the poor in Islam.

Index

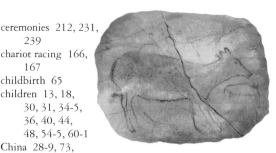

lucky gods 33
luxury 22-3

M

maize (corn) 72, 74, 75,
    122, 124
make up 131, 136, 137
Marduk 196
markets 74, 98, 99, 107,
    110, 124
marriage 30, 34, 40, 41,
    50, 54, 64, 65, 68-9
Mars 226
martial arts 160
masks 174, 241, 242-5,
    247
masons 89, 126
Maya 62-5, 122-5, 172,
    186, 187
merchants 92-3, 107,
    116-17, 124-5
meat 32
medicine 35
medicines 237, 241
Medusa 164, 165
memorial stones 48, 51
Mesopotamia 18-19, 74,
    76, 82-3, 148,
    178-9, 196-9
messages 228, 243
metalwork 154-5
millet 94
Minotaur 164
mirrors 136, 138, 140,
    148-9
missionaries 234
Mithras 227
Mohammed 208

money 72,
    73, 98,
    100-1
monkey-gods
    243
monks 234
monsters 165
mosaics 156, 157
mosques 209, 215
Mother Goddess 191
motherhood 18
mud bricks 16, 17, 19,
    20, 21, 62, 66
mummies 202, 203,
    205
murals 154
music 130, 162-3,
    170-1, 176, 247
musical instruments
    162-3, 170-1, 174,
    176
Muslims 26 (see also,
    Islam)
mythology 164
myths 242-3

N

Neanderthal people 194
Nebuchadnezzar 199
necklaces 131, 134-5
Nefertiti, Queen 136
netsuke 154, 155
Nile, River 20, 84, 86-7
noblewomen 30, 31
Noh theater 174, 175
nomads 13
North American Indians
    52-5, 118-19,
    168-9, 236-9
number systems 186, 187
Nut 200

O

oats 112
Odin 232, 233
Odysseus 165, 224
offerings 218, 220, 224,
    225, 228, 244, 245
Ogham 184-5
olives 104
Olympic Games 167
oppida (towns) 114-15
ornament 130, 134-5,
    138-9
Osiris 201
ovens 17

P

paintings 130, 131
palaces 24, 148
Pantheon 226, 227
paper 182
Parthenon 220, 223
patterns 130, 131
peasant farmers 73, 85,
    92-3
Pegasus 165
percussion 162-3
Perseus 165
Persia 102
pharaoh gods 200-1
pharaohs 22-3, 84, 85, 90,
    91, 136, 151
Picts 185
picture-writing 133, 169,
    180-1, 186
pictures 156-7
pigs 78, 94, 112
pilgrimage 213
plaster 63
plows 73, 84, 94, 95,
    104, 105, 112
poetry 152, 153, 170-1,
    182
Popol Vuh 242
porcelain 152, 154
Poseidon 106
    pottery 17, 18, 45,
        67, 89, 90, 93, 109,
        124, 150
        precious
        stones 147,

151
priests 204, 205, 218,
    220, 227
printing 182-3
printing on fabric 102-3
punishments 64
Punt 90, 91
puppets 174
purifying rites 238-9
pyramid temples 244-5

Q

Qin Shi Huangdi 74, 98
querns 47, 77, 85
Quetzalcoatl 242, 243

R

Ramadan 212
rattles 237, 239
rice 73, 76, 77, 94-5
ridges and furrows 110-11
riding 107
rituals 204, 212, 218,
    238, 246
role play 54
Roman Empire 38-43,
    110-11, 156-7,
    166-7, 226-7
roof charms 29
Rosetta Stone 180

S

Saami costume 144-5
sacred books 193, 208,
    210, 211
sacrifices 220, 228, 229,

Acknowledgments

This edition is published by Hermes House

Hermes House is an imprint of Anness Publishing Ltd
Hermes House, 88–89 Blackfriars Road,
London SE1 8HA
tel. 020 7401 2077;
fax 020 7633 9499;
info@anness.com

Publisher: Joanna Lorenz
Managing and Contributing Editor: Gilly
Cameron Cooper
Project Editor: Rasha Elsaeed
Editorial Reader: Joy Wotton
Authors: Daud Ali, Jen Green, Charlotte
Hurdman, Fiona Macdonald, Lorna Oakes,
Philip Steele, Michael Stotter, Richard Tames
Consultants: Cherry Alexander, Nick Allen,
Clara Bezanilla, Felicity Cobbing,
Penny Dransart, Jenny Hall, Dr. John
Haywood, Dr. Robin Holgate, Michael
Johnson, Lloyd Laing, Jessie Lim, Heidi Potter,
Louise Schofield, Leslie Webster
Designers Simon Borrough, Matthew Cook,
Joyce Mason, Caroline Reeves, Margaret Sadler,
Alison Walker, Stuart Watkinson at Ideas Into
Print, Sarah Williams
Special Photography: John Freeman
Stylists: Konika Shakar, Thomasina Smith,
Melanie Williams
Production Controller: Don Campaniello

Previously published as four separate volumes: *Home, Family &
Everyday Life Through the Ages*; *Work, Trade & Farming Through the
Ages*; *Art, Culture & Entertainment Through the Ages*; *Gods, Beliefs &
Ceremonies Through the Ages*.

Printed and bound in China

10 9 8 7 6 5 4 3 2 1

NOTES

NOTES

NOTES

NOTES

NOTES

NOTES

NOTES

NOTES